Jakob and Charlotte Rippert:
Nubia to Nuriootpa

Paul Kiem

Klaus Rippert

For Judy and Heike
who shared the pilgrimage

Jakob and Charlotte Rippert: Nubia to Nuriootpa

copyright © Paul Kiem and Klaus Rippert, 2026

ISBN: 978 - 0 - 6454459 - 1 - 6

First published 2026
Bolton Church, Newcastle NSW, Australia

Contents

Abbreviations	iv
Foreword	v
Prologue	vii
1. Jakob Rippert	1
2. The First World War, 1914-1918	5
3. Sudan Pionier Mission	13
4. Charlotte Wolter	19
5. Egypt and Nubia, 1924-1931	27
6. Palestine, 1931-1941	43
7. Tatura, 1941-1944	59
8. Peace and Repatriation, 1945-1947	77
9. Germany, 1948-1950	89
10. Migration and Compensation	103
11. Hermannsburg, 1950-1955	119
12. Nuriootpa, 1956-1975	135
Epilogue	151
Appendices	
A. Charlotte Wolter: 'Report 1', 1913	155
B. Charlotte Wolter: 'Report 2', 1913	155
C. Jakob Rippert: 'Departure and First Impressions on the Mission Field', 1925	156
D. Jakob Rippert: 'From the Mission Field, Ramadan', 1925	160
E. Jakob Rippert: 'My First Trip to Nubia', 1926	162
F. Jakob Rippert: 'First Nile Journey of the *Ischimbul*', 1927	167
G. Charlotte Rippert: 'Travel Diary During the Nubia Trip', 1929	170
Bibliography	173
Index	177

Abbreviations

AWM	Australian War Memorial, Canberra, Australia
EMO	Evangeliumsgemeinschaft Mittlerer Osten, Wiesbaden, Germany (Evangelical Middle East Ministries)
FRM	Finke River Mission Archives, Alice Springs, Australia
HHStAW	Hessisches Haupstaatsarchiv Wiesbaden, Germany
HStAD	Hessisches Staatsarchiv Darmstadt, Germany
LAA	Lutheran Archives Australia, Adelaide
NAA	National Archives of Australia
NAZI	Nationalsozialistische Deutsche Arbeiterpartei (NSDAP) (National Socialist German Workers' Party)
PKI	Paul Kiem
RPA	Rippert/Probert Family Collection, Australia
SPM	Sudan Pionier Mission
TAM	Tatura Irrigation and Wartime Camps Museum, Tatura, Australia
TSA	Temple Society of Australia Archives

The Authors

Paul Kiem (www.paulkiem.net) is a former history educator and past president of the History Teachers' Association of Australia. He researches Australian and European social history and has published numerous articles and book chapters. In 2024 he received the Ivan Barko Award from the Institute for the Study of French Australian Relations for his article 'The Huybers and Loureiro Families: A Case Study in the History of Australia's French Connection', published in *The French Australian Review*. Most recently, he contributed a chapter, 'Why Should Public Men be Held up to Ridicule?', to Scully, Fernandes and Khanduri's *Cartoon Conflicts* (2025).

Karl Klaus Rippert, a former engineer, is vice-chairman of the Hessian Family History Association (www.hfv-ev.de) and has been involved in genealogy for many years. He has published two books: *Chronik der Familie Ripper(t)* (*Chronicle of the Ripper(t) Family*) and *Familie Hufenbach aus Ostpreußen* (*The Hufenbach Family from East Prussia*). He writes regularly for *Hessische Genealogie,* journal of the Hessian Family History Association.

Foreword

Klaus Rippert is German; Paul Kiem is Australian. The two authors met online when, during 2023, Paul sought assistance from the Hesse Family History Association (*Hessische familiengeschichtliche Vereinigung e. V.*) with some family history research. Later that year Klaus came back with a question for Paul — could he find out anything about a person named Jakob Rippert? Klaus had just discovered Jakob, a descendant of a distant family branch, and was surprised to find that he was buried in Nuriootpa, South Australia.

Initially, it was difficult to find out much about Jakob from accessible web-based sources. Within a few weeks, however, the few clues easily found on the internet began to intrigue us. Research gathered momentum as snippets of information found in Germany and Australia were shared and began to reveal the outline of an unusual life. A breakthrough came when, around the same time, we discovered and were given generous access to two large collections held by family members, one in Australia and the other in Germany. Both collections comprised an extraordinary number of written sources, photographs and artefacts, richly documenting the lives of Jakob Rippert and his wife Charlotte.

The family collections provided much of the information for the story that follows. This information was supplemented or given context using secondary works and what turned out to be a surprising number of references found in sources located in a range of archives in Germany and Australia. These sources are acknowledged in the endnotes. The following sources were either especially important or have been referred to frequently:

Brandt Report	Karl Brandt, *Report on the Value of Secular Real Estate in Israel Owned by Former Residents of German Nationality or Extraction*, 1957, NAA: B1365, 1, (NAA).
Der Sudan Pionier	The journal of the Sudan Pionier Mission (SPM), published 1901-1928 and, as *Der Pionier*, 1929-1939.
EMO I, EMO II	Eberhard Troeger's unpublished histories of the Sudan Pionier Mission and Evangelical Middle East Ministries, c. 2024 (EMO). Eberhard Troeger was Director of EMO from 1975 to 1998.
Kahn Testimonial	Testimonial written by Albert Kahn in support of Jakob Rippert during his denazification hearings (HHStAW, Bestand 520/02, Nr. 10797).
Lebenslauf	*Entnazifizierungsakte Lebenslauf* — Jakob's account of his life submitted to a German Denazification Tribunal on 11 February 1948 (HHStAW, Bestand 520/02, Nr. 10797).
Memoir	An incomplete life story written by Jakob Rippert in 1971 (HStAD O 59 Rippert).

Acknowledgements

This history could not have been written without the support of Louise Rippert in Australia and Christiane Kessler in Germany. These two custodians of the Rippert family collections provided access to the materials that allowed us to reconstruct Jakob and Charlotte's remarkable lives. Partly as an outcome of this research project, the German collection has recently been lodged with the Hesse State Archives in Darmstadt (HStAD), where it is temporarily catalogued as 'HStAD 0 59 Rippert'. In our endnotes, the Australian family collection is referenced as RPA and the German family collection as HStAD.

Others who have been generous with their expertise or who shared material, advice or memories, include: Olga Radke, Finke River Mission Archives; Doris Frank, Temple Society Australia Archives; Bethany Pietsch, Lutheran Archives, Adelaide; George Ferguson, Tatura Irrigation and Wartime Camps Museum; Claudia Sosniak, Bensheim City Archives; Eberhard Troeger, EMO; Reinhold Strähler, EMO; Leo Glockemann; Garry Stoll; Glen Auricht; Walter and Brigitte Stoll; Herb Meinel; Anne Scherer; Ariel Hadari; Gil Gordon and Jacqui Salter. A special thank you to our German editor, Claudia Becker-Schäfer, and our English editor, Tracey Edstein.

Image Credits

Australian War Memorial (AWM): 7.13; Chris Drymalik Collection: 8.4; Finke River Mission Archives (FRM): 11.14; Fuchs family: 9.7; George Aubrey Aria: 8.1; Hessisches Haupstaatsarchiv Wiesbaden (HHStAW): 9.5; Hessisches Staatsarchiv Darmstadt (HStAD): 12.8; Lutheran Archives Australia (LAA). 8.5, 10.1, 11.9; Namatjira Legacy Trust: 11.2; National Archives of Australia (NAA): 10.6; Paul Kiem (PKI): 2.1, 2.4, 3.1, 5.1, 5.9, 5.10, 6.1, 6.5, 7.1, 7.2, 7.5, 7.6, 7.14, 7.15, 8.3, 9.4, 11.1-11.4, 11.8, 11.10, 12.1-12.3, 12.5-12.7; Rippert and Probert families (RPA): front cover, 1.1-1.4, 2.2, 2.3, 3.2, 3.3, 4.1-4.6, 5.2-5.8, 5.11-5.13, 6.4, 6.6-6.12, 7.7, 7.12, 8.2, 9.1-9.3, 9.6, 10.2-10.5, 11.5-11.7, 11.11, 11.13, 11.14, 12.4; *Sydney Morning Herald*: 7.3; Tatura Irrigation and Wartime Camps Museum (TAM): 7.8, 7.9, 7.10; Temple Society of Australia Archives (TAS): rear cover, 6.2, 6.3, 7.4, 7.11; Teologische Bibliothek der Universität Hamburg: 3.4. Every effort has been made to identify and acknowledge copyright and image sources. The authors welcome information regarding any error or oversight.

Prologue – Auerbach, January 1948

Jakob Rippert sat at the small table in front of the empty fireplace in his mother's sitting room, rubbing his hands together in a futile gesture against the cold and contemplating the papers in front of him. He had just dated — 15 January 1948 — and signed the *Meldebogen*, the questionnaire the denazification authorities had asked him to complete. What would they make of his answers? Where had he lived since the Nazis came to power in 1933? In Palestine and Australia. He'd been truthful about his party membership and done his best to explain it. He smiled at the irony of struggling to remain *Reichstrue* during all the years behind barbed wired in Australia when, no sooner did he set foot in the ruins of the Reich, than he was being asked to explain his loyalty. It didn't matter that an Australian judge had already declared the obvious, that he and Charlotte were 'harmless'. The interrogations had begun all over again.

Outside, the temperature had scarcely risen above freezing in the middle of the day. Inside his mother's home it was hardly much warmer. No coal had arrived this week and the small amount of wood they had collected was being saved for cooking the evening meal. Jakob could remember the harsh winter of 1916-1917, just before he had been conscripted, when they had survived on turnips, but he had become used to milder winters during his many years away from Germany. The neighbours might insist that this year's *Eiswinter* was not as severe as 1946-1947, but Jakob could only compare it with the cold in his first few weeks at the Tatura camp in 1941. There was no comparison. Food and heating made all the difference. In Australia they had never been hungry and, Jakob had ensured, there was always plenty of firewood. Now, in Germany, they had to stretch out the meagre amounts allocated on their ration cards and await the uncertain arrival of coal.

Fortunately, missionary friends from New Guinea had given them a generous gift of coffee beans when they were leaving Australia. At the time, they had no idea of their value. Now, only two weeks since their return, Charlotte had already exchanged some of the precious beans for potatoes. Jakob's mother had marvelled that they had had something of value to barter in the black-market. She would marvel again when friends in Australia responded to Charlotte's appeals to send food parcels.

It had been a grim homecoming. The long journey through devastated city wastelands, so many grieving families, the homeless and displaced wandering everywhere, the struggle for the most basic food items, terrible stories from the Russian zone and, impossible to keep in the background, the even more terrible stories about what Germans had done in the camps and occupied territories.

At least there had been the initial elation of their small family being reunited at long last. Even so, it was an awkward reunion. It was difficult to know what their son Reinhart had endured and not always easy to know what to say to him. The boy, the young man that he was now, seemed reluctant to talk about the past ten years. Jakob and Charlotte had been tested with their own difficulties in Palestine and Australia, but what about their only son, living alone with his grandmother after Jakob's father had been called home in 1940? The Red Cross messages they were allowed to exchange during the war had revealed very little about their son's life. Mercifully, Auerbach had been spared the devastation of Allied bombing and Reiny had been too young to be conscripted and sent off to the front, as Jakob had been in 1917. But Reiny had been forced to join the Hitler Youth. This was the only reason, surely, for the notice summoning him to Bensheim back in 1946 to be interviewed by the American intelligence soldier, Sergeant Kissinger. But why interrogate a child about what he had been forced to do? Strange enough that Jakob was being interrogated about Nazism when he had been nowhere near Germany for the past twenty years.

Reiny was reticent with his parents about his life under the Nazis. He was also determined. Determined to master English, dedicated to completing his schooling and asking about the opportunities for pursuing a medical career in Australia. The commitment to education was all that parents could wish for and the ambition to become a doctor, a missionary doctor, was a special joy for his mother. Still, Jakob struggled to reconcile the reticence and determination of the grown Reinhart with the always smiling boy he remembered from their happy years in Palestine. The memory and the lost decade since then ached far deeper than the bitter cold of his ruined homeland.

These thoughts needed to be put behind. Completing the *Meldebogen* and writing the *Lebenslauf*, the account of his life he was also required to submit, had brought on an introspection that Jakob feared was becoming self-indulgent. Surveying his life as he had recorded it in his *Lebenslauf*, he was conscious of the many rich and interesting experiences he had been privileged to share with Charlotte. Even though, as missionaries, their lives had been dedicated to witnessing to God's great goodness and working for others, they had both enjoyed practising their profession and being part of close communities in places as diverse as Nubia and Palestine. Even while incarcerated in Australia, there had been a sense of achievement in contributing to maintaining a strong and healthy German community. God had also tested them. There was the separation from Reinhart, the years behind barbed wire and the long torment of not knowing what was happening with their beautiful farm in Palestine. And yet, ever since his miraculous survival on the Western Front in 1918, God had also provided the strength and protection to see through adversity. Inspired with this confidence, Jakob resolved to look to the future rather than dwell on disappointments and current hardships.

This future, Jakob felt sure, would not be in Germany. In the short term, he would look for work, perhaps up in the British zone where the Schnellers had their German headquarters. Already, however, he and Charlotte had begun making inquiries about returning to either the Middle East or Australia. Grim as it was, the economic situation in Germany had little to do with this decision. Rather, for both, it was a desire to return to the mission field of their youthful endeavours. Regardless of the state it was in, the old homeland had never had any hold over them once they had dedicated themselves to a missionary calling.

Auerbach, January 1948

In the meantime, Jakob returned to the task in front of him. He looked at the papers on the table and gathered them into neat piles. The last pile consisted of testimonials he had been asked to give to the denazification people. *Persilscheine* — whitewashing Persil certificates — the local people were calling these testimonials. Jakob didn't think of the seven testimonials he had collected in this cynical way. They were, he was proud to think, genuine attestations to his Christianity and good character. And they came from a variety of people: the Director of the Sudan Pionier Mission, two Australian soldiers, two pastors, even a Catholic priest. He was now planning to get one more.

That morning his mother had told him she had heard from the village women that Albert and Marie Clara Kahn had recently returned to Auerbach. At a time when so much news was about lost friends and shattered families, this was exciting. Albert and Marie Clara had fled Germany in 1933 after the Nazis came to power. When they arrived in Palestine with their son Harry, Jakob and Charlotte had given them refuge on their farm. The last time Jakob had seen Albert was in 1939, when the family was comfortably settled in Haifa. Before the Nazis came to power, the Kahns had been part of Auerbach's small Jewish population. By the end of the Nazi era there were no Jews left in Auerbach. Now the Kahns had returned to the village. Jakob's mood brightened as he looked forward to catching up with his old friends and sharing experiences of the last decade. They might even have news of the farm. He was also going to ask Albert to write the last of his testimonials. It would certainly not be a *Persilscheine*. Rather, Jakob was confident, it would give the denazification people all the answers they needed.

Jakob and Charlotte Rippert: Nubia to Nuriootpa

Chapter 1
Jakob Rippert

Jakob Rippert was born on 29 May 1899 in Auerbach, a village in the Bergstraße district in the south of the modern German state of Hesse. In 1899 Auerbach had a population of around 2000. In 1939 it was incorporated into adjoining Bensheim to form the largest town in the Bergstraße between the cities of Darmstadt in the north and Heidelberg in the south.

> **Jakob Rippert's Ancestral Line: 1695 – 1975**
>
> 1. **Johann Conrad Rippert**
>   Protestant, carpenter in Hochstädten,
>   b. 1695 Unter-Ostern, d. 1729 Auerbach
>   m. 1721 Auerbach, **Anna Barbara Müller**
>
> 2. **Sebastian Rippert**
>   Protestant, Beisass, master linen weaver,
>   b. 1728 Hochstädten, d. 1791 Hochstädten
>   m. 1753 Auerbach, **Anna Julian Wilch**
>
> 3. **Johann Christian Rippert**
>   Protestant, master tailor,
>   b. 1769 Hochstädten, d. 1851 Auerbach
>   m. 1794 Auerbach,
>   **Catharina Elisabetha Meinhardt**
>
> 4. **Johann Philipp Rippert**
>   Protestant, factory worker,
>   b. 1811 Auerbach, d. 1878 Auerbach
>   m. 1837 Auerbach, **Susanna Dorothea Krämer**
>
> 5. **Johannes Rippert**
>   Protestant, factory worker, 1884 well master,
>   b. 1842 Auerbach, d. 1889 Auerbach
>   m. 1868 Auerbach, **Sybille Katharina Kraemer**
>
> 6. **Johann Philipp Rippert**
>   Protestant, factory worker, carpenter,
>   b. 1872 Auerbach, d. 1940 Auerbach
>   m. 1898 Auerbach, **Eva Mohr**
>
> 7. **Jakob Rippert**
>   Protestant, carpenter, builder, missionary
>   b. 1899 Auerbach, d. 1975 Nuriootpa, Australia
>   m. 1927 Cairo, **Adelheid Augusta Charlotta Wolter**

Jakob was the eldest child of Johann Philipp (1872-1940) and Eva Rippert (1874-1957, nee Mohr). The family was Protestant and Johann Philipp was a factory worker and carpenter. At the beginning of the twentieth century, Ripperts had been living in the area between Bensheim and Darmstadt for almost two hundred years. Earlier, about 1520, family members had migrated, probably from Switzerland or southern France, to the district around Erbach in southern Hesse. From here they quickly spread.[1] The first Rippert to arrive in the Bensheim area was Johann Conrad Rippert, who moved from Unter-Ostern to Auerbach in 1724.

Johann Conrad Rippert married Anna Barbara Müller on 9 January 1721 in Auerbach. He worked as a carpenter in nearby Hochstädten until his death in 1729. All Ripperts in the area around Auerbach can be traced back to him. Jakob Rippert was a seventh-generation descendant. All of Jakob's forebears were Protestant and the men were either factory workers or tradesmen. Some were carpenters, the vocation Jakob pursued after leaving school.

Jakob Rippert had three siblings, Susanna Elisabetha Margaretha (1902-1922), Wilhelm (1905-1984) and Ludwig Immanuel (1914-1941). Little is known about Susanna, who died of illness when she was twenty. Even though

2   Jakob and Charlotte Rippert: Nubia to Nuriootpa

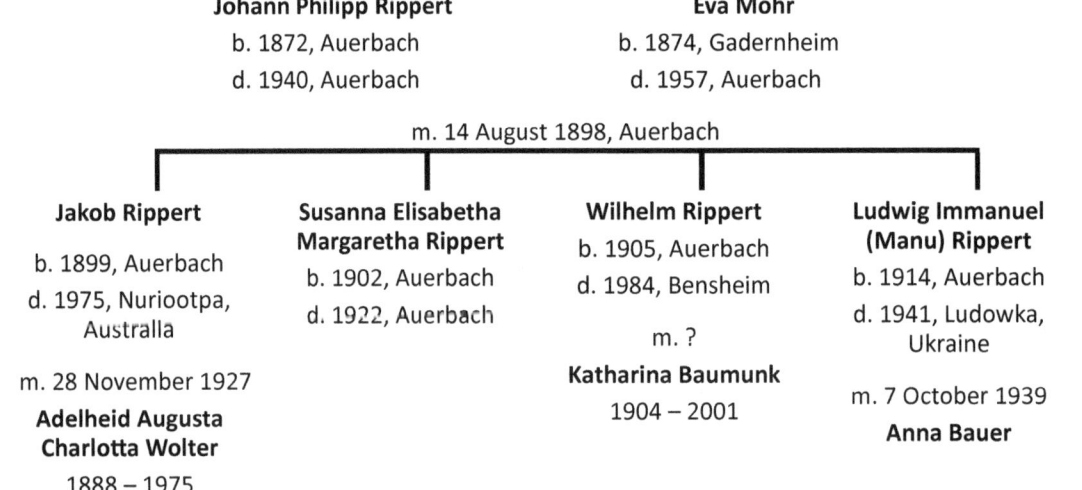

1.1 The Rippert family, c. 1915: Jakob at rear, Johann, Wilhelm, Susanna and Eva in the middle, and Ludwig Immanuel at front (RPA)

Johann Philipp Rippert
b. 1872, Auerbach
d. 1940, Auerbach

Eva Mohr
b. 1874, Gadernheim
d. 1957, Auerbach

m. 14 August 1898, Auerbach

Jakob Rippert	**Susanna Elisabetha Margaretha Rippert**	**Wilhelm Rippert**	**Ludwig Immanuel (Manu) Rippert**
b. 1899, Auerbach	b. 1902, Auerbach	b. 1905, Auerbach	b. 1914, Auerbach
d. 1975, Nuriootpa, Australia	d. 1922, Auerbach	d. 1984, Bensheim	d. 1941, Ludowka, Ukraine
m. 28 November 1927		m. ?	m. 7 October 1939
Adelheid Augusta Charlotta Wolter		**Katharina Baumunk**	**Anna Bauer**
1888 – 1975		1904 – 2001	

Table 1.1 The Rippert Family

they lived apart for most of their lives, Jakob and Wilhelm were close and, particularly in later life, kept in contact. Their detailed letters, preserved by Wilhelm, have been valuable sources for our research. Jakob was also close to Ludwig Immanuel, known as Manu, before the young man was killed on the Eastern Front during the Second World War.

Jakob attended Schlossberg elementary school, a new school built in 1911 in response to the growing population and economic development of Auerbach-Bensheim. From 1914 to 1917 he trained as a carpenter and passed his journeyman's examination before his education was interrupted by service in the First World War.

1.2 Evangelische Bergkirche, Auerbach, c. 1900 (RPA)

1.3 Jakob Rippert at left rear with his Bensheim Vocational School class, c. 1921 (RPA)

From spring 1919 to April 1921, Jakob worked as a journeyman carpenter while attending part time classes at Bensheim's Vocational School (*Gewerbeschule Bensheim*). Trade training had been established at Bensheim in the 1840s in recognition of the need for 'further and thorough instruction in the subjects necessary for the insightful operation of trade and commerce, which seems all the more urgent for Bensheim as almost a third of all residents are merchants and tradesmen'.[2] By the twentieth century, a strong tradition of vocational training had developed and Bensheim's popular vocational school offered courses ranging from technical drawing to painting to materials science.

Jakob specialised in building, structural and civil engineering. By the time he passed his final examination in April 1921, with a '*Sehr gut*' (very good), he had benefited from a sound technical education.[3] This provided a strong foundation for much of his life's work. Moreover, a commitment to technical education and skilled tradesmanship was one of two strong influences that were to shape Jakob's life. The other was his Christian faith.

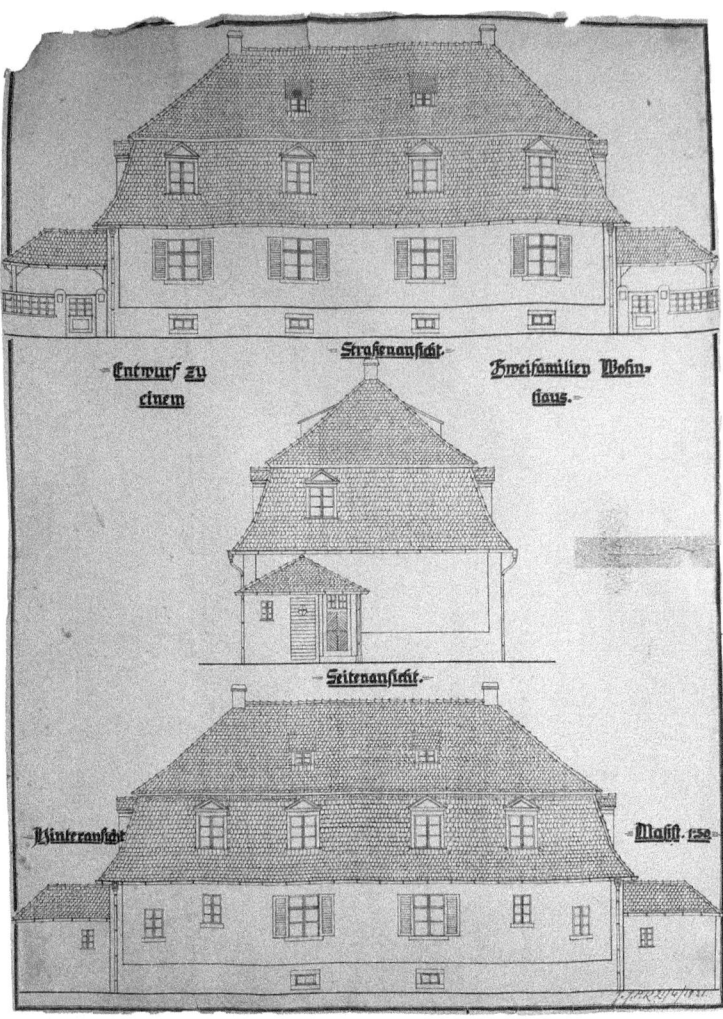

1.4 A technical drawing Jakob completed while he was a student in 1921. There is a similarity between these plans and an existing building he would construct at Cologne in the 1940s. (RPA)

Endnotes

1. See also Klaus Rippert, *Chronik der Familie Ripper(t)*, Gendi Verlag, Otzberg, 2022.
2. Peter Knapp, *1200 Jahre Bensheim*, Bensheim an d. Bergstr.: Magistrat, 1966.
3. Jakob Rippert, *Lebenslauf*, 1948, HHStAW, Bestand 520/02, Nr. 10797.

Chapter 2
The First World War, 1914 – 1918

More than a century after its conclusion, historians continue to debate the causes of the First World War. The event that sparked the outbreak of war in August 1914 was the assassination of Austrian Archduke Franz Ferdinand in Sarajevo on 28 June 1914. In the weeks that followed, the statesmen of Europe proved incapable of stopping the spiral into hostilities as the Austro-Hungarian Empire moved to retaliate against Serbia for the assassination, Russia came to the defence of Serbia, Germany came to the aid of its Austro-Hungarian ally and, finally, France and Britain were drawn into the conflict on the side of their Russian ally.

The background to this was decades of tension as the traditional European great powers, notably France and Britain, struggled to come to the terms with the emergence of Germany as an economic and military power. Each nation responded to the perceived threat to the balance of power by building up its armed forces and establishing a system of opposing alliances. By 1914, on one side was the Triple Alliance or Central Powers, consisting of Germany, Austria-Hungary and Italy; on the other side was the Triple Entente or Allies, consisting of Britain, France and Russia. It was the operation of these alliances, as each power came to the assistance of its ally, that helped to turn the diplomatic crisis sparked by Archduke Franz Ferdinand's assassination into a European war.

After the war broke out, the Ottoman Empire and Bulgaria entered the conflict on the side of Germany and Austria-Hungary. Italy, which had failed to enter the war as a member of the Triple Alliance 1914, joined the Allies in 1915. Britain and France were supported by their global empires and in 1917 the United States entered the war on the Allied side. Not only were nations and individuals from outside Europe drawn into the war, but fighting took place in German colonial possessions in Africa and the Pacific and there were naval clashes between Allied and German ships in oceans around the world. Hence, the war became known as the First World War. Nevertheless, while there was fighting in different locations and several important theatres of conflict, including the Middle East, the main fighting took place in Europe and the outcome of the war was decided on the two major fronts, the Eastern Front between Germany and Russia and the Western Front between Germany and France.

On the Western Front, Germany had been unable to gain a quick victory over French and British forces in 1914. Instead, fighting became bogged down in a stalemate as each side dug into a line of trenches all along the front. Artillery bombardments and futile infantry assaults on these trenches resulted in enormous loss of life but neither side managed to gain a meaningful breakthrough before 1918. On the Eastern Front, the Germans won early victories but there was no complete victory over the Russians until after the Bolshevik (Communist) Revolution in late 1917. Under the strain of war, the Russian home front had collapsed and Bolsheviks took advantage of the situation to stage a successful revolution in November 1917. Once in power, the Bolsheviks were focused on the consolidation of their revolution rather than a continuation of war with Germany and in March 1918, in the Treaty of Brest Litovsk, Russia agreed to German terms for surrender.

In April 1917, the United States had entered the war on the Allied side. Still, it would take time before American troops could be trained and transported to Europe. This gave Germany an opportunity to win the war before American entry could have an impact. With Russia out of the war, German troops could be transferred from the Eastern Front. Bolstered by the arrival of these reinforcements, at the end of March 1918 German commanders launched a massive offensive on the Western Front, the *Kaiserschlacht* (Emperor's Battle or Spring Offensive). Initially, the Allies were taken by surprise, German armies achieved a breakthrough and, for a time, Paris was threatened. However, not only did the Allies recover, but the German advance had come at an enormous cost in casualties and, despite the reinforcements transferred from the Eastern Front, Germany no longer had the manpower to replace these losses. By mid-1918, on the other hand, American troops were reinforcing the Allied armies. On 15 July 1918, Germany's final assault of the *Kaiserschlacht* was launched, beginning the Second Battle of the Marne.

When the First World War began in August 1914 Jakob Rippert was a fifteen-year-old boy. At this time, many of those going off to war were confident of a quick victory and there was talk of being

2.1 Douaumont Ossuary on the former Western Front in France. A monument to the futility of the First World War, it contains the remains of 130,000 unidentified German and French soldiers who were among the 300,000 killed in the Battle of Verdun in 1916. (PKI)

home by Christmas. Instead of a quick victory, there was a long war of attrition which consumed thousands of lives every day. All the major powers needed to reinforce their armies and each year a new cohort of young men was conscripted and sent to the battle fronts. Jakob's turn came when he was conscripted into the German Army in September 1917. He served, with the rank of *Soldat* or Private, until the war ended in November 1918.[1]

Despite writing extensively about most aspects of his life, Jakob recorded very little about his time in the army until decades after the war. We have only been able to access a few documents from 1918 to shed some light on his experience of the First World War: a letter Jakob wrote to his family from the Eastern Front, two annotated photos he kept and his name on an army casualty list.

In the letter Jakob wrote from the Eastern Front on 1 February 1918, he revealed he had suffered a leg wound which was exacerbated while recuperating:

> … now I've been ordered by the battalion to build shooting ranges. I was cutting wood for 4 days and a beam slipped and hit my shin where my wound is. It's thick and festering, I had to have it bandaged.

In the same letter, we get an impression of Jakob's response to the experience of war, along with the reassurance he found in his Christian faith. This response is consistent with how he would deal with hardship and challenges throughout his life:

> But as he leads me, so will I go. His ways are often incomprehensible to us, but whatever he puts in our path is meant to serve us all. We often think that it should be the way we think it should be, but he always puts a spoke in our wheel and that is good… My heart is often heavy when there is no one to talk to. But I always have someone with me who stands by me in everything.[2]

The first of Jakob's photos relating to the First World War shows German troops standing around a troop transport train at an unknown railway station. A barely legible note on the back tells us that the train is transferring troops from Russia to France, with the journey taking place from 19-23 April, 1918. The note on the back is marked 'Schütze Rippert'. A second photo shows Jakob as a young soldier in uniform. A note on the back tells us this photo was taken in 1918 at Auerbach after Jakob had been wounded and given home leave.[3] In September 1918 Jakob's name appeared on a German Army casualty list, where he was described as 'lightly wounded'.[4] This second wounding was more serious than the official casualty list suggests.

From these few traces, we learn that Jakob served on both the Eastern and Western Fronts, that he was wounded twice and that he was among the German troops transferred from the Eastern Front to the Western Front in early 1918. From a letter written near the end of his life, we learn that on the Western Front Jakob participated in one of the decisive battles of the war and experienced the horrors endured during artillery bombardments and infantry attacks. Prompted by illness, which Jakob attributed partly to his wartime injuries, this letter was written in 1971 and sent from Australia to family in Germany.

In what may be the only time he wrote about his war service in any detail, he gave this account of a terrifying incident that took place during the Second Battle of the Marne:

> My right parietal bone was damaged in 1918 during the second offensive near Fismes. When I was in Koblenz and Mother came to visit me, I was pretty bruised up in the military hospital back then. My right shin was torn open, my back was bruised, I was gas-blind and my head was twisted so that Mother didn't recognize me and walked past my bed first. Anyway, it was God's mercy that I got out of the bunker. We were on the run. The black French were behind us. Our main troops had already withdrawn, and we were positioned with a few heavy machine guns on the Roman road to the right of Reims. That was when the retreat began. We had to run after preparing our machine guns for detonation. In a valley, a burning aircraft crashed in front of us. Two of my comrades ran into an old French bunker, and I followed them. Just as I entered, a shell struck above the bunker, causing the entire entrance to collapse over me. I lost consciousness. My comrades, who had been standing

2.2 Jakob on home leave in Auerbach (RPA)

2.3 Jakob's photo of soldiers at an unknown location while being transferred from Russia to the Western Front in April 1918 (RPA)

deeper inside, remained unharmed and dug me out. They took me to the first-aid station nearby, which was also in the process of being dismantled. That's how I managed to survive — because my comrades, standing lower on the bunker stairs, had to clear the collapsed entrance to get out, and in doing so, they had to dig me out as well.

My confirmation verse has proven true so often in my life — Psalm 91, verses 11 and 12. Time and again, our faithful heavenly Father has shown mercy upon me and allowed me to recover. This time, in early May, I was convinced that the Lord was calling me home, and I had fully resigned myself to that fate.[5]

The Bible verses Jakob referred to are:

> For he will give his angels charge of you
>   to guard you in all your ways.
> On their hands they will bear you up,
>   lest you dash your foot against a stone.

Written fifty years after the events described, Jakob's reference to his Christian faith echoes what he told his parents in the letter written from the Eastern Front in February 1918: 'I always have someone with me who stands by me in everything.' Both the submission to God's will and the confidence that he was in God's care were constants in Jakob's outlook throughout his life. His confirmation verse was always a guide and reassurance.

The Second Battle of the Marne took place between 15 July and 6 August 1918. It began when the Germans launched the *Freidensturm* (Peace Offensive), an attack on Allied lines across the Marne River between Reims and Soissons. The last major effort of the *Kaiserschlacht*, this attack was a final bid to achieve a breakthrough and force the Allies to agree to a peace on German terms. In the event, while the Germans made initial territorial gains and established bridgeheads on the opposite bank of the Marne, they suffered heavy casualties and the German onslaught soon flagged. Just three days after the start of the attack, the Allies, led by the French, began a long-prepared counter-attack. This Allied counter-attack caught German forces unprepared, forcing them back several kilometres. By 21 July the Germans had been ordered to retreat from the Marne and were pursued by the Allies.[6]

As with all major battles on the Western Front, the Second Battle of the Marne resulted in hundreds of thousands of casualties. For the French and their allies, at least there was the motivation of moving forward and sensing victory. For the Germans, overwhelmed, retreating and sensing not just defeat in the battle but the collapse of any prospect of winning the war, there was a loss of morale. The desperation is captured in Gunner Officer Herbert Sulzbach's account of 21 July:

> The word 'hell' expresses something tender and peaceful compared with what is starting here now… [You] can hardly keep going in this massed [French artillery] fire, you can hardly see anything because of the smoke and you have to keep throwing yourself flat on the ground and cannot understand each time why you have not been hit… The French have grown hugely in strength, energy and morale … Our division on the right flank has had to give ground … The telephone

hardly ever works, as the lines keep getting shot through. We receive a few messages by lamp signals too… [Our latest] order reads: 'The Army's situation requires every foot of ground to be contested. We must put up a tough defence, regardless of the consequences, until reinforcements arrive.'

Never have such demands been made of our men's strength of character, morale, and physical endurance as have been made in the last few days; brought in over long distances in forced marches, in hot weather and without rest, and after the failure of their own offensive on which they embarked with great expectations; now thrown into a defensive battle of gigantic scale; they do their duty, they fight and they keep going.[7]

In their different accounts of the Second Battle of the Marne, Herbert Sulzbach and Jakob Rippert were describing events at close to the same time and location. On the date of Sulzbach's account, 21 July, the Germans had been pushed back to the French town of Fismes, on the right of Reims in the German lines. At this time, some German units were in retreat while others were being asked to hold rearguard positions. France's Moroccan Division, consisting of Moroccan troops and Senegalese reinforcements, played a major role in the French offensive. The Senegalese were the 'black French' pursuing Jakob and

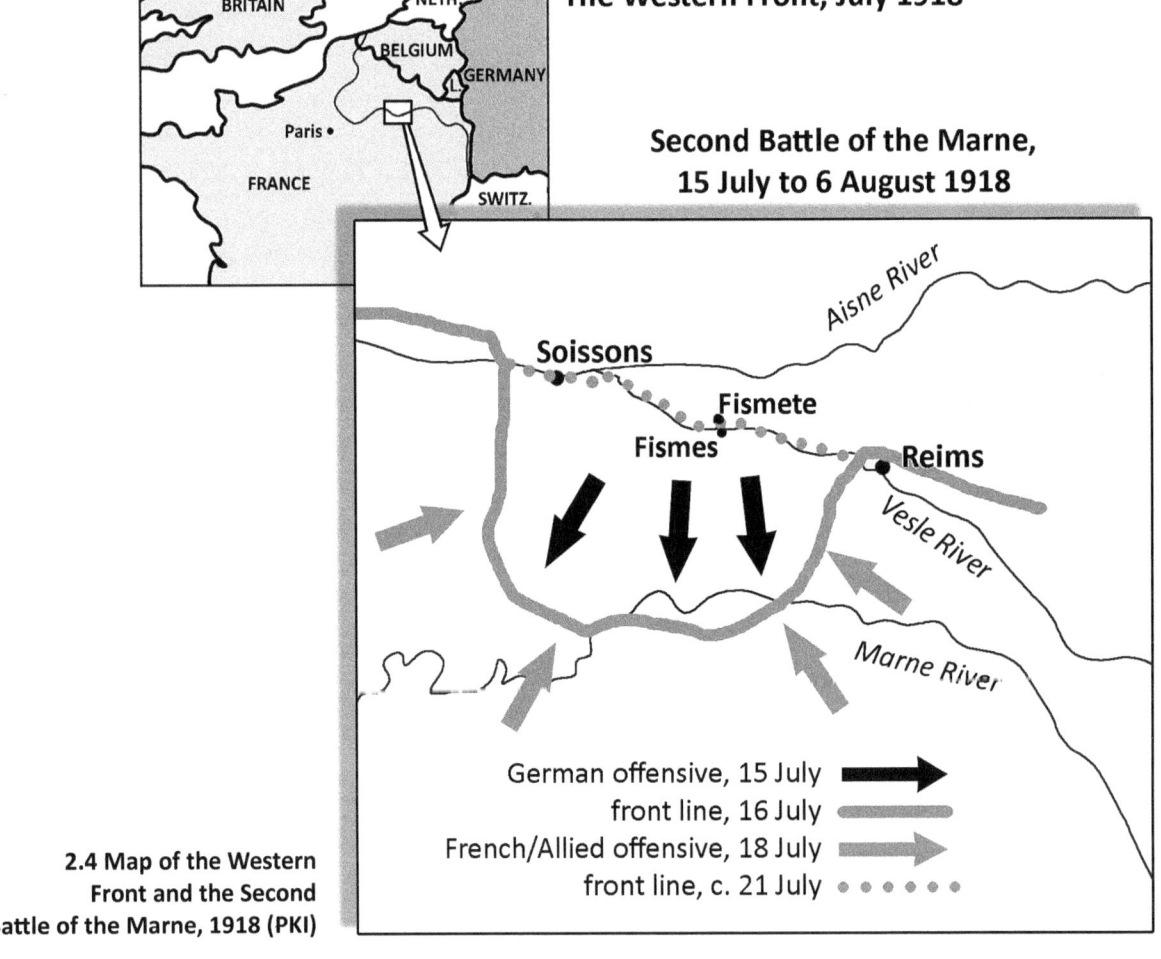

2.4 Map of the Western Front and the Second Battle of the Marne, 1918 (PKI)

his comrades at Fismes.[8] By this time, Jakob had endured the experiences described by Sulzbach — being brought up to the front in a long forced march and participating in the failed German offensive — and was now caught in the chaos of retreat. Unlike Sulzbach, Jakob was not lucky enough to avoid the French bombardment and, if not for the actions of his comrades, would have shared the fate of tens of thousands of soldiers on the Western Front in being buried alive. Fortunately, he was rescued and taken to hospital, but the injuries he sustained were serious and, we will see, caused recurring health issues throughout his life. At the time, he was only nineteen.

German defeat in the Second Battle of the Marne marked a turning point on the Western Front. It was quickly followed by another Allied victory in the Battle of Amiens in August 1918. With the German Army now on the verge of exhaustion and unable to supply reinforcements, the Allies launched their own major counter-offensive, which forced the Germans into retreat all along the Western Front. Hostilities came to an end when Germany agreed to an Armistice on 11 November 1918.

The devastation and loss of life resulting from the First World War had a profound effect on all the nations involved. Germans also had to deal with defeat and the imposition of a peace settlement requiring Germany to accept responsibility for having started the war. According to historian Gerd Krumeich, this meant Germans were denied the comfort of reassuring themselves that the sacrifices of the war had been in a noble cause. The deaths of nearly two million German soldiers and maiming of millions seemed meaningless. Unlike the populations of the victorious nations, Germans were not able to feel pride in their fallen heroes or undergo a process of collective healing through commemoration. As a consequence, many Germans remained embittered and angry. This anger manifested itself in the political and social divisions of the 1920s and, exacerbated by economic hardship, was one of the major reasons Adolf Hitler and his Nazi Party came to power in 1933. Hitler then set Germany on the pathway to an even greater tragedy.[9]

As a *frontsoldat*, front line soldier, Jakob Rippert experienced the worst of the brutality and seemingly worthless sacrifice of the First World War. He narrowly escaped being buried alive but sustained serious injuries. However, he did not react with anger, desperation or despair. Unlike many brutalised *frontsoldaten*, Jakob was not drawn towards extreme nationalist or militarist groups. He was not among the millions of Germans who reacted to the futility of the war by embracing hedonism, nihilism or political extremism. Instead, the experience of the First World War reinforced his Christian faith. Rather than responding with anger or cynicism, he developed an even deeper faith and a commitment to making a positive contribution to humanity.

The way in which his Christian faith expressed itself ensured Jakob would lead an eventful life that seems unconventional when compared with typical Germans from his class and era. Open to new experiences, he would live most of his life outside Germany and was always curious and eager to learn about other cultures. At the same time, he remained socially conservative and, while never overtly expressing political views, is likely to have retained a degree of nostalgia for the strength and apparent stability of the Germany of his youth — Kaiser Wilhelm II's German Empire. As a *frontsoldat*, Jakob had formed strong bonds with comrades who believed they were fighting in defence of their fatherland.

Even though this experience had not pushed Jakob in the direction of extreme nationalism, he remained a patriotic German war veteran. And although he would live most of his life outside Germany and eschew any obvious interest in politics, he retained an emotional and practical interest in seeing a strong Germany, restored to its position as a respected world power. Thus, while Jakob emerged from the First World War with a healthy moral resilience and largely avoided the impact of its aftermath in Germany's troubled inter-war years, his life would not be unaffected by the war and its consequences.

Endnotes

1. Jakob Rippert, *Lebenslauf*, 1948. According to his own recollection, Jakob was conscripted some months after his eighteenth birthday. At the time, sources suggest, Germany had reduced the conscription age to seventeen.
2. Letter, Jakob Rippert, in Russia, to his family in Auerbach, Germany, 1 February, 1918, RPA.
3. Photos from Jakob and Charlotte Rippert's collection, RPA. On the back of the photo of the train from Russia, '1917' has been written over an original illegible year date. The correct year date, given Jakob's period of service, is assumed to be 1918.
4. Prussian Casualties, list 1252, side 26533, page 26546, 26 September 1918: https://wiki.genealogy.net/Verlustlisten_Erster_Weltkrieg/Projekt
5. Letter, Jakob Rippert in Australia to family in Germany, 31 July 1972, HStAD. Fifty years afterwards, Jakob recalled these events as happening in 'early May'. He had gone up to the front line in May, but the fighting around Fismes occurred in late July as part of the Second Battle of the Marne.
6. Ian Passingham, *The German Offensives of 1918: The Last Desperate Gamble*, Pen & Sword Military, Barnsley (UK), 2008, pp. 123-125.
7. Quoted in Passingham, pp. 125-126.
8. Michael S. Neiberg, *The Second Battle of the Marne*, Indiana University Press, Bloomington, 2008, pp. 120-121, 130-132.
9. Gerd Krumeich, 'Der Erste Weltkrieg', in *Der Erste Weltkrieg in 100 Objekten*, Deutsches Historisches Museum, Berlin, 2014. p. 19.

Chapter 3
Sudan Pionier Mission (SPM)

In common with other European countries at the time, the missionary movement was strong in German states and the German Empire in the nineteenth and early twentieth centuries. By 1900 there were numerous missionary societies in Germany supporting the work of dedicated missionaries in locations throughout the world. The movement was driven by a mix of religious zeal and humanitarian ideals. The primary goal was evangelism, the winning of converts to Christianity, but missionaries also sought to improve the material welfare of those they worked with through education, provision of health care and assistance with infrastructure. Enabled by European imperialism and operating in European colonies or spheres of influence, missionaries were imbued with notions of European superiority and saw their role as not just saving heathen souls but sharing the benefits of European civilisation with the backward peoples of the world. Regardless of their primary motivation and sense of racial and cultural superiority, individual missionaries were often highly trained, in languages or a range of technical skills, had a genuine regard for the well-being of those they devoted their lives to and formed relationships that allowed for cultural interchange.

The Sudan Pionier Mission (SPM) was founded in 1900 by a diverse group consisting of the influential Irish evangelist Dr Henry Grattan Guinness (1835-1910), his daughter Lucy Guinness (1865-1906), the German Hermann Karl Wilhelm Kumm (1874-1930), Samuel Ali Hussein (1860-1927), a Nubian Christian, and the German pastors Julius Dammann (1840-1908) and Theodor Ziemendorff (1837-1912). Kumm was passionately committed to emulating the missionary zeal of St Paul in preaching the gospel where no one had yet preached it. Kumm, Henry Guinness and Lucy Guinness were the inspirational figures who established the SPM when they came together at Aswan, Egypt, in January 1900. Although based on earlier discussions about the need for a mission to reach the people of remote central Africa, Henry Guinness has described the SPM's foundation as almost spontaneous:

> …we met at Assuan [Aswan], seven hundred miles up the Nile. Dr. Kumm coming in from an evangelistic tour among the Arabs of the Sahara to visit us there. During our stay at Assuan the conditions of the Bishareen [Bishari nomads] of the neighbouring desert, and of the Nubians, whose country begins at the first cataract and stretches five hundred miles up the Nile, attracted our attention. Dr. Kumm collected from the Bishareen a vocabulary of the principal words in their language, and I secured the services of a Christian Copt to teach in a school, and of Ali Hissein [Hussein], a Nubian, who had trained in our College to evangelize Nubians. We gathered a number of the wild Bishareen into a building we hired for a school, and began a work which subsequently grew into the Sudan Mission.[1]

Guinness referred to the first cataract, a stretch of low water or rapids on the Nile River south of Aswan. It would soon be the site of the Aswan Low Dam. He also mentioned the early recruitment of Samuel Ali Hussein (Ali Hissein), who would become a revered figure within the SPM. Guinness went on to record a significant family event coinciding with the SPM's foundation:

> It was on this occasion that I gave my consent to my daughter's marriage with Dr. Kumm. As a token of their consent their hands were joined above the clasped hands of two of the Bishareen, on January 11th, 1900. They were married on February 3rd, at Cairo... From this time onward to her death Lucy gave herself heart and soul to the evangelization of the Sudan ...[2]

During the remainder of 1900, Guinness and the newly married Kumms spent months travelling about Germany enlisting support for their new mission. Initially, their most enthusiastic supporter was Pastor Julius Dammann and a first SPM office was set up where he was based in Eisenach. By 1902 the SPM's headquarters had been relocated to Wiesbaden, where Pastor Theodor Ziemendorff became the organisation's chair and played an important part in promoting the mission, attracting donations and inspiring young people to train for a missionary role with the SPM. One method used to spread the news about the mission's work was the formation of support groups, Helper Unions or Circles of Friends, at centres throughout Germany.[3] One of the most active of these groups was located at Halle where, we will see, it may have influenced a young Charlotte Wolter to devote her life to missionary work.

The SPM was part of a later wave of 'faith based' German missions which were inter-denominational, rather than tied to a church institution, and focused on bringing the message of the Christian gospel to previously 'unreachable' non-Christians in the most remote locations. As its name implies, the SPM was formed with the goal of Christianising the people of Sudan, a term then applied to a large area of central Africa south of Egypt. Sudan could be reached, it was envisaged, by travelling up the Nile River, using recently established steamer and rail routes, from a base in southern Egypt at Aswan. This original plan was never realised. The SPM's missionaries were unable to extend their operations beyond Nubian villages to the south of Aswan in Upper Egypt. The SPM has undergone a number of name changes and today its successor organisation is the *Evangeliumsgemeinschaft Mittlerer Osten* (EMO — Evangelical Middle East Ministries). It continues to operate in Egypt and the Middle East. In 2025 the

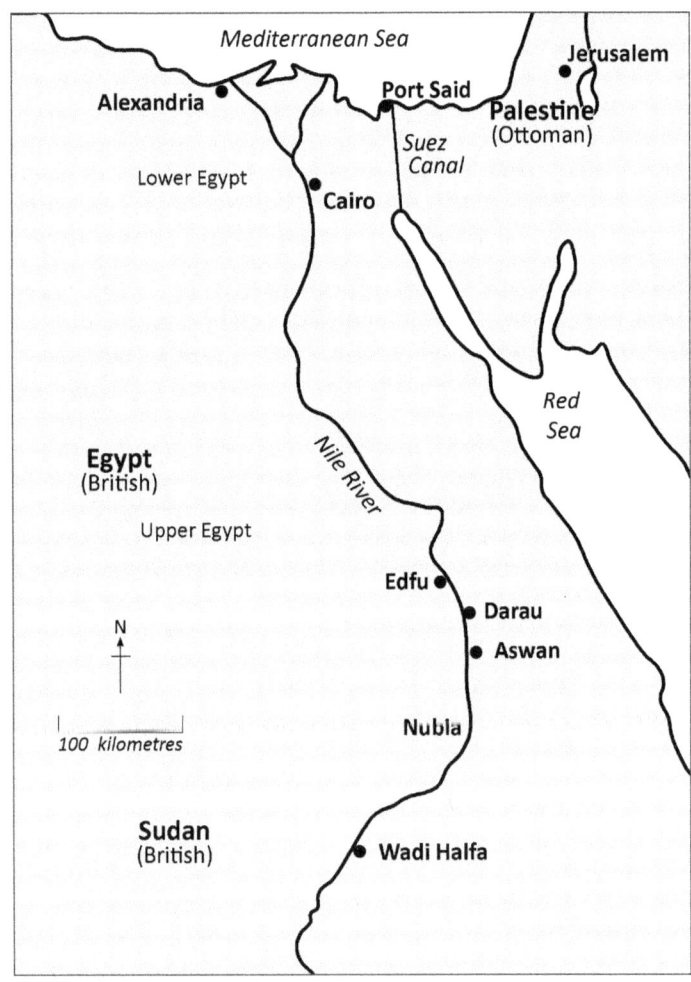

3.1 Egypt c. 1900 (PKI)

EMO published a book celebrating 125 years since the foundation of the Sudan Pionier Mission: *Nach dem Sandsturm Klart es auf: 125 Jahre erlebte Treue Gottes Geschichte und Geschichten* ('After the sandstorm clears: 125 years of experienced faithfulness of God with history and stories').[4]

In 1921, following his graduation as a builder from the Bensheim Vocational School, Jakob Rippert applied to join the SPM. Various factors contributed to this decision. Jakob later recalled being interested in mission work as a child and being particularly attracted to the idea of working in Africa. Along with being brought up in a religious household, this was probably linked to his mother, Eva Rippert, being an early supporter of the SPM. She made handicrafts to assist with fundraising and is likely to have received literature which promoted the mission's work, such as the SPM's journal *Der Sudan Pionier*. Beyond his family, Jakob had the example of one of the SPM's missionary recruits, Pastor Edgar Schäfer (1887-1956), who came from Auerbach. After completing his missionary training and being ordained at Wiesbaden in 1912, Schäfer was sent to Egypt to work with the senior missionary Pastor Enderlin at the SPM's Darau mission station. Coincidentally, as reported in *Der Sudan Pionier*, Schäfer was sent to Egypt along with another new missionary, Charlotte Wolter, Jakob Rippert's future wife.[5]

From his application to the SPM, we have a record of the responses Jakob provided to questions about his motivations for wanting to be a missionary.[6] For example:

> Which church or community do you belong to?
> > 'The Hessian Lutheran regional church.'
>
> What Christian work have you been involved in since your conversion?
> > 'Christian association of young men.'
>
> Do you have good reason to believe that you have been used by the Lord as an instrument of conversion for the conversion of others?
> > 'I can only say that I was able to show many a young man the way to the freedom of the kingdom of God.'
>
> Why are you signing up for missionary service in Sudan?
> > 'Because I want to serve my God out of gratitude for his great goodness, which he produces in me anew every day, with my profession and strength among the Mohammedans…'
>
> Which mission field did the Lord put in your heart from the beginning?
> > 'Egypt, the working field of the Sudan Pionier Mission.'
>
> When and under what circumstances did you come to faith?
> > 'I grew up in a religious home, but only came to the right faith and conversion during the barrage of the Western Front.'
>
> What are the names of your referees?
> > 'Pastor Esslinger, Auerbach, Hesse
> > Architect Kappler, Bensheim, Hesse
> > Peters, master builder, Borsfleth, Holstein
> > Eisenhardt, head teacher at the Bensheim Vocational School'

Jakob's answers reflect the personal values and world view he remained committed to for the rest of his life. His religious faith was genuine and profound, nurtured by a religious upbringing and galvanised by his experience of fighting on the Western Front. As a young man, he was engaged with both his local church and the 'Christian association of young men', *Christlicher Verein junger Männer*, the German version of the Young Men's Christian Association (YMCA) which was founded in Berlin in 1883. The YMCA's original mission statement, the 'Paris Basis' dating from 1855, could have been formulated with the young Jakob in mind:

> The purpose of the Christian Associations of Young People is to bring together those young people who acknowledge Jesus Christ as their God and Saviour according to the Holy Scriptures, who want to be his disciples in their faith and life, and who together seek to spread the kingdom of their Master among young people.[7]

The referees Jakob nominated in his application are significant. One is his Auerbach pastor but the other three are professional referees from the building profession. This is consistent with Jakob's future role as a 'technical missionary'. His religious faith found expression in practical work. His technical expertise was fundamental to his personality and shaped the way in which he interpreted his missionary calling.

3.2 Bishari tribesmen photographed by Jakob. Bishari had been present at the foundation of the Sudan Pionier Mission in 1900. (RPA)

3.3 The Sudan Pionier Mission House in Aswan c. 1925 (RPA)

Jakob's application to become a missionary with the SPM was successful and he has left the following summary of the training period that followed:

> I received my technical training in this profession from 1921 to 1924. Among other things, I attended the missionary seminary of the Rhenish Mission in Barmen, where I had to carry out technical work alongside my studies in missionary sciences and languages, and at the same time worked as an assistant to the director of the mission's ethnological museum. At the seminary of the Sudan Mission in Wiesbaden I had to study Arabic and Islamic studies, as well as carry out technical construction work. In October 1924, I was seconded to Upper Egypt as a specialist missionary by the regional bishop in Wiesbaden.[8]

His involvement with the mission's ethnological museum was a minor role at the time but it involved an experience which was to assume greater significance when Jakob remembered it in a very different context nearly two decades later.

There is one more interesting detail in the application Jakob submitted to the SPM in 1921. At the time, he was engaged to a young woman called Anna Rothermel. Anna was born in Auerbach on 2 October 1900 to Johann Adam and Katharina Rothermel.[9] We know nothing more about Anna. It is possible the relationship came to an end due to his commitment to missionary work.

By September 1924 Jakob had completed his training and was preparing to be assigned to Egypt. At this point, his war wound flared up again and he had to spend three months undergoing treatment in Wiesbaden, where doctors and nurses covered the cost of his treatment as a contribution to the SPM. In February 1925, following a full recovery and after being farewelled from the mission's headquarters, Jakob finally set out for Egypt, travelling overland to the Italian port of Naples, from where he sailed across the Mediterranean to Port Said at the northern end of Egypt's Suez Canal.[10]

3.4 Cover of SPM's *Der Sudan Pionier*, published 1901-1928 and, as *Der Pionier*, 1929-1939 (Theologische Bibliothek der Universität Hamburg)

We have a detailed account, written by Jakob, of this journey to Egypt and his first impressions of the mission field. This was published in the SPM's *Der Sudan Pionier* during 1925. It was the first of multiple long articles Jakob contributed to the journal. Together, they now form a collection of important historical sources, providing a fascinating insight into the missionary experience in Egypt in the early twentieth century. Of course, they are written from Jakob's perspective and influenced by his Christianity and European concepts of superiority that were typical of his age and inherent in the missionary movement. Rather than being a shortcoming, these authentic features of the author's voice add to the value of the articles as historical documents. In any case, they are well written, by an author who was an astute and reflective observer. They tell us a good deal about Jakob, revealing a personality that was earnest and self-consciously Christian but also displaying humour, humanity and, notwithstanding the occasional jarring judgement, an open-mindedness which embraced the people and new experiences he encountered.

Der Sudan Pionier's readership included Jakob's superiors, colleagues and the SPM's supporters at home in Germany. No doubt he was addressing all three groups, but his writing would have had special appeal for those in Germany whose interest in the mission was vital for its funding and ongoing recruitment of new missionaries. For these readers he had the narrative skill and travel writer's eye for detail to provide stories about exotic places and missionary adventures which inspired interest and highlighted the relevance and challenges of the SPM's work.

In the first of Jakob's contributions to the *Der Sudan Pionier* (Appendix C), he recounted his travels, described his first impressions of the mission and included a long description of a dhikr, a Muslim religious exercise. His interests appear wide-ranging, but in Aswan he was primarily interested in the condition of the mission's buildings. When Jakob arrived in 1925, the SPM had only recently resumed its work after being forced to leave Egypt in 1914. For ten years, there had been no care or maintenance of facilities. As the mission's new technical expert, Jakob's immediate task was to assess the buildings and begin a program of maintenance and repairs. This gave rise to comments about the need to ensure good German workmanship and gain access to quality German tools for the work ahead. Within a short time, this would result in Jakob establishing a relationship with the German community in Palestine.

Endnotes

1. H. Grattan Guinness, *Lucy Guinness Kumm, Her Life Story*, Morgan & Scott, London, 1907, pp. 17-18; Reinhold Strähler and Joachim Paesler, *Nach dem Sandsturm Klart es auf: 125 Jahre erlebte Treue Gottes Geschichte und Geschichten*, EMO, Wiesbaden, 2025, pp. 264-269.
2. Guinness, pp. 18-19; Strähler & Paesler, pp. 269-270.
3. Christof Sauer, 'Reaching the Unreached Sudan Belt: Guinness, Kumm and the Sudan Pionier Mission', Doctor of Theology thesis, University of South Africa, 2001, pp. 159-166.
4. Evangeliumsgemeinschaft Mittlerer Osten e.V., www.emo wicsbadcn.de/index.php/de/ (25 June 2005).
5. *Der Sudan Pionier*, April 1925, p. 46, May 1925, p. 58, October 1912, p. 85, November 1912, p. 84.
6. Jakob Rippert, Personalfragebogen der SPM, Zentrale Eisenach, c. 1921, EMO.
7. YMCA History, www.ymca.int (1 July 2025).
8. Jakob Rippert, *Lebenslauf*, 1948, HHStAW, Bestand 520/02, Nr. 10797.
9. Jakob Rippert, Personalfragebogen der SPM; Ortsfamilienbuch Auerbach, Familienbericht Rothermel, Anna.
10. *Der Sudan Pionier*, February 1925, p. 24; Eberhard Troeger, 'EMO II: 1914 to 1950', unpublished history, EMO, 2024, 7.2.3 & 11.5.1.

Chapter 4
Charlotte Wolter

Jakob Rippert's future wife, Charlotte Wolter, was already an experienced missionary while he was still in training for the vocation they would share for much of their lives. Ten years older than Jakob, Adelheid Augusta Charlotta (Charlotte) Wolter was born in Leipzig in 1888, the eldest child of Karl Albert Wolter (1856-1931) and Ida Wolter (1862-1930, nee Lippold). Charlotte had a younger sister and brother, Emma Margaretha Gertrud Wolter (1889-1974) and Rudolf (1892-1918).

During her childhood the family lived at Magdeburg but later moved to Dresden, where her father was a successful businessman. Surviving photos of the family home show a grand villa at Comeniusstraße 62 in Dresden's fashionable Streisen district. Even though Karl Albert's business may have suffered when the Great Depression hit in 1929, the Wolters children were brought up in comfortable circumstances.

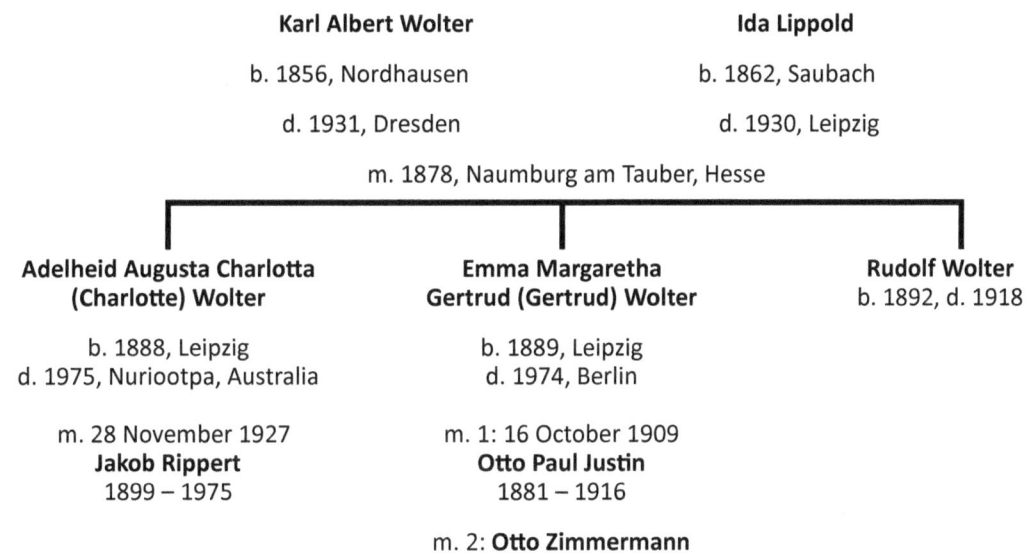

Table 4.1 Charlotte Wolter's Family

We know little about Charlotte's early life. However, it appears she became estranged from her father because of her vocational and marriage choices. On the back of a postcard depicting the Comeniusstraße villa is a handwritten note: 'Reiny's grandfather's house in Dresden. He was into importing/exporting. Didn't agree with Reiny's mother marrying his father as he was a commoner.'[1] 'Reiny' was Charlotte's son, Reinhart. The note was probably written by his wife.

We do have an unusual letter Charlotte wrote to her family in 1935:

Haifa, 6 February 1935

My dear brothers and sisters!

In view of the fact that after my death you will naturally be somewhat astonished by my small estate, the following lines are intended to enlighten you:
Dear brothers and sisters! You have long known about my inner attitude towards the earthly goods entrusted to me by God. You also know that from a young age I have never made much effort to become rich.

I have always followed my inner urge, as a single person, to think all the more of others and to alleviate their hardship, according to my own free will and discretion, where it so often confronted me. If one of my physical siblings had had to struggle with material hardship, as thousands upon thousands have, I would certainly have considered it my first duty to help the person concerned. But God has saved you from this and given you enough to get by without worrying, and that is a great mercy from Him. Surely each of you has so much understanding and heart that you recognize my actions without expressions of displeasure, and you are not angry with me because my inheritance from you is so small…

Finally, I ask you to focus more and more on that which remains eternal and to consider that our earthly life will come to an end and we must depart. Gather treasures in heaven![2]

It is not a straightforward letter. Charlotte's father, Karl Albert, had remarried prior to his death in November 1931 and his will had favoured his second wife and her children rather than Charlotte and her surviving sister, Gertrud. In 1935, when she addressed this letter to her step-siblings and Gertrud, Charlotte needed finance to fund a land purchase in Palestine. Hence, the letter was simultaneously a disavowal of her bourgeois origins and a not always subtle appeal for financial help. On this occasion the appeal to family was unsuccessful, but it would not be the last time when Charlotte's self-conscious disdain for the material world would need to be

4.1 The Wolter family in 1897: Albert, Ida, Charlotte, Gertrud and Rudolf (RPA)

Charlotte Wolter 21

4.2 The Wolter family home at Comeniusstraße 62 Dresden, c. 1920s. At times the house was shared with others. During the 1920s, for example, it was also the address of former Dresden Lord Mayor Otto Beutler (1853-1926). The house is likely to have been destroyed in the Allied bombing of Dresden in 1945. (RPA)

4.3 Charlotte in Germany c. 1912 (RPA)

4.4 Charlotte sailing to or from Egypt, c. 1914. In the background is German author Elisabeth Franke, 1886-1931. (RPA)

underwritten by charity or loans from others. Nevertheless, the values she espoused were sincere. As she wrote, 'from a young age', Charlotte turned away from earthly values and developed a deep commitment to active Christianity. This led her to reject the conventional middle-class world of her upbringing as she embraced a life of service to others as a nurse and missionary. Along with considerable hardship, this was to guarantee her not only a spiritually rewarding life but adventure and diverse experiences.

In 1905 Charlotte was enrolled in a teacher training course in Halle. Coincidentally, it was in this city that the Sudan Pionier Mission (SPM) had one of its active Friends Circles. In a further coincidence, like Jakob Rippert's mother, Charlotte's mother was involved with the SPM and is likely to have influenced her daughter to consider a missionary vocation. At some stage Ida Wolter appears to have separated from her husband, dedicated herself to Christianity rather than capitalism and become one of the SPM's most ardent supporters. When she died in 1930 her death was reported in the SPM's journal, where she was described as a 'faithful praying woman' who, even in old age, made a vital contribution to the mission's work by distributing literature and raising funds.[3]

By 1908 Charlotte had abandoned teaching and begun to train as a missionary at the SPM's headquarters in Wiesbaden. Her missionary training included an introduction to Arabic and she acquired a lifelong interest in studying non-European languages. Alongside her missionary training Charlotte worked as a nurse at the Wiesbaden hospital of eminent ophthalmic surgeon Dr Hermann Pagenstecher (1844-1932). This was followed by further study at Kassel in 1910 and at the University of Tubingen's Women's Clinic in 1911. By 1912 she was qualified as a nurse and midwife and had some experience as a pharmacist. In October 1912 she was sent by the SPM to Egypt where, as a twenty-four-year-old, she began working at the mission's new hospital in Aswan.[4]

During 1913 *Der Sudan Pionier*, the SPM's journal, published Charlotte's accounts of her first year of work (Appendices A and B). Inevitably, like Jakob Rippert's writing, these articles reveal the attitudes and prejudices of a European Christian missionary of the early twentieth century. At the same time, they are well-written, observant, insightful, largely optimistic and suggest not just a fixed outlook but a degree of open-mindedness and genuine regard for the people Charlotte had come to serve, above all the women. Similar to the long reports Jakob Rippert would publish in *Der Sudan Pionier*, Charlotte's writing offers fascinating glimpses into the world around her.

While Charlotte was working at Aswan prior to the outbreak of the First World War, the SPM missionaries would take a break from their work during the hottest time of the year, when temperatures rose to over 50 degrees celsius. Some went to Europe but most spent their vacation in Lebanon or Palestine, where they continued their studies in Islam and Arabic. During the summer break in August 1914, those in Lebanon and Palestine heard about the outbreak of the war in Europe. When they attempted to return to Aswan they were stopped at Cairo by British authorities. Despite lengthy negotiations, they were denied permission to return to Aswan and forced to take an old Italian cargo steamer to Europe. Charlotte was among those sent back to Europe. Not being able to return to Aswan was disappointing for the missionaries, but at least they were not interned by the British as enemy aliens for the duration of the war.⁵ Looking back, Charlotte may have felt fortunate to escape such a fate on this occasion.

Back in Germany, according to the mission's historians, 'the missionary brothers and sisters soon sought and found a ministry. The men were drafted into military service and the sisters worked in military hospitals'.⁶ Charlotte was one of those who worked in military hospitals, including in Wiesbaden, caring for those who had been wounded, gassed or maimed. She kept photos from this period which show her sitting with colleagues or patients at the hospital. Charlotte experienced the hardships of the home front, where there were food shortages in the last years of the war, and shared with millions of other Germans the loss of family and friends. Her brother-in-law, Otto Paul Justin, was killed on the Western Front in 1916 while serving as an officer with a Grenadier Guard regiment.⁷ Her younger brother, Rudolf Wolter, died in late 1918, although it is unclear if his death was war-related.

In common with Jakob Rippert, the experience of the First World War seemed only to reinforce Charlotte's Christian faith and determination to return to missionary work. While in Germany, she attended classes on the History and Culture of the Orient, took courses in Arabic and Turkish and helped to promote the SPM's work and form support circles in Hamburg and Saxony.⁸

4.5 Charlotte, seated in the front row above where she has marked an X, with staff and patients at a German military hospital in Wiesbaden during the First World War (RPA)

Ein heiliger Christabend in Palästina, 1923
Charlotte Wolter

Now it was here, the holy Christmas Eve. A cold winter's day had preceded it. The snow-covered summit of Mount Hermon, which towers above the lower foothills of Lebanon, was a wonderful sight when we stepped outside our house, which lay between gardens on the northern edge of Acre. Now that night had fallen, the sky shone with the twinkling of the approaching army of stars. The silhouette of the ancient city of Acre with all its minarets and the beautiful domes of the Djezzar Mosque with its crescent moons stood out in blue-black ink on the horizon, not far away from us. The muezzin's call rang out to us from the highest minaret, audible from afar through the clear air.

Was it really Christmas Eve, Christmas night? Wasn't that when Muhammad's fame was proclaimed and the faithful called to night prayers in the mosque of Allah? Wasn't there a place for the Christ Child anywhere in this city? There was at least one place, in our modest little house on the outskirts of Acre, the much-contested site of the Crusaders in the Middle Ages. Only a few Arab Christians lived half-hidden and shyly in the corners of the city, which had become a bastion of Islam. We had only recently moved into our house in the middle of a Mohammedan area to begin our missionary work. But the light that once shone from the manger in the stable in Bethlehem was with us.

On Christmas Eve, we lit the candles of our little Christmas tree, a small pine. We had prepared cakes, tea and Arabic coffee, and now we went 'out onto the country road' and invited anyone who passed by. Soon we had our small living room full of astonished, somewhat embarrassed people. With the help of the coffee so beloved by the Arabs, which is sipped comfortably from tiny cups, their oriental tendency to socialize and talk eloquently, and probably also their curiosity, soon gained the upper hand and a lively questioning began. How easy it was for us to tell our dear guests the message of the child in the manger. Our hearts really opened up on that first Christmas Eve in Acre. I felt as if all the Christians from five parts of the world were celebrating with us that evening. We three missionaries felt like the hosts of future Christianity. I felt as if we were surrounded by people who, like the shepherds in the field and the wise men from the East, had come to seek and find the child in the manger.

Who had accepted our invitation? There were our neighbours, a young Muslim couple with a baby. Husband and wife in the picturesque dress of Palestinian farmers. They came from a mountain village in Galilee and could neither read nor write. After every sentence from the Gospel that we told them, their astonished 'Allah' rang out. They listened willingly and without inner resistance. They had never thought about God and their souls; no one had ever talked to them about it. They returned to their hut late, thanking us and kissing our hands in the oriental peasant way. We often visited them there later.

Another neighbour had also come, a man from far away, a Kurd. This proud man, from the warlike tribe of the Kurds, had recently bought an orange garden. He looked down a little at everyone present, a somewhat motley crew. He was sitting next to an Armenian who had come with his mother, wife and five children. Hardly any of those present knew the others. Most of them were new to our region and town. Some of them also talked about their lives and experiences that evening.

Our Kurd was the proudest speaker. Among other things, he boasted about how many Armenians he had killed with his own hand during the Armenian persecution in the First World War. Only gradually did he realize that one of the Armenian families who had fled to Palestine, much hounded and plundered, was sitting next to him. Then came the message of Jesus Christ, the Saviour from sin and guilt, which he was probably hearing for the first time in his life. He became increasingly quiet and thoughtful. When he said goodbye after many thanks, he took an Arabic New Testament home.

Apart from our Christian Armenian family, all our guests were Mohammedans. Friend and foe were united under the heavenly message of peace.

British authorities in Egypt would not permit the SPM to send its missionaries back to Aswan in the years immediately after the First World War. Rather than leave them idle, the Karmel Mission, which operated in Palestine, invited the SPM to send some of its experienced missionaries to assist with its work. As a result, in 1923 three SPM missionaries began working with the Karmel Mission at Acre and Haifa in northern Palestine. These missionaries were Samuel Jakob Enderlin and his wife Elisabeth and Charlotte Wolter. All three were able to communicate in basic Arabic and Charlotte eventually gained the trust of the local women she worked with.⁹ In Acre, she made home visits and, sometimes accompanied by Elisabeth Enderlin or an evangelist from the Karmel Mission, visited the nearby village of Manshîya weekly, where she treated the sick and held religious discussions. Once she had gained British recognition for her German qualifications, Charlotte worked with a local doctor to open a women's clinic in Acre. Within a month of the practice opening in January 1924, she was fully occupied at the clinic during the morning and with home visits in the afternoon.¹⁰

Charlotte has left a remarkable story about Christmas Eve in 1923. Entitled *Ein heiliger Christabend in Palästina* (A Holy Christmas Eve in Palestine), it is a response to her experience of a first Christmas in the Holy Land and reflects her deep Christian faith and missionary zeal. As with her reports in *Der Sudan Pionier*, the language and the attitudes conveyed are of their time, but the observations are eclectic and interesting. Even if embellished in recollection, there is a special quality to the way in which Charlotte captures a unique moment when a German Christmas Eve was celebrated with a diverse group on the edge of ancient Acre more than a hundred years ago.¹¹

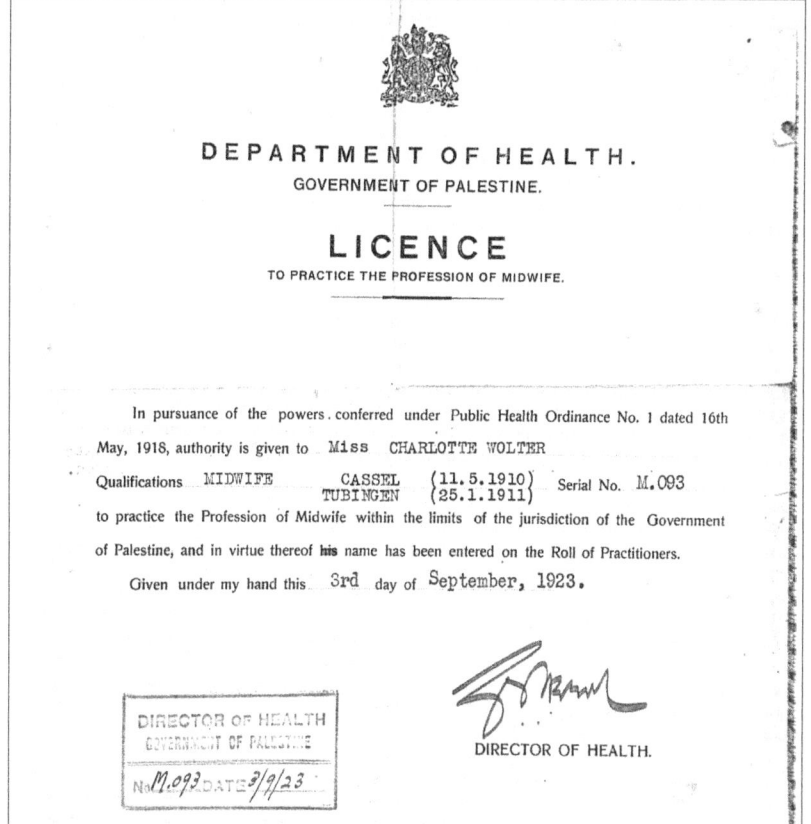

The three SPM missionaries remained in Palestine until late 1924, when they were allowed to return to Egypt. When the mission inspector Johannes Held reported on these events in 1925, he noted that the Enderlins and Charlotte would be returning to the 'greater tasks' in Egypt, but that they would soon be aided by those who had recently completed their training, including the 'young missionary Rippert'.¹²

4.6 Charlotte's licence to practise midwifery, issued by the British Palestine authority in 1923 (RPA)

Endnotes

1. Postcard showing Comeniusstraße 62, Dresden, c. 1920s, RPA.
2. Letter, Charlotte Rippert to family, written in Haifa on 6 February 1935, RPA.
3. Reinhold Strähler and Joachim Paesler, *Nach dem Sandsturm Klart es auf: 125 Jahre erlebte Treue Gottes Geschichte und Geschichten*, Evangeliumsgemeinschaft Mittlerer Osten e. V. (EMO), Wiesbaden, 2025, pp. 172-173; *Der Pionier*, May 1930, p. 79.
4. Strähler and Paesler, pp. 279-280; Charlotte Wolter's education certificates, RPA; Eberhard Troeger, 'EMO I: 1900 to 1914', unpublished history, EMO, 2024, 6.2.3.
5. Eberhard von Dessien, Ulrich Ehrbeck, Eberhard Troeger, *Wasser auf dürres Land: 85 Jahre Sudan-Pionier-Mission/Ev. Mission in Oberägypten*, Verlag der Evangelischen Mission in Oberägypten, Wiesbaden, 1985, pp. 28-29.
6. Von Dessien et al., p. 27.
7. German World War I Casualty Lists, List 1183, Vol. 1916 XIX, 30 September 1916.
8. SPM Board Minutes, 16 October 1919, p. 261, EMO.
9. Johannes Held, *Anfänge einer deutschen Muhammedanermission: Rückblick auf die ersten 25 Jahre der Sudan-Pionier-Mission 1900-1925*, Verlag der Sudan-Pionier-Mission, 1925.
10. Eberhard Troeger, 'EMO II: 1914 to 1950', unpublished history, EMO, 2024, 9.2.3.
11. Charlotte Wolter, manuscript, 'Ein heiliger Christabend in Palästina', HStAD.
12. Johannes Held, *Anfänge einer deutschen Muhammedanermission*, 1925.

Chapter 5
Egypt and Nubia, 1924 – 1931

From the mid-1920s, when British authorities allowed the Sudan Pionier Mission (SPM) to resume its work in Egypt, experienced missionaries such as Charlotte Wolter returned and new missionaries such as Jakob Rippert arrived from Germany for the first time. The SPM's priority was to quickly re-establish its facilities and services after a decade of neglect. In the meantime, there were issues in the background. Funding was limited and dependent upon maintaining support among European donors. While securely based in Aswan, an overriding goal was to expand southwards to work among the Nubian people. At the same time, the completion of the Aswan Low Dam in 1902 and subsequent increases in the height of the dam's wall meant that the Nubians along the Nile were gradually losing their land as it was submerged under the rising waters behind the dam. It was in this environment that Jakob and Charlotte worked, often in the same area, he as specialist builder/engineer and she as a nurse. While in Egypt, as a result of Charlotte's past connections and Jakob's need to source building materials and specialist services, the pair developed relationships with a German community in Palestine. This would be important for the next phase in their lives following their marriage in 1937.

Charlotte Wolter was welcomed back to Aswan in November 1924 after spending the previous year with the Karmel Mission in Palestine. Along with her missionary colleagues Elisabeth Enderlin and Gertrud von Massenbach,

5.1 Egypt in the 1920s (PKI)

she began working with Bishari nomads who lived in a camp outside the city. In January 1925 they were able to reopen the SPM's Aswan clinic. It was soon visited by up to 150 women and children each day. Charlotte's medical skills and caring nature won the affection of the Arab, Nubian and Sudanese women. As Charlotte and Gertrud von Massenbach became more proficient in the Nubian language, it was noted, 'every Nubian word' opened hearts and doors. Nubian women began to address them as 'Nubians'. In April, after her intense work in Palestine and Aswan, Charlotte was sent back to Germany on home leave. In Germany she was able to report to the SPM's supporters on the resumption of the mission's work in Aswan.[1]

When Jakob Rippert arrived in Aswan in February 1925, his principal task was to restore the mission's buildings in Aswan and Darau. To best use the meagre funds available for this work, he did much of the physical work himself, with the help of other missionaries such as Pastor Enderlin and Samuel Ali Hussein. He also employed a team of local bricklayers and labourers. As the early

5.2 Charlotte Wolter was a talented amateur artist who painted several Egyptian scenes, including this view of Luxor (RPA)

work took place during the Muslim fasting month of Ramadan, this meant the local workers had to cope with heavy physical work in Aswan's oppressively hot climate while they were fasting during daylight.²

Jakob's first experience of Ramadan in a Muslim country prompted him to write another long article for *Der Sudan Pionier* (Appendix D).³ His initial observations are on the impact fasting had on the effectiveness of his workers. He builds on this with the clear intention of creating a portrait of Aswan during Ramadan which is richly evocative of place, time and local character. Like his first article for *Der Sudan Pionier*, the description provides another colourful first-hand account 'from the mission field' for readers back in Germany who were eager for stories about the exotic places where missionaries laboured to save souls. At the end of the description, Jakob makes some harsh judgements about Islam, including statements excluded from the abridged version presented as Appendix D. In part, the vehemence of these judgements was undoubtedly aimed at translating interest in the story into support and funding for the SPM's desperate battle against the perceived hollowness and evils of non-Christian beliefs and practices. These judgements may have been sharpened by Jakob's own adherence to the Lutheran belief in salvation being received freely from God through Jesus Christ, rather than needing to be earned through ritualised practices such as fasting, something more associated with non-Protestant Christian denominations.

5.3 Jakob with workers at Aswan. He sent this photo to his parents with a message on the back: 'A Christmas greeting to you, dear parents, your Jakob and his brown and black construction workers. Bricklayers, carpenters, joiners, earthworkers, plumbers, sly rascals. Taken on the Saturday before 1st Advent, Aswan, Dec. 10, 1930 Your Jakob'. (RPA)

The stridency of Jakob's response to Ramadan did not prevent him from developing a regard for the men he worked with. Indeed, the relationships he established and the conversations that took place while working reinforced his view that his work was the most effective way for him to model Christianity and spread the good news of the Gospel. In time, he became especially close to the Nubians. He was described as having almost a 'father-son relationship' with Samuel Ali Hussein, the Nubian Christian who had been part of the SPM's founding group. When Samuel died on 8 March 1927, Jakob was at his bedside, Samuel having asked him to 'leave all your work today and stay with me, because today is my last day'. When Jakob was later asked to move to the mission station established in the Nubian village of Koshtamne, he responded 'I don't need to assure you that I love this people and that I am at home among them… and consider it the highest task to be a messenger of the Gospel here…'[4]

Charlotte Wolter returned to Aswan from home leave towards the end of 1925 to find much of the refurbishment work completed and commented on the new 'friendly' appearance of the buildings. This work, and later construction for which Jakob was responsible, was not accomplished without his needing to overcome various hurdles. Later, for example, when building a clinic there was much 'back and forth' between Jakob and the mission's board over details ranging from the dimensions of clinic examination rooms to the provision for staff toilet facilities. In 1930 he had to get special approval for the expenditure of 20 Marks on specialist literature about control of termites. Perhaps Jakob reflected on the continuity when, twenty-five years later, he found himself engaged in similar discussions with another mission board on the other side of the world.[5]

One of the biggest challenges Jakob faced was sourcing building materials, particularly wood, and quality tools to complete his work to the high standards he set. This challenge was overcome in a way that would have important long-term ramifications. During 1925, when he was taking a break in the milder climate of Palestine and possibly because it had been recommended to him by Charlotte Wolter, Jakob made contact with the German community in Haifa. Here he found German tradesmen and engineers, tools, workshops and the materials he was looking for. As he wrote in his memoir:

> From 1925 onwards, I came to Palestine almost every year to buy wood and building materials. I also made the windows and doors for my buildings in Upper Egypt and Nubia in my friend Appinger's workshop because I didn't have any woodworking machines in my workshops there.[6]

Gottlob Appinger (1876-1960) was a member of a prominent family in Haifa's German colony. He operated a well-equipped carpentry workshop and imported timber from Europe. Appinger would prove to be a generous friend to both Jakob and the SPM.

In January 1926, Jakob accompanied Pastor Enderlin on a journey up the Nile. Their destination was the village of Koshtamne, about 100 kilometres south of Aswan, where the mission had been offered two houses for rent. Using these houses to establish a mission station would be a fulfilment of the mission's long cherished goal of reaching out to the Nubian people who lived along the Nile south of Aswan. Jakob's account of the journey, published in *Der Sudan Pionier* in 1926 (Appendix E), is interesting for several reasons.[7] Typically, he recorded detailed observations of the landscape and the people encountered. At the beginning, he painted a vivid picture of the steamship which sailed between Shellal and Wadi Halfa. As humble missionaries, he and Enderlin travelled third class and were looked down upon by the notables in first class. Sailing up the river, they stopped at Gerf Hussein, the location of an ancient Egyptian rock cut temple which would eventually be submerged under the rising waters created by the damming of the Nile. At Koshtamne, Jakob's builder's eye was drawn to the houses and thoughts about how they might be adapted for European use as a mission station. At the same time, there was strong resistance to the mission's expansion from the Nubian villagers, or at least from the male village leaders with whom Enderlin negotiated.

Despite the resistance, Enderlin managed to arrange a lease on the two houses and on 9 April 1926 four missionaries arrived in Koshtamne to establish the SPM's first mission station in Nubia. Like many similar Nubian villages, Koshtamne occupied both banks of the Nile and the mission station was set up on the more populous east side. The four missionary pioneers were Gertrud von Massenbach, Gertrud Noack, Charlotte Wolter and Jakob Rippert.[8] Gertrud von Massenbach has left this account of their arrival:

> As we sailed through Nubia by boat, all three of us [women] were discouraged. All around us there was nothing to be seen but a desolate rocky desert, and here and there a little village stuck to the mountains, whose houses were the same colour as the stone on which they hung. Finally, a wide valley opened up in front of us, and it was said: 'Look, here lies Koschtamne!' There are also stones and rocks on the eastern shore, but they are not as high and do not look as inhospitable as further north. As we sailed slowly along the village, we saw with great joy that the children are dressed as cleanly as in Aswan on feast days.
>
> The news that the *Hakima* — doctor, meaning the nurse Charlotte Wolter — was on the ship had spread and so we were watched with great interest by the people on the shore, and a few times the women waved to us in a friendly way.
>
> Finally, we moored in front of our new house. Some men were standing on the shore. After a friendly greeting, we walked towards the house. We had already seen from the river that in the two narrow alleys that led directly along the house, there were a lot of women who were half hidden. When we entered the courtyard, a crowd of women streamed in through the small side door. It was our neighbours who had come to greet us.
>
> Our house is a real Nubian homestead: three rooms and a fairly large courtyard. These rooms are of quite a nice size, not too low, so they can be quite airy. What is missing is a proper roof, windows and doors. But Mr Rippert helps us to do this. He also wants to build us a proper kitchen, and a mat tent for the polyclinic and schoolwork. So we will probably be able to start the work very easily. The house has one major advantage: all windows open to the north. We will be able to get every cool breath of air in the heat, and also have a wonderful view over the wide water surface of the Nile, to the yellow sand mountains on the other bank, in front of which a narrow green strip stretches.

Now we can say with great joy: We have made the beginning of a new work in the Nubian country and now we ask our friends to stand behind us in faithful intercession, so that God can give us the gift of standing among the people with the full blessing of the Gospel.⁹

Resistance to the missionary presence at Koshtamne was gradually overcome. The benefits of Charlotte Wolter's medical clinic were soon recognised, specifically by the village women. Meanwhile, Jakob set to work improving the facilities, developing good relations with the local men as he worked with them.

The establishment of the mission station at remote Koshtamne exposed the need for the mission to have access to its own reliable transport for travel up and down the Nile. Jakob came up with an ambitious proposal to meet this need — with the assistance of his friend Gottlob Appinger in Haifa, he would build a small motorboat and bring it back to Aswan. The proposal came to fruition when, after his summer leave in Palestine in 1926, Jakob stayed in Haifa to superintend the building of the boat in Appinger's Haifa workshop.¹⁰

5.4 SPM missionaries in Aswan c. 1930: left to right, Hermann Schönberger, ? Farraj, Gertrud Noack, ? Mansur, Käthe Gauer, Gertrud von Massenbach, Ilse von Dewitz, Lina Marthaler, Charlotte Weimann, Hans Merklin, Elisabeth Herzfeld, Charlotte Rippert, Jakob Rippert (RPA)

Named the *Ischimbul*, 'Messenger of Truth', the boat was transferred aboard a steamer from Haifa to Alexandria after it was completed in December 1926. Jakob then set out on an epic journey, sailing all the way up the Nile River from Alexandria to Aswan. There was great celebration when he reached Aswan with the *Ischimbul* in April 1927. The boat gave the mission access to its mission stations up and down the Nile and its value was quickly recognised. The only drawback was that if Jakob was absent there was no one on hand to maintain the boat's engine. One of these absences occurred later in 1927 when his war wound troubled him yet again and Jakob was forced to undergo surgery at the Victoria Hospital in Cairo.[11]

Jakob produced one of his most compelling narratives when he told the story of the first stages of the *Ischimbul*'s 1000 kilometre journey up the Nile. The account was published in two instalments in *Der Sudan Pionier* during 1927 (Appendix F).[12] Accompanied by a friend from Haifa, Mr Kaltenbach, and with the dubious help of a hired helmsman from Alexandria, Jakob set out with the *Ischimbul* towing a barge loaded with supplies and a small sailing vessel. After negotiating a narrow canal connecting Alexandria with the Rosetta branch of the Nile, the party sailed up the Nile Delta, through Cairo and on towards Aswan. Navigating the busy waterway, with its barrages, locks, lifting bridges and sandbanks, was a formidable undertaking for a European who was unfamiliar with the river and its many challenges. It proved to be a highly eventful adventure that, in Jakob's skilful retelling, shifts backwards and forwards between impending disaster and a comedy of errors. On at least one occasion Jakob had cause to give thanks once again for 'God's kind preservation'. A disappointment is that he only recorded the first part of this great journey — the narrative ends at Beni Suef, 100 kilometres south of Cairo.

An interesting aspect of the *Ischimbul* account is Jakob's response to the frustrations he experienced with his hired boatmen. His European prejudices are evident. So too, after his time living in Upper Egypt, are some curious locally acquired attitudes. Thus, he contrasts the religious observance of decent Muslim sailors he is familiar with in Upper Egypt with the depravity of non-observant sailors from the Nile Delta. His helmsman is incompetent and cheeky because, of course, that is what you would expect from an Alexandrian. On the other hand, his Nubian donkey boy could not have stolen a donkey simply because 'Nubians don't steal'.

During 1927 Jakob Rippert and Charlotte Wolter announced their engagement and on 24 November they were married in Cairo. In the following year they were given home leave and lived at Wiesbaden briefly while Jakob used a promotional film to present talks on the mission's work. Sadly, when they were in Wiesbaden the couple had to mourn the birth of a stillborn son on 9 October 1928.[13]

Jakob and Charlotte returned to Egypt in 1929 and now worked together. One of their first tasks, carried out in February-March, was to take the SPM's mission inspector, Pastor Johannes Held, on an exploratory trip up the Nile with the *Ischimbul*. Charlotte kept a diary of this expedition and published it in *Der Pionier* (Appendix G).[14] A touching moment she records was when, on her arrival at Koshtamne, the Nubian women 'said kind words to me about the loss of our child' and, as a gesture of love and trust, mothers asked her to hold their babies.

5.5 An invitation to the launch of the *Ischimbul* in Haifa (RPA)

5.6 The *Ishimbul* ready to be taken to the harbour in Haifa. Jakob sent the photo to his father and wrote on the back: 'Ernst Appinger [Gottlob Appinger's son] and my Abdalah, Nov. 26, other pictures will follow and father keep them all safe.' (RPA)

5.7 The *Ischimbul* in its first Nile lock. Jakob is on the left. (RPA)

Charlotte's account of the trip up the Nile to Abu Simbel in 1929 takes us on a journey into a lost world that now lies beneath the waters of Lake Nasser. The purpose of the trip was to explore where 'in the drowning country' it might be possible to establish a mission station to replace Koshtamne after it was submerged following completion of work to raise the level of the Aswan Low Dam's wall in 1932. There was concern about further dislocation for the Kenuzi Nubians, with whom the missionaries had been working at Koshtamne. There were hopes that the Kenuzi might be able to relocate south to the lands of the Fadija Nubians. Subsequently, the building of the Aswan High Dam in the 1960s, and the resulting creation of the vast Lake Nasser behind it, would drown all the villages the missionaries visited on this trip.

While Nubian villages and farmland disappeared as Lake Nasser rose, during the 1960s some of the ancient Egyptian treasures along this section of the Nile were rescued and reconstructed on higher ground. The most remarkable of these conservation efforts involved the United Nations supported project to dismantle and relocate the magnificent rock cut temples of Abu Simbel. Charlotte's report mentions prehistoric drawings along the Nile's bank, which are now under water, and her party's visit to the Abu Simbel temples at their original site. At the time, for Europeans to visit this remote location

5.8 Jakob and Charlotte's wedding in Cairo on 24 November 1927. The celebrant is Pastor Karig and in the background are deaconesses of Cairo's Kaiserswerth Institute, a German Protestant medical charity. (RPA)

5.9 Map showing some of the villages visited by the SPM's missionaries on their 1929 expedition to Abu Simbel. Shading shows the area now inundated by Lake Nasser. (PKI)

5.10 Pharaoh Ramesses II's temple at Abu Simbel. Along with the nearby temple of Queen Nefertari, during the 1960s it was cut into blocks and reassembled on higher ground under a specially constructed dome. (PKI)

of one of ancient Egypt's most spectacular and intriguing monuments was a rare privilege, deserving of more than the few lines Charlotte devotes to it.

More generally, what is suggested in Charlotte's descriptions of the travelling and camping arrangements of the Nile expedition is a high degree of gender equality among the missionaries. This was in keeping with how they carried out their missionary work as a whole. Also of interest, at one of the camp sites Jakob Rippert was bitten by a scorpion. Fortunately, the party included a doctor who was able to administer an anti-venom serum he had brought along. It may have been another occasion when Jakob thought of his confirmation verse and the angels who were on hand in moments of danger.

After returning from their trip up the Nile, the Ripperts took over the running of the Koshtamne mission station. When visiting people up and down the Nile, he and Charlotte lived in the *Ischimbul*'s enclosed cabin for weeks at a time.[15] In October 1929, Jakob took charge of a project to drill for underground water in a bid to supply the village with clean drinking water. It was easy enough to find Nile water that had filtered into the ground near the river, but bores and pumps located near the river were subject to flooding. Jakob took on the challenge of drilling for groundwater on the higher, rocky ground. When, after ten days of drilling, he found good drinking water seeping down from the mountains, there was great rejoicing. As Jakob wrote:

> We have received this water as a gift from God, and our hearts are full of praise and thanksgiving for it. There is great joy among the workers and also in the whole village, and many come to see the miracle… water from the rock![16]

Jakob's grandfather had been a 'well master' back in Auerbach in the nineteenth century. He had now drilled the first successful deep well in Nubia. Always learning on the job, he had developed expertise that would prove highly useful in his next role.

There was even more rejoicing the next year when, on 15 April 1930, Charlotte gave birth to a son, Reinhart, at the Deaconess Hospital in Cairo.[17] SPM published the following announcement in its retitled journal, *Der Pionier*:

> God's goodness gave the Rippert couple a healthy baby son on April 15. In order to counter the particular danger posed to small children by the climate, the parents decided to take their child home after just a few months and place him with his grandparents. Although this step must have been difficult for them — after all, this is where the parents' great sacrifice in the mission lies — we are nevertheless pleased about this brave attempt to solve this question, which is so important for the further steady development of the missionary work…[18]

Without any provision to support her taking a break away from Aswan, Charlotte had taken Reinhart to be cared for by Jakob's parents in Auerbach while she returned to continue her contribution to the mission's work. In robbing Charlotte and Jakob of precious family time with their son, the sacrifice involved was certainly significant, even more so when considered in hindsight.

5.11 Jakob and Charlotte at Koshtamne in 1928 (RPA)

5.12 The *Ischimbul* with SPM passengers on the Nile River in the late 1920s (RPA)

At the end of 1931 Jakob and Charlotte made a decision to leave Egypt and their work with the SPM. At least four factors influenced this decision. Firstly, the SPM had always battled to finance its operations and by the 1930s the situation had reached a crisis point due to a decline in financial support and the onset of the Depression in 1929.[19] As a result, the mission struggled to pay its missionaries and was forced to curtail activities. It was decided to shut down all technical operations until the financial situation improved. This came at a difficult time when, with the raising of the Aswan Low Dam, the Koshtamne mission station was destined to be submerged and the SPM would need to fund the development of a new centre if it meant to continue operating in Nubia.

5.13 Jakob and Charlotte with their son Reinhart after his birth in April 1930 (RPA)

The decision to stop technical operations left Jakob without his familiar role but he rejected a suggestion that he retrain as a 'theological missionary'. As he later recalled:

> I was supposed to leave all this behind [his work] and my mission suggested that I should go back to Germany and study theology for a few more semesters in order to continue working as a theological missionary in the field in Nubia. However, as I already had too much technology in my blood from my father and grandfather, I couldn't decide to do this.[20]

Secondly, Charlotte had begun to suffer from health problems attributed to the years of work in the extreme heat of Egypt. These conditions had also separated Jakob and Charlotte from their only child, Reinhart. It is likely that they were looking for missionary work that would allow their small family to be together.

A third reason for the Ripperts' departure from Egypt was discord within the SPM that had a particular impact on Jakob. By the end of the 1920s, the interventions of the SPM's missionary inspector, Pastor Johannes Held, were generating tension. Held made his first visit to Egypt in 1929, when he had been taken on an investigative journey up the Nile River by the Ripperts. The recommendations Held made after his inspection were poorly received by the mission's management in Germany. According to one of the SPM's historians, Eberhard Troeger:

> In 1929, during his long and first trip to Egypt, Inspector Held developed proposals for the establishment of economic ventures in Upper Egypt in order to open up additional sources of income for the mission. He proposed the establishment of an agricultural farm north of Aswan and the drilling of wells in Nubia. The Wiesbaden working committee rejected both proposals as illusory, risky and not financially viable. As a matter of principle, the mission should not act as a commercial enterprise. The proposal to erect wind turbines in Darau also found no sympathy in Wiesbaden.[21]

Not only did Inspector Held's proposals cause unrest at board level, they provoked a strong reaction from Jakob. On 9 September 1930, in a long letter marked 'Confidential', he revealed these thoughts to his brother Wilhelm:

> I'm done with Held in Wiesbaden, absolutely done, because he's always tried to pull me in over the last few years when he's messed something up …
>
> Ever since I rejected all his crazy technical ideas as unworkable in our poor country, I've been in his way. The Arab says *malesh*, which means I don't care …
>
> I am counting on God, and if it is his will and I stay healthy, we will not perish, he certainly still has tasks for us. Maybe we'll start a job somewhere in the Orient [Middle East], a farm or a plantation, so that we can continue our Mohammedan mission and earn our own daily bread.[22]

Evident in this response was a consciousness that Jakob was now the breadwinner for a family and this needed to be balanced against the sacrifices he and Charlotte had always been prepared to make for their missionary work as individuals. The final, and probably decisive, reason for the Ripperts leaving

Egypt and the SPM was that Jakob had found another situation where he could continue to work in a technical area associated with missionary work in the Middle East, but in a location that was more amenable to family life. This opportunity came about due to the relationships he and Charlotte had formed in Palestine.

The Ripperts' departure from Egypt in October 1931 was not easy. As Jakob later wrote, 'we loved the country and the people on the Nile and we had both received our special training for this country'. His and Charlotte's resignation was accepted with great reluctance by the SPM's board. Not only had the Ripperts' work been vital in a number of areas, from health care to maintenance and transport, but as individuals they were held in high regard by their missionary colleagues and the Arab and Nubian people they had worked closely with. Their contribution to the SPM's work in Egypt and Nubia in the 1920s is extensively documented in *Der Sudan Pionier* and, in 2025, was highlighted by Strähler and Paesler in their 125 year history of the SPM and its successor organisations.[23]

During 1935 the village of Koshtamne and its mission station disappeared under the rising waters of the Nile River.

Endnotes

1. Reinhold Strähler and Joachim Paesler, *Nach dem Sandsturm Klart es auf: 125 Jahre erlebte Treue Gottes Geschichte und Geschichten*, EMO, Wiesbaden, 2025, pp. 306-307; Eberhard Troeger, 'EMO II: 1914 to 1950', unpublished history, EMO, 2024, 10.2.1-10.2.3.
2. Strähler and Paesler, pp. 311-312; Troeger, 'EMO II', 11.5, 12.1.
3. Jakob Rippert, 'From the Mission Field, Ramadan', *Der Sudan Pionier*, July 1925, pp. 83-88.
4. Troeger, 'EMO II', 3.6.5, 14.5.3: 1929/30.
5. Troeger, 'EMO II', 12.1.
6. Jakob Rippert, Memoir, 1971, HStAD.
7. Jakob Rippert, 'My first trip to Nubia', *Der Sudan Pionier*, April 1926 pp. 38-42 and May 1926, pp. 51-55.
8. Strähler and Paesler, pp. 303-304, 318-319; Troeger, 'EMO II', 14.5.1.
9. Gertrud von Massenbach, 'First days in Koschtamne', *Der Sudan Pionier*, May 1926, pp. 58-60. (Abridged version translated from Strähler and Paesler, pp. 72-73).
10. *Der Sudan Pionier*, March 1926, p. 32; Troeger, 'EMO II', 12.5.7.
11. Troeger, 'EMO II', 11.5, 14.5.3: 1926/1927. 'Ischimbul' is possibly a German translation of a Nubian term for 'Messenger of Truth'.
12. Jakob Rippert, 'First Nile journey of the Ischimbul', *Der Sudan Pionier*, June 1927, pp. 77-80 and July 1927, pp. 94-96.
13. *Der Sudan Pionier*, November 1928, p. 135; Troeger, 'EMO II', 11.5.1.
14. *Der Pionier*, May 1929, pp. 71-74 and June 1929, pp. 84-87.
15. Jakob Rippert, Memoir.
16. Jakob Rippert, *Der Pionier*, January 1930, p. 7, quoted in Troeger, 'EMO II', 14.5.3: 1929/30.
17. Troeger, 'EMO II', 11.5.1.
18. *Der Pionier*, May 1930, p. 67.
19. Troeger, 'EMO II', 5.4.2.
20. Jakob Rippert, Memoir.

21. Troeger, 'EMO II', 16.1.
22. Letter, Jakob Rippert to his brother Wilhelm Rippert, 9 September 1930, HStAD.
23. Jakob Rippert, Memoir; Troeger, 'EMO II', 11.5.1; Strähler and Paesler, pp. 309, 311-312.

Chapter 6
Palestine, 1931 – 1941

After their work with the Sudan Pionier Mission came to an end in October 1931, the Ripperts moved to Palestine. Here, Jakob began work with the Syrian Orphanage and the couple established their own farm near Acre in northern Palestine. They were already familiar with the area from visits during the 1920s and had friends and good support from within Palestine's unique German community. The Ripperts' farm prospered, Reinhart was brought back from Germany to live with his parents and the family shared in the pleasant lifestyle enjoyed by Palestine's Germans in the inter-war decades. Nevertheless, they had chosen to live in an area that would soon become the focus of complex international tensions and the outbreak of the Second World War in 1939 brought an end to this settled period in their family life.

In the 1920s and 1930s, Palestine was governed by Britain on behalf of the League of Nations as a mandated territory. Before the First World War, it had been a part of the Ottoman Empire. With the defeat of Germany and its Ottoman ally in 1918, the Ottoman Empire was broken up and its former Middle Eastern territories were assigned to the victorious powers, Britain and France, as mandates. As it did with former German colonies around the world, the League of Nations entrusted these Middle Eastern territories to Britain and France on the understanding that they would be prepared for eventual independence. This was consistent with undertakings Britain had given to Arab allies during the First World War. In 1917, however, Britain made a contradictory commitment when, according to the Balfour Declaration, it agreed to support Zionist plans to establish a Jewish homeland in Palestine. These contradictory commitments, along with Palestinian resistance to Jewish immigration and settlement, led to increasing conflict between Palestinians, Jews and the British during the inter-war period. In 1948, when the British Mandate formally ended, this conflict culminated in the outbreak of full-scale war between Palestinians and Jews. Jewish victory in this war resulted in the foundation of the modern state of Israel.

During the First World War, the British army which defeated Ottoman and German forces in the Middle East was made up of contingents from throughout the British Empire. In the important British victory at Beersheba in October 1917, for example, units of the Australian Light Horse played a key role in overcoming Ottoman defences. Two weeks after this battle, there was an interesting encounter as Australian columns moved northwards along Palestine's coastal plain in pursuit of the retreating enemy. At Wilhelma, situated about fifteen kilometres east of Jaffa, the Australians found a German agricultural settlement. Its inhabitants had just witnessed the departure of Ottoman-German forces and were now waiting anxiously to see how they and their property would fare under the victorious British army. As recalled by one of the residents, Friederike Imberger, the British behaved impeccably and were happy to pay for fresh farm produce. Among the Australian troops, moreover, were German speaking descendants of nineteenth century German immigrants. According to Imberger, one of these

Australians had looked at the kitchen in the family's home and exclaimed, in German, 'Oh, just like at home at our place in Australia!'.[1] It is a story with relevance to Jakob and Charlotte Rippert's future.

The Germans living at Wilhelma in 1917 were Templers, members of a small religious group that emerged from within the Lutheran Church in the early nineteenth century. Templers advocated for a purer form of Christianity, free from the dogmas, rituals and hierarchies of the institutionalised Church and more focused on the simple message of love thought to have guided original Christian communities in the Holy Land. In 1861, following a formal break with the Lutheran Church, the German Temple Society (*Der Deutsche Tempel*) was formed under the leadership of Christoph Hoffman (1815-1885). Together with Georg David Hardegg (1812-1879), Hoffman promoted the goal of building a Christian community, or spiritual temple, in the Holy Land. This led to the establishment of a first Templer settlement in Palestine at Haifa in 1868.

In time, seven major Templer settlements were created in Palestine. Templer 'German Colonies' at Haifa (1868), Jaffa (1869) and Jerusalem (1873) became distinctive enclaves within these growing urban centres. In what are now the three Israeli cities, the term 'German Colony' is still used for these districts, and their heritage value celebrated, long after the Germans were displaced. Rural settlements were established at Sarona (1871), Walhalla (1892, an offshoot of Jaffa), Wilhelma (1902) and Betlehem (1906). Near Betlehem was another rural German settlement, Waldheim (1907), established by former Templers who had returned to the Lutheran Church.[2]

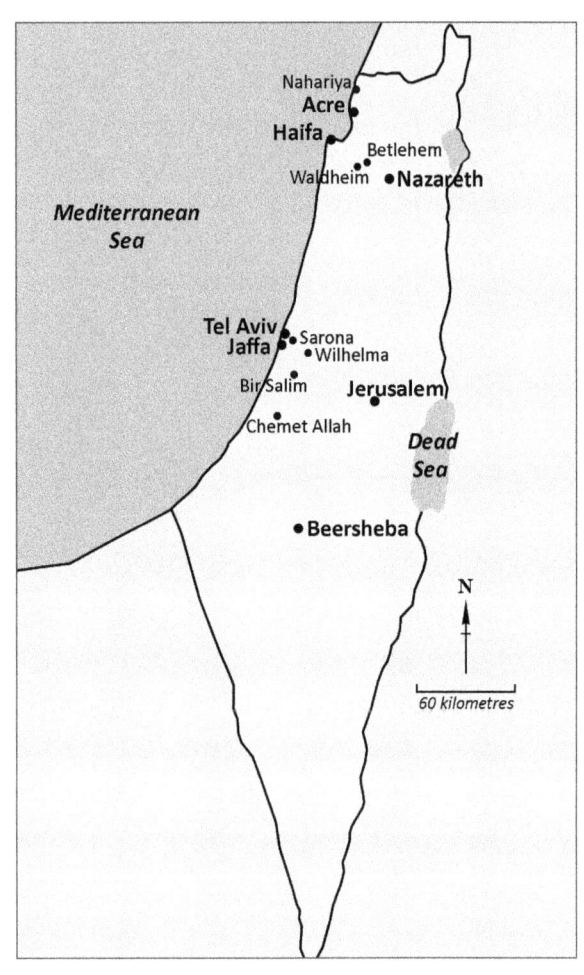

6.1 Palestine in the 1930s (PKI)

The German settlers in Palestine had to overcome many early challenges. In his 1973 study of the Templers, Israeli historian Alex Carmel described what he regarded as the pre-modern state of Palestine under Ottoman rule:

> Palestine had more locations that lay in ruins than ones that were inhabitable; its population was uncivilized and fanatic … The country did not have one single normal harbor and no railway; its roads were deserted; its forests denuded; its commerce negligible, its agriculture primitive; there was no modern industry.[3]

There is a widely held belief that the small population of Templers made a disproportionate contribution to addressing these shortcomings. Once their settlements at Haifa and Jaffa were on a sure footing, the Templers became involved in a range of activities in the manufacturing and service industries, including in trade, construction, transport and tourism, the latter catering for Christian pilgrims to the Holy Land. According to Carmel, it was hard to exaggerate the influence German culture and technical know-how had on accelerating progress in Haifa in particular.[4]

The successful Templer agricultural settlements provided an example of how communal farming, initiative and energy could make the seemingly marginal lands of Palestine productive. At Sarona, for example, the Templers pioneered the planting of Australian eucalyptus trees to help drain malarial swamps. Eucalyptus trees are now widespread and often identified as an 'Israeli tree'. Sarona Templers were also the first to market Jaffa branded oranges, destined to become an iconic product of Palestine and Israel. The Templer experience had a strong influence on later Jewish settlers, with leading Zionist thinkers promoting the German agricultural settlements and practices as models for later Jewish settlements.[5]

From a Palestinian perspective, a simple progress narrative that has firstly the Templers and then Jewish settlers making a reality of the biblical land of milk and honey is selective. For example, Jaffa oranges may have been first marketed by Sarona Templers towards the end of the nineteenth century, but the fruit variety itself had been developed decades earlier by an Arab orchardist, Anton Ayub. And while the Templers had a reputation as successful farmers, Mahmoud Yazbak suggests, their hard work and technical ingenuity need to be considered alongside their shrewdness in buying up and then monopolising land close to existing water sources.[6] Once established, the success of the German farms was often heavily reliant upon Arab labour.

6.2 Gottlob Appinger's timber mill and carpentry workshop in Haifa, c. 1920s. This workshop was where Jakob Rippert built the *Ischimbul*. (TSA)

6.3 Templer marketing for Jaffa oranges (TSA)

By the beginning of the twentieth century, the Templers made up a small but distinctive and relatively prosperous expatriate group within Ottoman Palestine. Even though a growing number had been born in Palestine and never been to Germany, they retained a strong German identity and when the First World War broke out most of the young men enlisted in the German army. With German defeat and the establishment of the British Mandate, in 1918 the Templers were looked upon with suspicion by the British and many were deported to internment camps in Egypt. When they were allowed to return to their homes, farms and businesses in 1920, they found their properties damaged or neglected. Renewed hard work ensured a relatively quick return to prosperity, albeit in a new environment where they had to navigate increasingly challenging relationships with Arab or Jewish neighbours, employees or clients. What remained unchanged was the Templers' unsustainable commitment to both their German nationality and their Palestinian homeland. By the late 1930s there were 2000-2500 Germans in Palestine, of whom nearly 1300 were Templers.[7]

Jakob and Charlotte Rippert were devout Lutherans, not Templers. Histories of this period often blur the distinction by using the term Templer to refer to all Palestine Germans. As we will see, Jakob and Charlotte's lives did become intertwined with the larger Templer story for much of the 1930s and 1940s. When they arrived to settle in Palestine at the end of 1931, they had both had earlier contact with the Mandate and its German communities, Templer and Lutheran. Charlotte had worked for the Karmel Mission in Palestine in the early 1920s and Jakob had worked with Germans in Haifa, including when he built the *Ischimbul*, while he was in Egypt.

During one of his visits to Palestine Jakob established contact with Jerusalem's Syrian Orphanage and its Director, Pastor Hermann Schneller (1893-1993). Fortuitously, around the time the SPM was forced to wind back Jakob's technical work in Egypt, Jakob was offered work as a 'farmer/engineer' with the Syrian Orphanage. It was a position that matched Jakob's passion and expertise and, after accepting it, he and Charlotte could look forward to bringing Reinhart back from Germany and living as a family in Palestine.[8]

Established in Jerusalem in 1860 by Johann Ludwig Schneller (1820-1896) and named for the origins of its first orphans, the Syrian Orphanage was dedicated to looking after orphans and providing them with an education and trade training that would equip them to lead productive lives and contribute to the building of Christian Arab communities. By the 1930s the Syrian Orphanage was a highly respected German Lutheran institution in Palestine. Presided over by three generations of the Schneller family, its alternative name was the Schneller Institution. In addition to the main orphanage in Jerusalem, during the early twentieth century three annexes were opened in other parts of Palestine: an agricultural settlement and school at Bir Salem (1906), the Galilee Orphanage in Nazareth (1910) and a second agricultural settlement at Chemet Allah (1930). Bir Salem, now part of Kibbutz Netser Sereni, was south of Tel Aviv and Chemet Allah was further south, near the modern Israeli town of Kiryat Malachi.[9]

Jakob began working for the Syrian Orphanage in Jerusalem after his arrival in Palestine in November 1931. In Jerusalem, he formed a close attachment to the Director, Pastor Hermann Schneller, the founder's grandson. Later, for most of the 1930s, Jakob worked at the Bir Salem and Chemet Allah agricultural settlements. At these settlements he did construction work on buildings, bored for water and created irrigation systems. He refined his skills as a water boring expert. Jakob also took the opportunity to learn about citrus and banana cultivation from Mathias Spohn (1866-1935), Bir Salem's manager. Spohn was a German agricultural expert who lived at Bir Salem for forty years, so long that the site became known as Spohn's Farm, a location name still appearing on recent maps.[10]

Jakob's work for the Syrian Orphanage was seasonal and left him time to pursue a new venture — developing his own farm. The Ripperts' friend Gottlob Appinger, the Haifa timber merchant whose carpentry workshop Jakob had used, owned land about four kilometres north of Acre in northern Palestine. During 1932, after Jakob had drilled for water on Appinger's property and found a good source of underground water, the Ripperts decided to buy their own property nearby. Once again, Jakob found water and constructed a deep well. With a reliable water supply guaranteed, and advised by Appinger and Mathias Spohn, Jakob and Charlotte then set about developing an orange orchard and banana plantation. Because it would take 6-8 years for the orchard to become profitable, throughout the 1930s they relied upon income from a dairy herd and poultry to sustain themselves and generate funds for reinvestment.[11]

By his own account, Jakob's farm was 'built up from wasteland'. This has echoes of a familiar Templer/Zionist narrative about making neglected marginal lands bloom. In this case, the Ripperts' farm does appear to have been developed and become productive in a relatively short time. A German Jewish visitor, Albert Kahn, described it as 'built from fallow land' and remembered it being 'considered a model farm in northern Palestine'. Family photographs from the mid to late 1930s support this assessment. They show substantial buildings, well-established trees and signs of a range of farming activities. Clearly evident are some of the thousands of cypress trees Jakob planted as windbreaks between fields. A map of the farm, drawn by Jakob to support a later compensation claim, shows a complex layout of fields and an irrigation channel flowing from the deep well he had constructed.[12]

How was the farm developed so quickly? Firstly, Charlotte lived on the farm and was involved with many aspects of it, including the lucrative poultry operation. Secondly, the Ripperts employed up to sixteen Arab workers. Thirdly, Jakob's youngest brother, Ludwig Immanuel (Manu) Rippert (1914-1941), came from Germany to work on

6.4 Jakob's youngest brother, Ludwig Immanuel (Manu) Rippert. The photo was taken at Sawides Studio, Haifa in 1937. (RPA)

the farm. From 1932 to 1936, he assisted with much of the planting and construction work. In 1936 he returned to Germany to do compulsory service with the *Reichsarbeitsdienst*, the Third Reich's Labour Service. In early 1937, Manu returned to manage the farm when Jakob was absent for much of the time, presumably working for the Schneller Orphanage in southern Palestine but possibly assisting neighbours around Acre as well. Manu had to return to Germany for another period of labour service in September 1937. Despite investing in a farm of his own, referred to below, he never returned to Palestine.[13]

Where was the Ripperts' farm located? We know it was four kilometres north of Acre, along the main road between Acre and the Lebanese border. Its precise location remains uncertain, but it is likely to have been at the northern edge of Kibbutz Shomrat. In *All That Remains*, a book documenting the fate of former Arab villages, there is a reference to an early Jewish settlement, ha-Yotzerim, occupying land in this area 'that had belonged to the German Templars (sic)'. This is an example of where 'Templers', incorrectly spelt, has been conflated with 'Germans'. The German property referred to can only have been the Ripperts' farm or one of a handful of nearby German farms. Sketch maps drawn by Jakob, of the area and of his farm, match this location. We also have a photograph of Reinhart and another child with an 'Ottoman' Aqueduct in the background. This aqueduct is a striking feature in the landscape immediately north of Shomrat. As it approaches Shomrat, the aqueduct reduces to a ground level

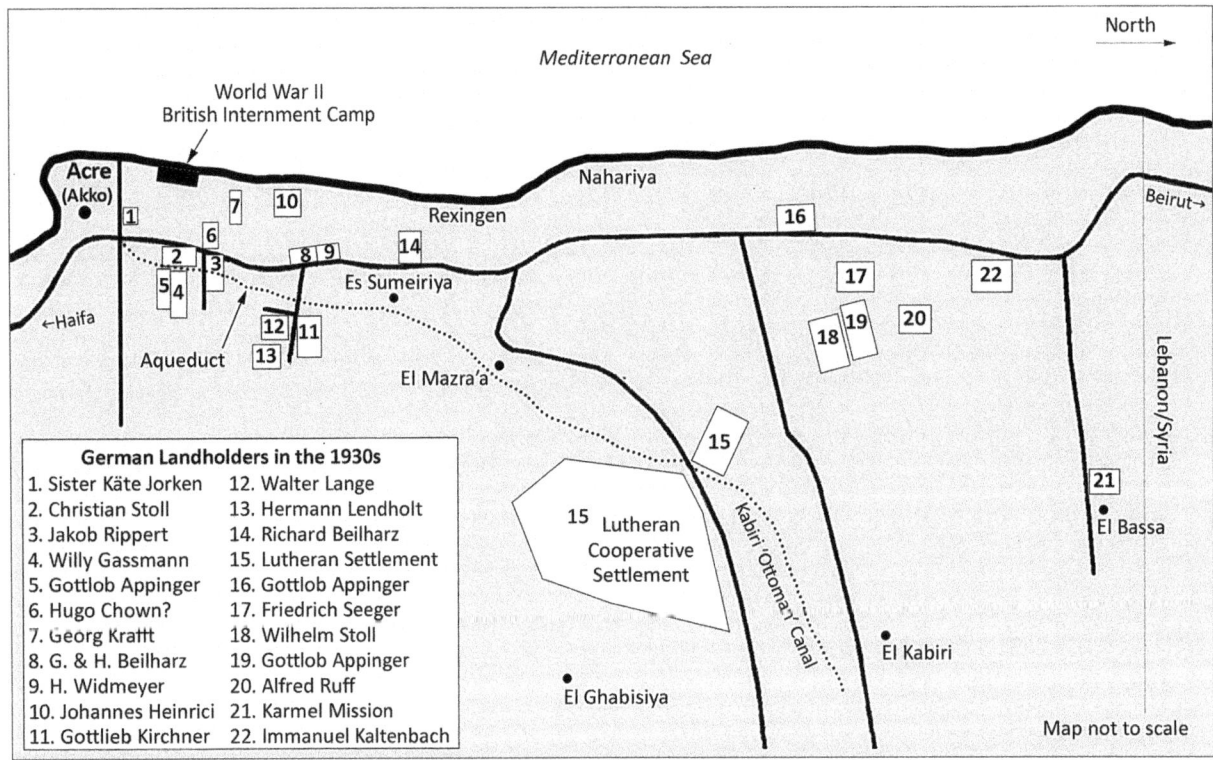

6.5 Sketch map of German landholdings north of Acre in the 1930s. This version is adapted from an original held by the Templer Archives, Australia. The original was prepared by Helmut Ruff in 1953, based on advice from Jakob Rippert. (PKI)

canal. This canal was shown on Jakob's map, running through the back of his farm. In 2025, Shomrat's archival website has photos of a 'German cowshed', demolished in 2016, and refers to it as 'one of several Templar (sic) buildings' in the area. The website refers to the Stolls, the Ripperts' neighbours, as 'one of five families who bought land in the Western Galilee'.[14]

According to Jakob, he was the first German to establish a farm north of Acre. In the years after 1932, others quickly followed and by 1939 there were more than twenty German properties between Acre and the Lebanese border. One of the German landholders was Christian Stoll (1904-1982), who ran a florist shop in Haifa. He developed a successful flower nursery on a property next to the Ripperts' farm. Unlike the Ripperts, the Stolls lived in Haifa rather than on their farm, but the two families became close, establishing a relationship that would be important to the Ripperts decades later in Australia. Christian's brother, the Haifa baker Wilhelm Stoll (1894-1976), also established a fruit and vegetable farm north of Acre after successfully discovering water on a property. It is likely this was done with Jakob's assistance.[15]

During the mid-1930s Jakob became involved as a board member in setting up a German Evangelical Settlement Cooperative, modelled on the Lutheran agricultural settlement at Waldheim. The goal was for the co-operative to provide farming opportunities for up to sixteen young Germans. Jakob purchased a share for his younger brother, Manu. The exact location of the property purchased for this co-operative is uncertain but it was about five kilometres northeast of the Rippert farm, somewhere between the Arab villages of Ghabisiya and Mazra'a. This venture was probably never fully realised. It is poorly documented and, like the German farms north of Acre in general, is overlooked in histories.[16]

Jakob was busy beyond his farm. Apart from his work with the Syrian Orphanage, he shared his expertise as a 'water expert' with all his neighbours, German, Arab and Jewish. For example, he advised Dr Soskin and Dr Rubins on the development of Nahariya, a neighbouring Jewish settlement on the Mediterranean coast. Soskin was a leading Zionist, agronomist and promoter of Jewish agricultural settlements. He was one of the founders of Nahariya and, as reported in the *Palestine Post*, in 1937 he described two years of successful work at the site. This work included the laying down of '14,000 metres of pipes for irrigation purposes'.[17]

One of the chapters in *Nothing Can Make Them Stumble*, Herb Meinel's history of the Stoll and Meinel families, is entitled 'The Fabulous 1920s and 30s'. It describes the families' time in Palestine when, after the setback of the First World War, the German community quickly recovered, prospered in a growing economy and came to relish their lifestyle, whether in cosmopolitan Haifa or on one of the agricultural settlements. The Stolls and Meinels who grew up in Palestine in this period looked back on it as the 'fabulous years' of their lives. It was a sentiment widely shared by children who were part of a unique German community but who viewed Palestine as their homeland and who were likely to have Jewish, Arab and English friends. The Ripperts were the same. As Jakob would later recall, 'we loved our home near Acre very much, the country and the people'. After Reinhart was reunited with his parents, he spent his early childhood years with them on the farm, with family photos capturing a simple but happy rural lifestyle.[18]

6.6 The view north from the roof of the Rippert farm-house. On the right is the Ottoman Aqueduct and on the left the main road north skirts a high point. Indistinct, directly north from the roof, are the tents of a British army camp located on the current site of Kibbutz Lohamei HaGeta'ot. These features help to locate the farm in the vicinity of Kibbutz Shomrat. (RPA)

6.7 The farm, showing extensive development, including the cypress trees planted by Jakob (RPA)

6.8 A gathering at the Rippert farm on the 50th anniversary of the founding of Haifa's Lutheran community. The tall, bearded man at centre left is Pastor Detwig von Oertzen (1876-1950), Pastor in Haifa and Waldheim in the 1920s and 1930s. Charlotte Rippert is standing in the middle, facing her left. (RPA)

Palestine, 1931-1941 51

6.9 Reinhart on the family farm in 1933. Written on the back is a caption: 'Reinhart on forbidden paths'. (RPA)

6.10 Reinhart with neighbouring children in the mid 1930s. Left to right, Ruth Stoll, Walter Stoll, Reinhart Rippert, Herta Stoll, unknown. (RPA)

Unfortunately for the Palestine Germans, by the mid-1930s there were two signs that their cherished interlude in Palestine might be coming to an end. The first was Nazism. The second was growing Arab opposition to Jewish immigration.

During the 1930s around 19% of Palestine Germans joined the Nazi Party. Others were active in Nazi associations such as youth groups. By comparison, in 1945 only about 10% of the population of Germany were party members and membership among overseas Germans in general was as low as 5%. Why did Palestine Germans appear to join or support the Nazi Party in disproportionate numbers? Paul Sauer, author of the most comprehensive history of the Templers, has explained that they 'fell under the spell of patriotic euphoria' and, as a vulnerable overseas community, welcomed the arrival of a strong German government and 'became enthusiastic about the strong national community conjured up by National Socialism'. The 'dark side' of Nazi methods and ideology, he suggests, 'remained largely concealed from Germans abroad'.[19]

German historian Heidemarie Wawrzyn, in her book *Nazis in the Holy Land 1933-1948*, has challenged what she sees as Sauer's 'excessively sympathetic' view of the Templers. After extensively documenting Nazi related activities of Palestine Germans as a whole and providing a long list of party members and their details, Wawrzyn argues that they 'excelled at ignoring the Nazi regime's persecution of its Jewish population'. This persecution was made clear by Nazi race laws, the violence of *Kristallnacht* in 1938 and the mass emigration of Jews from Germany to Palestine after the Nazis came to power. Even after the full extent of Nazi evil became known, Wawrzyn suggests, Palestine Germans 'displayed a shocking lack of sensibility and responsibility for having welcomed the totalitarian, racist Nazi regime and having participated in the organizations and celebrations of the NSDAP [Nazi Party] in Palestine'.[20]

As Wawrzyn concedes, as well as support, there was opposition to Nazism from what may have been a silent majority whose members, for a variety of reasons, failed to assert themselves. One of those reasons was intimidation. *Die Warte des Tempels*, the Templer publication, reflected some of the tensions created by Nazism for Germans in Palestine. In its December 1933 issue, *Die Warte* expressed pride in the actions of Hitler in eliminating 'class disorder' and communism, but it also reminded readers to tolerate a diversity of views and not call into question the patriotism of those who retained reservations about Nazism. In early 1935, due to disquiet in Palestine about the way in which it was presenting Nazism, editorship of the *Die Warte* was transferred from Germany to Palestine. A subsequent issue highlighted the contradiction between the Templers' preservation of 'the purity of our German national character' in Palestine, which appeared to align with Nazi ideals, and misgivings of a religious nature: 'One cannot reconcile the superiority of one race with one's belief in God the Father of all men.'[21]

Jakob Rippert was a member of the Nazi Party. His membership can be used to illustrate how difficult it is to form judgements about those who were party members. With a membership apparently dating from 1934, it might be assumed that he was an enthusiastic 'early joiner'. This needs to be viewed beside the fact that in 1933 the Ripperts had given refuge to a Jewish family from Auerbach who had fled Germany after Hitler came to power. Albert Kahn, his wife Marie Clara and their son Harry stayed with the Ripperts on their farm until Jakob helped Albert to find work and accommodation in Haifa.

In 1948 Albert Kahn wrote a detailed reference describing Jakob's actions and Harry Kahn remained in contact with Jakob and Charlotte until the 1960s.[22]

Apart from this single documented act of kindness towards Jewish refugees from his home village, Jakob appears to have worked well with his Jewish neighbours, including when assisting with the early development of Nahariya. Moreover, he was a prolific writer of letters. In these letters, across decades, his passionate commitment to Christianity is almost always evident. Nazism, by contrast, is never mentioned, other than to express shock at what was revealed after the Second World War. There is simply no evidence, in his writings or actions, to show Jakob was in any way committed to Nazism or even vaguely interested in politics. Why, then, did he join the Nazi Party? It was a question he would have to answer before a denazification tribunal when he returned to Germany in 1948.

Ultimately, there were probably few fanatical Nazis in Palestine, many whose party membership was not indicative of a strong commitment to Nazism and a significant number whose opposition to Nazism is easily overlooked. Even so, the prevalence of Nazi Party membership and activity in Palestine continues to be a controversial subject. Beyond Sauer's explanation involving poorly informed colonial patriots being seduced by the apparent return of old-fashioned values and strong government in Germany, it remains difficult to account for. After all, most of the Palestine Germans, Templer and Lutheran, were committed Christians. The following thoughts, written in 1995 by German Templer Brigitte Hoffmann, seem an appropriate reflection for those Palestine Germans who, whatever their intentions, appeared to endorse Nazism:

> If National Socialism built its ideology on the thesis of a master race and other inferior races (and granted the master race the right to turn the other, inferior races into labour slaves), then there was an unbridgeable gap between this doctrine and that of Christianity and even more so that of the Temple. It did not take much understanding to see this unbridgeable gap. And yet we ourselves have failed in this.[23]

Some Germans were alert to the longer-term implications of Nazi racial policies for their own position in Palestine. In the late 1930s, a more immediate danger was posed by the Arab uprising of 1936-1939. During the 1920s and early 1930s there had been outbreaks of violence as Arabs began to react against ongoing Jewish immigration and settlement. In 1933, the advent of Hitler's government in Germany gave further impetus to this immigration as Jews fled Nazi anti-Semitic policies. Between 1931 and 1939, the Jewish population of Palestine increased from 175,000 to 460,000. This resulted in the Arab share of the population dropping from 82% to 70% in less than a decade.[24] In 1936, this influx of Jewish settlers, along with the realisation that the British mandatory government supported Zionist aims for the creation of a Jewish homeland, prompted an Arab revolt against British rule and Jewish settlement.

Despite feeling they generally had good relations with their Arab neighbours, the Germans in Palestine became caught up in the period of protracted violence lasting from 1936 until the revolt was suppressed in 1939. The area north of Acre, where the Ripperts lived, was affected by security concerns. In January

1937, the *Palestine Post* reported the murder of a German, Jacob Speker, on his farm near Nahariya. Evidence of the wider insecurity in the area is contained in a letter written by the German Consul in November 1938 about an 'Arab gang' threatening German settlers near Acre.[25]

In his history of the Templers, Paul Sauer describes how in 1936 and 1937 'young German settlers established a protection service for their widely scattered countrymen near Acre'.[26] This appears to be referring to the individual farms north of Acre and aligns with Jakob's recollection of his role at the time:

> In the uprising years from 1936 to 1939, my position was particularly difficult and my struggle for existence endangered by the raids and shootings among Arabs, Jews and Englishmen. Proof that the English authorities knew and respected me is the fact that during those years I was sworn in as a volunteer policeman to protect the German settlement against insurgent Arabs with 5 rifles and ammunition for myself and my employees. The District Commissioner, as well as the highest officials of the Agricultural Authorities were in and out of my farm, as well as the High Commissioner Sir [Arthur Grenfell] Wauchope, who was my guest several times.[27]

In July 1938, the violence came very close to home when it directly affected Christian Stoll, the Ripperts' neighbouring farmer. Living in Haifa, where he ran his florist's business, Stoll travelled backwards and forwards to his nursery, which was operated by Arab employees. In early July, he was returning to Haifa in his car, accompanied by his 5-year-old son Walter, when the car was stopped by an Arab mob which had gathered after a bomb explosion in the city's Arab market. The car was surrounded. Stoll was hit by a rock and forced to abandon the car while attempting to protect his son. The pair were only saved when one of the crowd recognised Stoll and stepped in to protect them, assuring everyone that he and Walter were German, not Jewish. A Jewish driver travelling just ahead of them had been shot dead. The incident occurred on one of the most violent days of the uprising, with the *Palestine Post* reporting at least twenty-three dead and many more injured in Haifa.[28]

Only a month before this outbreak of violence had threatened the lives of their neighbour and his son, the Ripperts had sent their own son, 8-year-old Reinhart, back to Germany to stay with Jakob's parents. Given the ongoing insecurity and their exposed position on their isolated farm, it seemed like a sensible precaution for Reinhart to stay with his grandparents in the relative safety of Auerbach until the situation in Palestine improved. At the time, the experience of Christian and Walter Stoll can only have confirmed the wisdom of this decision. What could not be anticipated was the impact of looming global events and the serious consequences they would have for the Ripperts as a family. Separated from his parents, Reinhart would grow up with his elderly grandparents in wartime Nazi Germany. It would be ten years before he would see Jakob and Charlotte again.

The suppression of the Arab Revolt in 1939 did not bring security for the Ripperts or other Germans in Palestine. It was a prelude to even more difficult and prolonged challenges. Nazi Germany's invasion of Poland on 1 September 1939, followed by Britain and France's declaration of war on Germany two days later, marked the beginning of the Second World War. As Paul Sauer notes, 'this signified the beginning of the end' for the Templers, along with other Germans, in Palestine.[29]

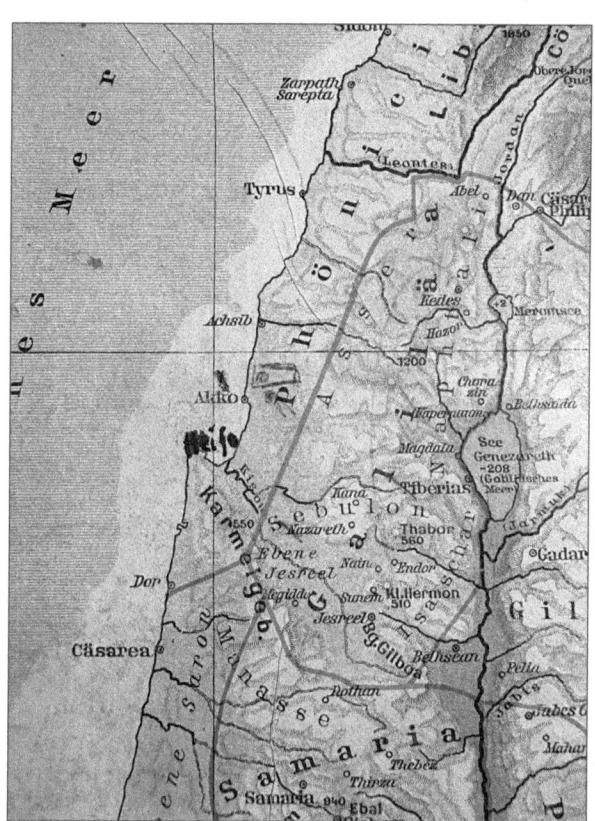

6.11 While at school in Germany, Reinhart marked the location of the family farm in his school atlas, just above Akko/Acre (RPA)

6.12 Charlotte and Reinhart with his grandparents, Johann and Eva Rippert, when Charlotte took Reinhart to Germany in 1938 (RPA)

As had happened in 1914, prior to the outbreak of hostilities hundreds of young German men left Palestine in August 1939 to enlist in the German military. Among those who felt obliged to fulfil their military obligations as German citizens were Christian Stoll and his brother-in-law Martin Meinel (1904-1986). Both Stoll and Meinel survived the war and would meet up with the Ripperts again in the 1950s in Australia's Barossa Valley. On the other hand, in 1939 Jakob's younger brother Manu was already in Germany, where he had returned to complete his second period of labour service and marry. Drafted into the army, he was killed on the Eastern Front, in Ukraine, on 18 July 1941.[30]

As soon as war was declared, the British authorities in Palestine took measures to deal with the security risk posed by what they saw as potentially dangerous enemy aliens living in the Mandate. German men up to the age of 50 were arrested and taken to an internment camp near Acre. German women, children and the elderly were confined to their homes or guarded settlements. As a male considered fit for military service, Jakob was interned on 2 September. Charlotte was allowed to continue managing their farm for a short time but in early 1940 all German property was taken over by the Mandate's Custodian of Enemy Property and in May 1940, along with family groups, she was confined to the German rural settlement at Waldheim.[31]

The camp where Jakob and other German men were interned was located on the Mediterranean coast, a few kilometres north of Acre. A former labour camp, it was known as Internment Camp No. 1 or Mazra'a Internment Camp. Jakob was employed as the camp's quartermaster. This was presumably due to his previous good relations with British authorities. While there is no direct evidence for the relationship, it is possible that he was on friendly terms with one of the senior British officers, Inspector Michael Higgins (1897-1967), who was married to a Templer, Luise Wächter.[32]

One of the roles of the quartermaster was to assist British authorities in processing new internees. In his 1971 memoir Jakob recorded two minor stories in relation to this role which came to assume prophetic significance. Firstly, years earlier, when he was studying missiology in Germany in the 1920s, he had come across a display case in Frankfurt's *Völkermuseum* which caught his attention. In the case was a book entitled *Kultur und Religion der Aranda und Laridja in Zentral-Australien* by the missionary Carl Strehlow (1871-1922). Another open book in the display case showed a portrait of Strehlow. The books and the portrait lodged in Jakob's memory and for a long time remained one of the few details Jakob knew about Australia. Secondly, as quartermaster of the Acre camp, in 1939 Jakob was asked to process Oskar Liebler (1888-1943), 'a little old man with a full white beard' who had been working as a missionary among Bedouins in Jordan. In one of the books Liebler had in his suitcase, Jakob found a portrait he recognised as Strehlow. The book, Liebler explained, was a biblical story and songbook translated into the central Australian Arrarnta language by Strehlow. For a brief period, 1910-1913, Liebler had worked at the Lutheran Church's Hermannsburg Mission in Central Australia where, from 1894-1922, Carl Strehlow had been the renowned Pastor. In 1939, as Jakob reflected in his 1971 memoir, there was no possibility of him imagining that one day he would be responsible for building the Carl Strehlow Memorial Hospital at Hermannsburg in remote Central Australia. Looking back, he saw the coincidences linked across decades as evidence that 'God's ways are strange and wonderful'.[33]

In the meantime, Jakob and Charlotte had no idea how long their internment would last or where it would take them. Like most of the Palestine Germans, they had not yet come to the realisation that their Palestinian idyll had come to an end.

Endnotes

1. Paul Sauer, *The Holy Land Called: the story of the Temple Society*, (trans. Gunhild Henley), Temple Society of Australia, Melbourne, 1991, pp. 131-132; *Memories of Palestine: narratives about life in the Templer communities 1869-1948*, Temple Society of Australia, Melbourne, 2005, pp. 63-64. Wilhelma was located outside the north-eastern corner of what is now Ben Gurion International Airport. The former German settlement is now an Israeli moshav, Bnei Atarot, and the Imberger house is one of several surviving German buildings.
2. 'Spuren des Tempels: Die württembergischen Templer im Heiligen Land', www.tempelgesellschaft.de/de/geschichte.php (21 February 2025). Betlehem was also called Bethlehem Galilee and should not be confused with the more well-known Bethlehem south of Jerusalem. Small groups of Templers lived in other locations in Palestine such as Nazareth and Neuhardthof, on the coast south of Haifa. Even though 'Templer' is often misspelt in English as 'Templar', Palestine's nineteenth and twentieth century German Templers have no connection with the medieval Knights Templar who were associated with the Holy Land during the crusades.
3. Alex Carmel, *Die Siedlungen der württembergischen Templer in Palästina, 1868-1918*, W. Kohlhammer, Stuttgart, 1973, p. 4, quoted in Mahmoud Yazbak, 'Templars (sic) as Proto-Zionists? The "German Colony" in late Ottoman Haifa', *Journal of Palestine Studies*, 28:4, 1999, p. 41.
4. Alex Carmel, *The History of Haifa Under Turkish Rule*, Yad Itzhak Ben-Zvi, Jerusalem, 1977, p. 116, quoted in Danny Goldman, 'The Architecture of the Templers in their Colonies in Eretz-Israel, 1868-1948 and their Settlements in the United States 1860-1925', Thesis, The Union Institute and University, Cincinnati, 2003, p. 3.
5. *Fabric of Society, The Templer Journey: an embroidered history*, Temple Society of Australia, Melbourne, 2009, p. 62; Sauer, pp. 51, 95; Jana Gur, 'The Rise and Fall of Israel's Oranges', *Tablet*, 15 December, 2020, www.tabletmag.com (21 February 2025); Salman H. Abu-Sitta, *Atlas of Palestine 1917-1966*, Palestine Land Society London, 2010, p. 40; Yossi Ben-Artzi, 'Religious ideology and landscape formation: the case of the German Templars in Eretz-Israel', in Alan R. H. Baker and Gideon Bigger (eds), *Ideology and Landscape in Historical Perspective*, Cambridge University Press, 2006, pp. 93-94, 103.
6. Jana Gur, 'The Rise and Fall of Israel's Oranges'; Mahmoud Yazbak, 'Templars (sic) as Proto-Zionists?', pp. 40-54. For a contrary view of Templer achievement and contribution to the development of Palestine, see Salman Natour and Avner Giladi, '"Eraser" and "Anti-Eraser" – Commemoration and Marginalization on the Main Street of the German Colony: The Haifa City Museum and Café Fattush', Mahmoud Yazbak and Yfaat Weiss (eds), *Haifa Before & After 1948: Narratives of a Mixed City*, Republic of Letters Publishing, Dordrecht, 2011, p. 160.
7. Sauer, p. 227; Heidemarie Wawrzyn, *Nazis in the Holy Land 1933 – 1948*, De Gruyter Magnes, Berlin & Jerusalem, 2013, pp. 73-74.
8. Jakob Rippert, Memoir, 1971, HStAD.
9. Gil Gordon, 'Die Schneller Dynastie – Drei Generationen protestantischer Missionsarbeit im Orient', H. Goren and J. Eisler (eds), *Deutschland und Deutsche in Jerusalem, Eine Konferenz in Mishkenot Sha'ananim, März 2007*, Mishkenot Sha'ananim, Jerusalem, 2011, pp. 117-136.
10. Jakob Rippert, Memoir.
11. Ibid.
12. Jakob Rippert, *Lebenslauf*, 1948; Albert Kahn, Testimonial, 5 February 1948. Both documents are from Jakob Rippert's Denazification file, HHStAW, Bestand 520/02, N: 10797.
13. Jakob Rippert, Memoir; Ludwig Immanuel (Manu) Rippert, Memoir, c. 1940, HStAD.
14. Walid Khalidi (ed.), *All that remains: the Palestinian villages occupied and depopulated by Israel in 1948*, Institute for Palestine Studies, 1992, p. 23; Archion Shomrat, www.archionshomrat.co.il (16 March 2025). The Archion Shomrat website's reference to a 'German cowshed' in the location dating from 1906 casts some doubt on Jakob's claim to be the first German farmer north of Acre. The information on the website may not be precise but there are some indications that at least one German family was farming in the area before the Ripperts arrived.

15. Herb Meinel, *Nothing Can Make Them Stumble: The Story of the Stoll/Meinel Family*, Adelaide, 2016, pp. 92, 100-101.
16. Jakob Rippert, Memoir; Manu Rippert, Memoir.
17. Jakob Rippert, *Lebenslauf*; Jakob Rippert, Memoir; *Palestine Post*, 22 September 1937, p. 8.
18. Meinel, pp. 111-118; Robert Rockaway, 'The Screwy History of the Modern Knights Templer', *Tablet*, 22 March 2021, p.5 www.tabletmag.com (21 February 2025); Jakob Rippert, Memoir; letter, Charlotte Rippert to her sister Gertrud Zimmermann, 3 February 1932, HStAD. Charlotte's letter suggests that Reinhart did not join his parents until after their first summer in Palestine. Charlotte told her sister two interesting things in this letter. Firstly, she revealed that she and Jakob had borrowed money to purchase their farm. Secondly, along with caring for Reinhart in 1932, Jakob's parents appear to have been looking after a '14-year-old orphan girl' and a 'young Nubian'. How this worked for Jakob's parents in Auerbach in Depression era Weimar Germany is unclear. Charlotte did ask her sister to send children's clothes to her mother-in-law. We have no further detail about the reference to a 'young Nubian'.
19. Wawrzyn, pp. 73-74, 135; Sauer, p. 198.
20. Wawrzyn, pp. v, 144.
21. Wawrzyn, p. 67; Sauer, p. 207; *Die Warte des Tempels*, 15 December 1933 and 15 August 1935, quoted in Francis R. J. Nicosia, 'National Socialism and the Demise of the German-Christian Communities in Palestine During the Nineteen Thirties', *Canadian Journal of History/Annales Canadiennes d'Histoire*, 14: 2, 1979, pp. 241-242.
22. Albert Kahn, Testimonial, 1948.
23. Brigitte Hoffmann, 'Unsere Verantwortung in der Welt Gedanken über die Haltung der Tempelgesellschaft zum Nationalsozialismus', Der besondere Beitrag Beilage der *Warte des Tempels*, No. 2, 1995, https://www.tempelgesellschaft.de/posts/der-besondere-beitrag-414.php (17 March 2025). Only a small number of Palestine Germans were Catholic and few of these joined the Nazi Party.
24. Benny Morris, *1948: A History of the First Arab-Israeli War*, Yale University Press, New Haven, 2008, p. 14; Simon Sebag Montefiore, *Jerusalem, the Biography*, Weidenfeld & Nicholson, London, 2024, pp. 538-539.
25. *Palestine Post*, 28 January 1937, p. 5; letter, Consul Wilhelm Melchers to Auswärtiges Amt, Berlin, 23 November 1938 (Yad Vashem Archives, R 3/30) quoted in Wawrzyn, p. 96.
26. Sauer, p. 224.
27. Jakob Rippert, *Lebenslauf*.
28. Meinel, pp. 121-122; Walter Stoll, Interview, 27 November 2024; *Palestine Post*, 7 July 1938, pp. 1-2.
29. Sauer, p. 231.
30. Nicosia, p. 254; Meinel, p. 125; Manu Rippert, Memoir. Sources quote different figures for the number of Germans who returned for military service in 1939, ranging from 200 to 400.
31. Sauer, p. 231; Jakob Rippert, *Lebenslauf*; *Palestine Post*, 8 February 1940, p. 2 and 30 May 1940, p. 2.
32. Jakob Rippert, *Lebenslauf*; Danny Goldman, 'Fences of Hope: Headcount and a Daily Massage, Following Sketches of an Anonymous Detainee in Mazra'a Detention Camp', *Et-Mol*, 153, 2000, pp. 14-17.
33. Jakob Rippert, Memoir; M. Lohe, F. W. Albrecht, L.H. Leske, *Hermannsburg: A Vision and Mission*, Lutheran Publishing House, Adelaide, 1977, pp. 23-30. The title of the Strehlow publication is as quoted in Jakob Rippert's memoir. It was one of several volumes published in Frankfurt from 1907 onwards.

Chapter 7
Tatura, 1941 – 1944

In mid-1941, with Rommel's Axis armies advancing across North Africa from the west and fighting between Allied and Vichy French forces only a few kilometres to the north, the British decided they needed to remove potentially dangerous enemy aliens from Palestine. In June, German men who had been interned in the camp near Acre, along with women and children who had been confined to agricultural settlements, were brought together at Lydda (Lod), near Jaffa, where they were put on board a train. Only older German men and women were allowed to remain in Palestine. At Lydda, there was joy as families were reunited after being separated since September 1939, but there was also anxiety about where the journey they had been made to hurriedly prepare for would end.

This journey made a vivid impression on thirteen-year-old Helmut Ruff, who later wrote an account entitled 'Transported to the End of the World'. On 31 July 1941, after saying goodbye to his grandfather and elderly relatives, he and his family were put on a train from Haifa to Lydda, where they were joined by other internees. From Lydda, all the internees spent an uncomfortable night on another train heading south and then across the top of the Sinai. On the next morning, they reached Kantara (El Qantara) where they crossed the Suez Canal on a ferry. The young Helmut Ruff was conscious of stepping on to a new continent, Africa. During the day they were put on another train which took them down the west side of the Suez Canal. The internees then realized they were destined for the port of Suez on the Red Sea. This led to speculation about the British taking them to one of their east African colonies.[1]

Near Suez, Ruff recalled, their train was passed by a north bound troop train with 'soldiers stripped to the waist in the heat' yelling and waving at the internees. These were Australians heading north to fight Rommel's forces. They had arrived at Suez on the *Queen Elizabeth*, the ship the internees would board the next day. The train then passed a large encampment of German prisoners of war (POWs) who would also be put on board the *Queen Elizabeth*. Launched in 1938, this ship was Britain's most modern passenger liner but with the onset of war it had been converted into a troopship, with multiple bunks squeezed into the luxury cabins to double its passenger capacity to 5000.

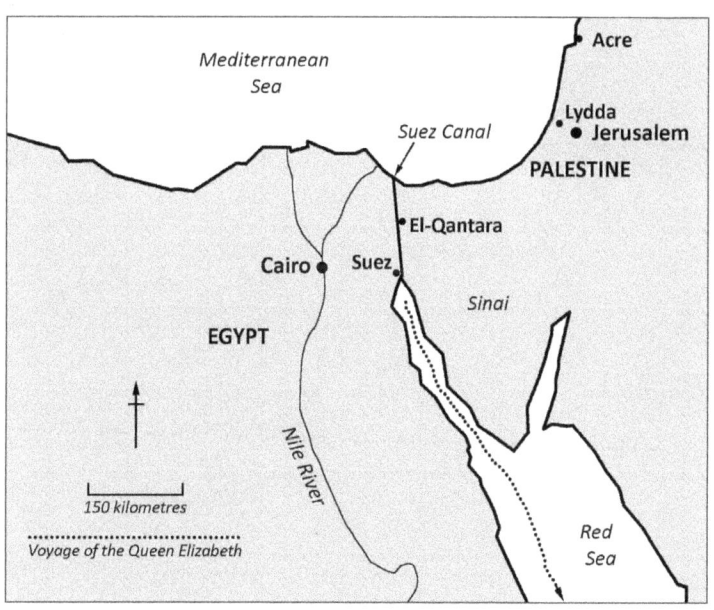

7.1 Palestine and Egypt, 1941 (PKI)

During 1941 it sailed between Australia and Suez four times, bringing Australian troops to the Middle East and transporting internees and German and Italian POWs to Australia on some of the return voyages.²

Because of the danger from German air raids and submarines, the *Queen Elizabeth* was anchored far out in the Gulf of Suez and surrounded by escort ships. The civilian internees and POWs were taken out to the massive liner on small boats which were dwarfed as they approached what Jakob Rippert described as 'one of the most beautiful and largest British passenger ships'. Once they reached the *Queen Elizabeth*, male internees were put to work stowing their luggage well below decks. Assigned quartermaster for the internees, as he had been in the Acre internment camp, Jakob was put in charge of this operation. In the extreme heat of an Egyptian summer, he described it as exhausting work for men who had just spent almost two years of inactivity behind barbed wire in Palestine.³

While the luggage was loaded, the German and Italian POWs and civilian internees from the Middle East were taken on board. The civilian internees being deported consisted of 170 Italians and 665 Germans from Palestine. The German group was made up of 536 Templers, 84 Lutherans (Evangelicals), 32 Catholics and 13 Jewish Germans.⁴

Late on Saturday 2 August 1941 the *Queen Elizabeth* weighed anchor and began to sail southwards down the Red Sea. On board, the POWs were confined to cabins on the lowest decks; on the higher decks male internees were separated from females and family groups. The cabins were hot and cramped. Due to security concerns, the portholes were often sealed and lighting prohibited at night. The groups were given some time above deck and came together at mealtimes, which were organized by the German POWs. The POWs provided welcome entertainment by leading the singing of German folk songs. Helmut Ruff remembered the Jewish police guards who accompanied them from Palestine being unhappy about this singing but, like other internees, described Australian soldiers who guarded the POWs as 'relaxed and friendly'. From a different perspective, among Jewish guards there was resentment about what

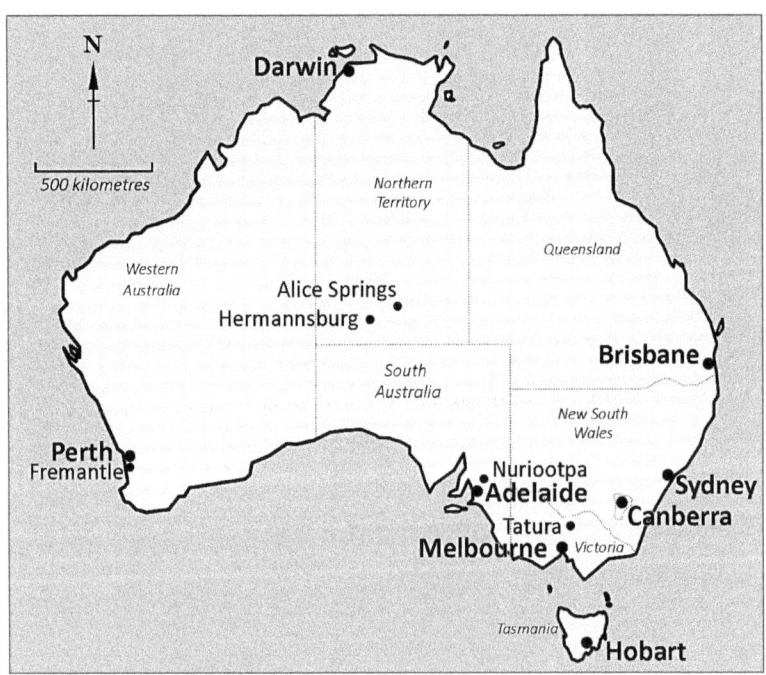

7.2 Australia, with key locations (PKI)

they saw as favourable treatment of the Germans by the British. The Germans had to move their own luggage because, when first directed to do so at Kantara, the Jewish guards had refused.[5]

When the *Queen Elizabeth* turned east after leaving the Red Sea, speculation resumed about its destination. Only after it left Ceylon (Sri Lanka) and took up a south easterly course did the internees realise they were being taken to Australia. This was confirmed by the Australian guards. The further south the ship headed, the colder it became and, after enduring the heat of the tropics, the Palestine internees found themselves ill-prepared for the cold weather as they approached the Southern Ocean. They stopped briefly in Fremantle, where Australian authorities took over. During a rough crossing of the Great Australian Bight, Helmut Ruff was annoyed to learn he had missed a sighting of whales.

On 23 August 1941, after a voyage lasting three weeks, the *Queen Elizabeth* entered Sydney Harbour. Despite the hardships they had endured and the uncertainties ahead, the stunning setting lifted spirits. As Helmut Ruff remembered: 'We admire the beautiful scenery, the lush vegetation coming right down to the water's edge, the many bays and above it the mighty harbour bridge.'[6]

Sydney's *Daily Telegraph* reported on the arrival of internees as a human-interest story, describing how Australian soldiers helped families as they were ferried ashore to a waiting train. It also captured images of children clutching the few possessions they had been able to bring from Palestine:

> Australian garrison soldiers carried babies and pushed prams when German and Italian internees from Palestine were landed in Sydney. The ferry-load of internees included many parents with young children and babies in arms. A few weeks' old German baby, wrapped in a patched shawl, was carried ashore by a grinning Australian private. 'I know all about it. I've got one of my own', he said.
>
> The same man helped a German mother with her twin daughters, aged three, who were dressed alike in scarlet woollies. Suitcases, bundles, cane baskets, and water bottles were carried, from the ferry to the train for internee mothers. Some of the small girls wore dark blue ski suits and carried school bags strapped to their backs. Younger girls nursed dolls and teddy bears. One boy, in a brown Tyrol suit, carried a bucket and a hobby horse.[7]

The *Sydney Morning Herald* published photos of POWs and a family as they disembarked. While the adults in the family 'wore solemn faces', the *Herald* observed, 'the children smiled a cheerful greeting to the new land in which they would live for the duration of the war'.[8] It was an insightful observation which contrasted the anxieties of the adults torn from their established lives with the cheerful optimism of children who were embarked on a long adventure from which they would emerge with surprising resilience.

In Sydney, the internees were put on a train for the last stage their long journey. Even though the train was more comfortable than the one that had taken them from their homeland to Egypt a few weeks before, this final leg seemed to go 'on and on' as they passed, firstly, Sydney's 'single storey houses set in their own gardens', then the countryside, with its little towns, farmhouses and native bush and, on the following morning, 'open country with fields stretching to the horizon'. When they reached the Murray River border between New South Wales and Victoria at Tocumwal, the internees were surprised to have to change trains because the two states had different rail gauges, a legacy of the railways being built in separate colonies during the nineteenth century. The Victorian train took them to a siding near Rushworth, where armed soldiers supervised their transfer to buses. Late on 25 August 1941 these buses drove into a nearby camp surrounded by barbed wire and delivered the internees to what, for most, would be their home for the next five to six years.[9]

Helmut Ruff has given us this description of his family's first night in their new home:

> We are surrounded by barbed wire, guard towers and searchlights…
> We have been allocated two small rooms. The only furniture they contain are beds made of timberframes with wire mesh nailed to them. On top lie straw palliasses and several grey army blankets. It is freezing cold in the unlined rooms. The outside walls are corrugated iron,

7.3 Photograph appearing in the *Sydney Morning Herald* when it announced the arrival of the Palestine Germans on 25 August 1941. In front are Gottlob and Berta Beck and their daughters Hannelore, 11, and Gudrun, 6. (Information, Doris Frank TSA; photo, *Sydney Morning Herald* and National Library of Australia's Copies Direct)

> internal walls are of thin masonite sheets, the ceiling is formed by the corrugated asbestos-cement roof. Along the length of the outside walls, under the eaves, is a 30 cm open strip covered only with chickenwire.
>
> We crawl into our beds in our warmest clothes and with extra socks on, trying to get warm, when the lights go out in all the huts. Only the powerful lights along the perimeter fences and the searchlights in the watchtowers light up the night. What are they doing to us? Have we deserved this? Did they bring us almost one third around the globe to finish up in a place like this? We feel like the convicts 'transported at the King's pleasure to the end of the world'. Are we the last convicts to be deported to Australia?[10]

Even after the first few months, when they had adjusted to camp routines, internees were still getting used to their new environment:

> Everything is very strange, of course. The only trees we see are eucalypts, the grass appears to be a different green, some of the birds seem to laugh at us, the sheep we sometimes see have no tails and the horses pulling the army wagons are so much bigger and more powerful than the ones we knew in Palestine. The moon seems to hang upside down in the night sky, the stars are different and the sun stands in the north at noon.[11]

The German family groups from Palestine, along with Italian families, were housed in Camp 3. About 150 kilometres north of Victoria's capital, Melbourne, the camp was located roughly halfway between two small towns, Tatura and Rushworth. At different times, both these names were used to refer to the camp; only Tatura has been used in this account.[12] Although cold in winter and hot in summer, and for the internees appearing relatively featureless, isolated and sparsely populated, the landscape around Camp 3 consisted of gently undulating farmland and scattered bush in a pleasant part of rural Australia. A few kilometres to the east was a lake, the Waranga Basin Reservoir, where the internees would later be taken on picnic outings. Nearby were other camps, including those housing POWs and some of the 'Dunera Boys', a group of predominantly Jewish German refugees who had been interned in Britain as enemy aliens. In mid-1940, they were forced to endure a horrific voyage to Australia on the troopship *Dunera*, when many were mistreated by their British guards.[13]

In addition to the Italian and German families from Palestine, at various stages Camp 3 held 154 German nationals detained in Australia, 78 Germans from New Guinea who were mostly missionaries and their families, 6 German technical or academic experts who had been working in Iran, along with their wives, and 11 Germans who had been living in the Straits Settlement (Malaya). During the period of internment 91 children were born. Camp 3 was divided into four compounds, A, B, C and D. Jakob and Charlotte Rippert shared a hut with other families in Compound C. Helmut Ruff's father, Gottlieb, was elected leader of Camp 3 and Compound C. As in the Palestine camp and on the *Queen Elizabeth*, Jakob continued in his role as quartermaster, a job that kept him on his feet 'from early morning until evening'.[14]

At the time of their arrival in the Tatura camp, Australian Templer historians Doris Frank and Renate Weber have described the general view among internees as being 'that Germany would win the war and they would be able to return to Palestine'.[15] Over time, this view would need to evolve. Meanwhile, the internees set out with a determination to make the best of their situation by improving their basic living conditions, allocating roles to manage the daily routines of camp life and developing a wide range of community activities. In this they were given considerable autonomy and support by the Australian military authorities, who were more than happy for the internees to look after themselves, especially when it could be done with the quiet efficiency for which the Germans had a reputation.

As quartermaster, one of Jakob's first tasks was to work with the Australian guards to organize the internees' luggage when it arrived. An older Australian officer, Captain William Anderson Moncur (1896-1962), was impressed that Jakob knew most of the German families and was able to organize the luggage so efficiently. The two got along well and Moncur, a farmer, even raised the possibility of Jakob coming to work on his farm when the war was over.[16]

Moncur was also a member of the Victorian Parliament. On one occasion he brought a delegation of politicians and a wounded Australian army officer to visit the camp and introduced them to Jakob. The wounded officer, who Jakob described as having 'lost a leg fighting the Vichy French in Palestine in 1941' was Roden Cutler (1916-2002), one of Australia's most distinguished military figures and later a diplomat and long-term Governor of New South Wales. The action in which Cutler lost his leg, and for which he was awarded the Victoria Cross, took place in Lebanon in early July 1941. It was part of the Syrian

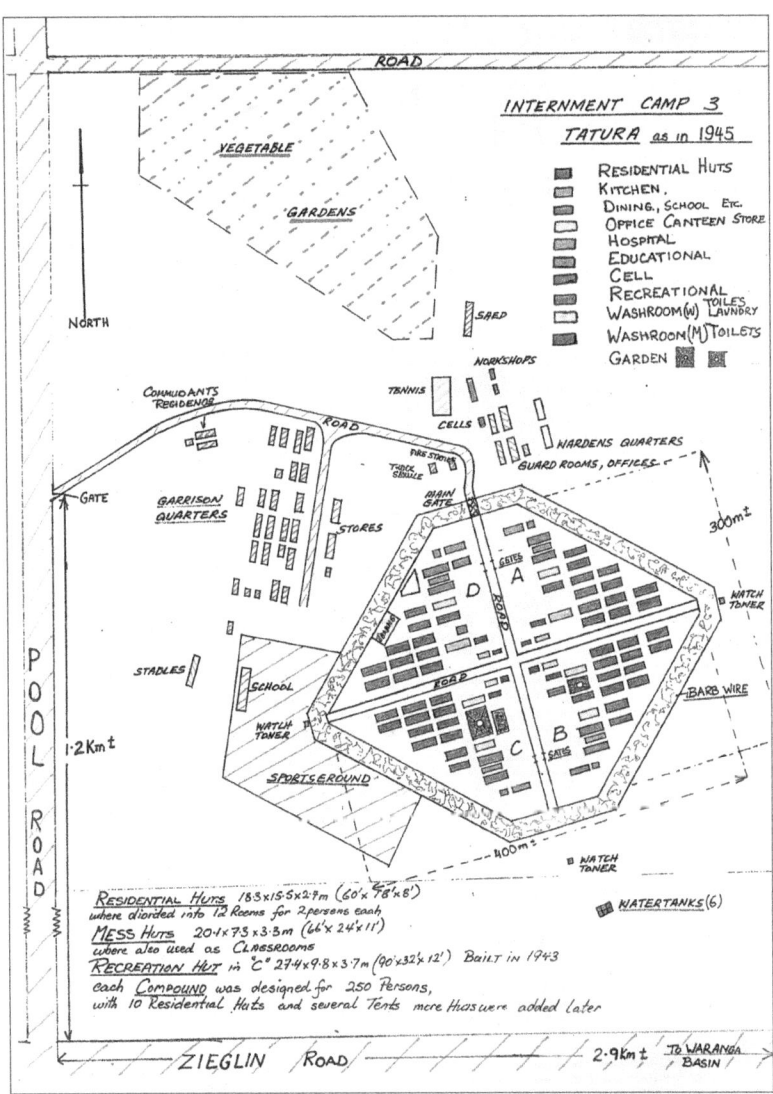

7.4 Camp 3 plan drawn by Helmut Ruff (TSA)

Campaign, fought on Palestine's northern border in June and July 1941, which had influenced the British decision to remove enemy internees from Palestine. According to Jakob's recollection of their meeting, Cutler told him he had visited the German settlements at Sarona and Wilhelma while he was recuperating in Palestine and been impressed with 'what German diligence had built'. Cutler followed this observation with an invitation: 'we want all your people to stay here in Australia and settle with us. We will help you get compensation from the Jews or whoever owns the land after the war.' Written by Jakob in 1971, this version of his conversation with Cutler suggests unusual insight and openness on the part of the young officer and future diplomat in relation to both Australian government policy and post-war developments in Palestine.[17] It is possible Jakob's recollection was influenced by hindsight and that he was recalling a conversation he had not with Cutler, but with one of the accompanying politicians, whom he does not name.

Roden Cutler visited the Tatura camp when he was serving as a member of the Aliens Classification and Advisory Committee, which had been set up by the government to report on conditions experienced by internees. Although mainly concerned with the classification and internment of enemy aliens from within Australia, the committee played a role in ensuring that all internees were treated as humanely as possible under wartime conditions. This committee was made up of some eminent figures and chaired by the

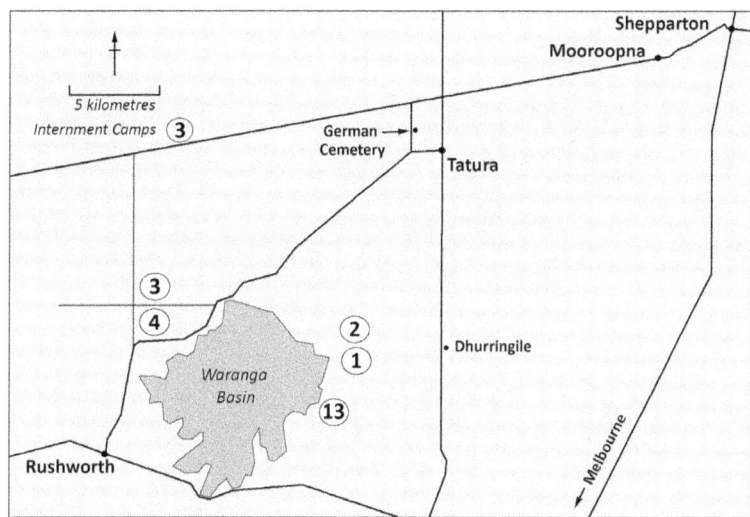

7.5 Map showing Tatura and Rushworth camp sites (PKI)

7.6 Camp 3 site today (PKI)

politician Arthur Calwell (1896-1973), who would go on to become Australia's first Minister of Immigration after the war.[18] It may be no coincidence that the conversation Jakob reported having with Cutler resonates with the vision Calwell developed for a major post-war immigration scheme.

Part of Jakob's role was to assist in organising various work groups to staff the kitchen, gather firewood, clean the common areas and operate a workshop. Within a short time, the internees requested and were supplied with additional equipment (from chamberpots for children to cleaning and writing materials), established a vegetable garden, set up a school, dental and medical clinics and used sheets of plywood to add internal lining to their basic huts. According to the diary of Camp 3's leader, Gottlieb Ruff, treatment by the Australian Army was 'correct and fair' and the food supplied was 'good and plentiful'. There was no shortage of food, as experienced by civilians in Germany during and after the war.[19]

By 1942, four kindergarten teachers were catering for 81 children aged from three to six. Towards the end of the year a total of 173 children were being taught by fourteen teachers. These teachers were all qualified internees or subject experts. Once senior classes were added, for sixteen to eighteen-year-olds, the camp's school offered matriculation courses which were later recognised in both Germany and Australia. Dental care was provided by one of the internees, Dr Xilo, who was supported by an Australian Army dentist. The Medical Clinic was run by Australian Army doctors while Dr Rubitschung, an internee whose German qualifications were not recognised, was permitted to act as a medical orderly.[20]

In Jakob Rippert's memoir he describes how Charlotte began to play music on her violin and sing with some of the young girls. The violin, originally a present from her father in Germany, had been brought to Australia from Palestine. These musical sessions were taken over by Pastor Schneller, who developed a chamber music orchestra. In time, in addition to this orchestra and a brass band, there was an accordion ensemble, a male voice choir and various groups who performed in concerts and plays. These performances took place in a meeting hall built under Jakob's direction and equipped with a large stage.[21]

With so many children in the camp and strong German traditions around its celebration, Christmas was an important time. Helmut Ruff's memory of Christmas 1941 is of days of 40ºC temperatures, along with a dust storm, making life in the camp's corrugated iron huts almost unbearable. On Christmas Eve, 'the few candles on the make-do Christmas trees made of eucalypt branches bent double in the heat'. Christmas 1943 was a much more joyful affair. The internees were allowed to collect pine branches to make Christmas trees, the 10.30 pm lights out rule was waived for Christmas and New Year celebrations and the camp canteen was permitted to buy enough kegs of beer to allow a ration of ½ a litre per adult. A busy few weeks of activities and entertainment concluded on New Year's Eve with separate Templer and Lutheran religious services followed by a concert in the meeting hall.[22]

For Helmut Ruff, a preserved program of the 1943 Christmas and New Year activities served 'as a reminder of how our parents and relatives, our friends and fellow internees, under adverse and often primitive conditions and after four years behind barbed wire did not lose their good spirits, their sense of humour and their dignity and "made the best of it"'. In his diary, Gottlieb Ruff made a curious observation regarding the uplifting, community building experience of the New Year's program. The motto for the evening, he recorded, was '*eine KDF-Fahrt*' (a Strength Through Joy Voyage). This was a clear reference to *Kraft durch Freude* (KdF – Strength Through Joy), a program of subsidised cultural and leisure activities, including sea voyages, the Nazi Party's Labour Front had established in Germany in 1933. In Nazi Germany, the purpose of the KdF program was to win over German workers and integrate them into the Nazi national community.[23]

A message from internee Wilhelm Fugmann in the 1943 Christmas program offers another perspective on the community values at work:

> Father Christmas from Germany (in the form of Red Cross parcels) seems to have been held up by the war and the blockade whilst children wait for him here with yearning eyes. All we can give to each other had to be made by ourselves. Scraps of wood, empty steel cans, silver foil and other materials have been utilised. The most precious material we had, however, was the good will, the love and the enthusiasm put into the preparations for this Christmas. For these there is no suitable thank-you. The greatest thanks must be the satisfaction of having contributed towards a festive Christmas.[24]

The resourcefulness contributing to a memorable Christmas in 1943 was evident throughout the long period of internment. This is demonstrated by the extensive collection of camp artefacts in the current exhibition at Tatura Irrigation and Wartime Camps Museum, where the internee experience is treated as an important aspect of local heritage. These artefacts include children's toys, models of camp buildings, embroidery and clothing made in the camp. A sewing machine on display is an ancient German Kayser model which had been owned by Christine Weiss in Palestine in the 1890s. She had taken it into internment in Egypt at the end of the First World War. When again forced into internment during the Second World War, the machine accompanied her to Tatura, where it was rostered for use by dressmakers, leatherworkers and sewing students. After internment the machine went with the Weiss family to South Australia before eventually being donated to the museum. Another wonderful exhibit is a set of puppets, with faces carved from fruit boxes and painted to resemble individual internees. These were used in puppet shows. The background scenes for these shows were painted by Italian artist Cesare Vagarini.[25]

Among a large collection of internee artwork held by the museum are several of Charlotte Rippert's paintings. An accomplished amateur artist, she painted portraits, images of camp life and scenes from Germany, Egypt, Palestine and Australia. A few of these paintings were exchanged within the camp as gifts on birthdays or other occasions. Some remain in private collections, but most appear to have later been donated to the Tatura Museum. One of Charlotte's paintings, Cairo Courtyard, was painted on the side of a butter box from Numurkah Butter Factory, one of the camp's suppliers. This painting was donated to the museum by the Glockemann family, who were German nationals interned in Australia. At Tatura they lived in the same hut as the Ripperts. Another of Charlotte's paintings, held by the Australian Templer Archives, depicts the Pross family's Haifa restaurant in a scene that is evocative of

1930s Haifa. The Bauhaus influenced restaurant building is instantly recognisable as the re-purposed but only slightly altered building on a roundabout at 17 Ben Gurion Avenue in modern Haifa. The Pross family was also interned at Tatura and Charlotte may have produced the likeness of its restaurant from a photograph they had brought with them.[26]

Cesare Vagarini was one of a handful of recognised artists interned in the Tatura camps. Another was a graduate and teacher from Germany's renowned Bauhaus design school, Ludwig Hirschfeld-Mack (1893-1965). Of Jewish heritage, he had fled Germany for England in 1936, only to be interned as an enemy alien in England after war broke out. In July 1940 he was transferred to Australia aboard the infamous *Dunera*. After being interned in camps at Hay and Orange, in New South Wales, Hirschfeld-Mack was moved to Tatura's Camp 2 in August 1941. He was released in March 1942 after James Darling, headmaster of Geelong Grammar, discovered that 'one of the best known art instructors on the [European] Continent' was an internee at Tatura. Darling arranged to have him released to work as an art master at Geelong Grammar. After proving to be an inspirational teacher, Hirschfeld-Mack subsequently settled in Australia, where he became a leading representative of the Bauhaus diaspora. During his internment, Hirschfeld-Mack taught classes and produced woodcut illustrations of the camps. In December 1941, he wrote this description of life at Camp 2, which was located about ten kilometres east of Camp 3: '… we are going swimming once a week, we are treated very decently, the climate is very healthy, the country beautiful, the food is excellent.'[27]

We have little evidence from which to reconstruct the day-to-day life of Jakob and Charlotte Rippert during their years at Tatura, but there are a few useful references scattered through official records, Jakob's 1971 memoir and the recollections of their fellow internees. As well as being a prolific artist, Charlotte studied a number of languages, including Japanese and Turkish, to complement her earlier Arabic studies; she taught Sunday school, contributed to the orchestra and gave painting and music classes to the children. In 1943 and 1944 she spent short periods in hospital on three different occasions, at the army hospital at Camp 1 and at the civilian hospital at nearby Mooroopna. This may have been related to gallbladder problems she had experienced on the *Queen Elizabeth*. Jakob was kept busy with his duties as quartermaster. These ranged from the routine, such as organising the collection of firewood, to major works such as superintending the construction of the 'great hall' or, in 1944, the renovation of the camp's septic tanks. He left the camp on at least two occasions. In 1943 he went to Camp 1 to see a dentist and in 1944 he was taken by car to Melbourne to be fitted with orthopaedic shoes. When he was released from the camp in 1947, Jakob was given a recommendation from Staff Sergeant Archibald Blackwood, who had known him for six years. Blackwood wrote: 'He has given every satisfaction and can be relied upon to use his initiative to the best advantage for his employer. He is reliable, honest and industrious, and I have no hesitation in recommending him to anyone requiring his services.' Major Edward Chapman, Camp Commandant in 1947, supported this assessment. 'As supervisor of internee work parties', he reported, Jakob had 'carried out his duty in the most efficient manner and has shown the utmost co-operation and willingness to help camp authorities in every way'. On the other hand, the Ripperts made contrasting impressions on the camp's children. While Charlotte was 'like a second mother', Jakob has been described variously as busy, 'very handy but severe' and 'pedantic', although not the 'fearsome figure' perceived by some.[28]

For the children in general, Camp 3 was a happy place. Frida Zerjal, an Italian from Palestine, referred to 'nothing but good memories' in a memoir published in 2003. She wrote: 'My memories of the camp are, strangely, of children being free. We were surrounded by lovely Australian guards who, I suppose, felt sorry for us children.' Her positive memories are echoed by Germans who spent much of their childhood in the camp. Though sometimes conscious of the anxieties their parents were dealing with, in many ways they had an ideal childhood in a supportive community, where parents were always around but so were numerous other children. Friendships formed often lasted a lifetime. All children lived equally in the same basic material circumstances, they benefited from an excellent education and they created their own childhood adventures in and around the camp. Garry Stoll remembers excursions to the nearby lake, led by a mounted soldier, and other unauthorised excursions outside the camp when the children absconded while a guard was asleep. If caught outside the camp, a child was confined in a special cabin for a day, an experience conferring a notoriety that was aspired to. Garry learnt some of his first English from the guards, including the word 'bloody', as in 'bloody kids' or 'bloody krauts'. On a darker note, along with the rich variety of religious and cultural activities organised by the adults, Nazi youth groups were active in the camp. Participation in these youth groups might amount to 'lots of running around and exercises' but, as in Germany, their purpose was to inculcate and sustain loyalty to the Nazi regime.[29]

The extent of commitment to Nazism among Palestine Germans, and the difficulty in drawing conclusions about it, were discussed in the previous chapter. Even when individuals were members of

7.7 Charlotte Rippert's painting of a Camp 3 scene, c. 1944 (RPA)

7.8 Rear of Charlotte Rippert's *Cairo Courtyard*, which she painted on the side of a butter box used by one of the camp's suppliers. (TAM)

7.9 Exhibits at Tatura Irrigation and Wartime Camps Museum. Top, three of Charlotte Rippert's paintings. Bottom, the Kayser sewing machine which had been taken into internment in Egypt at the end of the First World War and to Australia during the Second World War. The leather handbag at lower left was made on the sewing machine by Johannes Weiss. (TAM)

7.10 Charlotte Rippert's painting, *Cairo Courtyard*, c. 1944. The painting was donated to the Tatura Museum by the Glockemann family in 1988. The Glockemanns had shared a hut with the Ripperts in Camp 3. (TAM)

7.11 Charlotte Rippert's painting of Haifa's Pross restaurant and beer garden as it appeared in the inter-war years, 1946. The building still exists on Ben Gurion Avenue in modern Haifa's German Colony. (TSA)

the Nazi Party, the nature of their commitment varied greatly. For most, it is suggested, it was about German nationalism and cultural identity rather than fanatical Nazism or racial identity. Nevertheless, the outbreak of war intensified whatever nationalism was involved, particularly in a situation where many of the older males were First World War veterans and families had relatives serving with German forces in the Second World War. For example, Jakob Rippert was a First World War veteran and his youngest brother, Immanuel, was killed in action on the Eastern Front in 1941.

Internment only strengthened national bonds within the small German community and created circumstances where more committed Nazi Party members gained greater influence. Even though the Australian authorities adopted a relatively tolerant hands-off approach to internal camp governance during the war, the internees were closely monitored and there was an awareness of the depth of Nazi influence in Camp 3. In 1944, for example, an intelligence officer made the following comment on a letter written by Camp Leader Gottlieb Ruff which appeared to endorse Nazi-like attitudes: '… it portrays a sound insight into the doctrine which is preached to the many juvenile members of the camp. Evidence has never been lacking that these juveniles are being brought up in a complete Nazi atmosphere…'.[30]

Camp leadership positions were monopolised by prominent Nazi Party members, with Australian intelligence reports concluding this was the result of 'rigged' elections and bullying. Historian Paul Sauer mentioned the strong pressure to comply: 'Men and women who were critical of or even rejected

7.12 Camp 3 photo, 7 March 1945. Back row: Gretel Kaltenbach, Magdalene Kaltenbach, Immanuel Kaltenbach, Gotthilf Kaltenbach, Charlotte Rippert, Jakob Rippert. Front row: Helga Weinmann, Elfriede Kaltenbach, Anna Kaltenbach, Walter Weinmann. (RPA)

National Socialism (Nazism) had their difficulties.' Intimidation could work at different levels. The camp leaders, those with the best Nazi Party credentials, liaised with Germany's Nazi government by using the services of Melbourne's Swiss Consul. They played a role in ensuring the rights of all internees were looked after, but they also influenced the distribution of Red Cross parcels and pocket money supplied by the German government. Anyone perceived to be not *Reichstreue*, loyal to the Third Reich, might feel threatened by the possible withdrawal of these benefits. Longer term, in the event of a German victory, those who were not *Reichstreue* might fear retribution if their non-compliance was reported to the German government.[31] All of these factors are likely to have come into play in mid-1944, when the German internees of Camp 3 rejected an Australian proposal to allow individuals to leave the camp.

During May 1944 an investigative board, under the chairmanship of Justice Wilfred Hutchins (1884-1950), interviewed adult male and single female internees. All of those interviewed rejected any option to work outside the camp and said they were only interested in repatriation. In fact, the camp's Nazi Party leadership had orchestrated this apparently unanimous response. After a meeting to discuss the outside work option, they sent a letter to the Camp Commandant on 12 May 1944 to advise that internees only wanted to be repatriated and were not interested in working outside the camp. Some plausible reasons were given for rejecting the offer of supervised release. These included a fear of hostile Australians and the right not to assist an enemy during war time. With their own logic, the camp leaders put their case this way:

> The war aims repe[ate]dly expressed by the enemies of Germany who have declared [war] on the German Reich comprise the total destruction of the political, economical and cultural existence of

7.13 Students of Camp 3's Class I/A with their teacher, Mrs Gudrun Heider, in 1945. (AWM 030245/08)

the German Reich and the German nation. Consequently no loyal German can justly be expected to work for or contribute to the achievement of that goal.³²

An underlying reason for the prompt action in heading off the proposal was left understated by the camp leaders. Allowing individual internees or whole families to leave the camp and disperse into the Australian community would not only threaten the cherished cultural cohesion of the Germans, but it would undermine the ability of the camp's Nazi Party leaders to maintain a strict *Reichstreue* adherence within the Palestine group.³³

On 15 May a copy of the letter sent to the Camp Commandant was sent to the Swiss Consul, J. A. Pietzcker. This letter was accompanied by a list of the names of all those internees who supported the camp leaders' direction to reject the option of outside work. Also included was a list of the names of the handful of internees who had refused to support this decision. Jakob Rippert's name was on the list of those who had complied with the leaders, along with all but two of the Palestine Germans, Franz Nothbaum and Franz Skolar. German nationals interned from within Australia displayed more independence — twelve of this smaller group refused to support the position of the camp leaders. Consul Pietzcker was asked to submit a copy of the letter and the two lists of names to the Reich government as a record of how the Nazi

7.14 Grave of Jakob Decker who died at Tatura in 1946. The ashes of his wife, Johanna Frieda, are also interred here. Born in Jaffa, Palestine, in 1891, she died in Melbourne in 1992. (PKI)

7.15 Graves of two children of the Stuerzenhofecker family. They both died in tragic accidents at Camp 3 in 1946. (PKI)

The graves are located in Tatura's German Military Cemetery. It contains the graves of 250 Germans, internees and POWs, who died in Australia during the two world wars.

Party leaders within the camp had managed the issue. Attention was drawn to the list of names of those who had not supported the decision, with these individuals being labelled 'as of a different opinion than the by far greater number of the remaining inmates of this Camp'. In a subsequent Australian inquiry, Camp 3 leader Gottlieb Ruff rejected charges that up to 50% of internees had been intimidated into supporting the decision to reject outside work. When questioned about why the lists of names, including the few who had not supported the decision, were sent to Pietzcker, Ruff's response was translated as: 'For the reason that most of the people were getting the German pocket money. The Swiss Consul would determine who should get the pocket money, which meant who were true Germans and who were not.'[34]

If intimidation was a major factor in ensuring apparent Nazi solidarity in Camp 3, it may have had a lot to do with parents being anxious to avoid open hostility in what was very much a family camp. By contrast, Israeli historian Lior Yohanani has found evidence of open division between pro and anti-Nazi factions when only German men had been interned together back in Palestine. In their camp near Acre, the two factions had to be housed in separate huts and on one occasion there was an open brawl between the two sides. As Yohanani notes, this undermines extreme interpretations about the depth of adherence to Nazism among Palestine Germans.[35]

From the May 1944 interviews with internees, Australian intelligence officers formed the view that the 'Palestinian Templer Germans' were beginning to 'fear Palestine will be under the administration of Jewish Govt'. Thus, despite the apparent loyalty to the Third Reich suggested by their near unanimous compliance with the camp's Nazi leaders and the inclination always to reject adverse war news as Allied propaganda, it seems individual internees were beginning to develop a realistic anticipation of the outcome of the war and what this might mean for Palestine and their own expectation of returning to their former homes.[36]

Endnotes

1. Helmut Ruff, 'Transported to the End of the World', 1997, pp. 2-3, (TSA). 'End of the world', a phrase also used by Jakob Rippert in his memoir, highlights the enormity of the journey for the internees. Even though one was a child and the other an adult, Helmut and Jakob's memories of the journey are similar.
2. Ruff, 'Transported', p. 4; Chris Konings, *'Queen Elizabeth' at War: His Majesty's Transport, 1939-1946*, Patrick Stephens, Wellingborough, 1985, pp. 18-26.
3. Jakob Rippert, Memoir, 1971, HStAD.
4. Paul Sauer, *The Holy Land Called: the story of the Temple Society*, (trans. Gunhild Henley), Temple Society of Australia, Melbourne, 1991, p. 235; Ruff, 'Transported', p. 7.
5. Ruff, 'Transported', pp. 5-7; Jakob Rippert, Memoir; Garry Stoll, 'Transcript of Interview with Garry Stoll' (Interview), recorded by Meredith Campbell, 1996, Tape 1, Side A, p. 2, FRM; Lior Yohanni, 'Zionist identity and the British Mandate: Palestine's internment camps and the making of the Western native', *Nations and Nationalism*, 26:1, 2020, pp. 254-256.
6. Ruff, 'Transported', p. 7.
7. 'Internees Helped by Guards', *Daily Telegraph* (Sydney), 25 August 1941, p. 2.
8. *Sydney Morning Herald*, 25 August 1941, p. 6.
9. Ruff, 'Transported', p. 8.
10. Ibid., pp. 8-9.
11. Ibid., p. 9.
12. As a group, the camps were known as the 'Tatura camps', but Camps 1 and 2 were designated 'Tatura' and Camps 3

13. *Dunera: Stories of Internment*, State Library of NSW, 2024, pp. 8-10.
14. Doris Frank and Renate Weber (eds), *75 Years of Templers in Australia*, Temple Society Australia, Melbourne, 2016, pp. 7-8; Ruff, 'Transported', pp. 10-11; Jakob Rippert, Memoir, 1971. Of the 91 children born, 45 were to Palestine Germans, 17 to internees from Australia, 2 to those from Iran, 26 to those from New Guinea and 1 to those from Malaya (information from Doris Frank).
15. Frank and Weber, p. 32.
16. Jakob Rippert, Memoir; Moncur, William Anderson, Mobilization Attestation Form, NAA: B884, V5978, NAA.
17. 'William Anderson Moncur', Parliament of Victoria, www.parliament.vic.gov.au (15 November 2024); Jakob Rippert, Memoir; Colleen McCullough, *Roden Cutler, V.C.: The Biography*, Random House Sydney, 1988, pp. 109-149.
18. McCullough, pp. 186-188.
19. Ruff, 'Transported', pp. 11, 14, 16; Jakob Rippert, Memoir; Garry Stoll, Interview.
20. Jakob Rippert, Memoir; Ruff, 'Transported', pp. 14-15; Dietrich Ruff and Rolf Beilharz, 'Templers', in James Jupp (ed.), *The Australian People*, Cambridge University Press, 2001, p. 376.
21. Jakob Rippert, Memoir; Ruff, 'Transported', pp. 14-15.
22. Ruff, 'Transported', pp. 17-22.
23. Ruff, 'Transported', p. 21; Richard J. Evans, *The Third Reich in Power*, Penguin, London, 2006, pp. 465-466.
24. Ruff, 'Transported', pp. 21-22.
25. According to Tatura Museum's caption, the puppets were made by Alfons Konig, their costumes were made by Irmhild Beinssen and Gisela von Koch, and Alfons Kong and Cesare Vagarini painted backdrops for the puppet shows. Vagarini was an Italian artist. He and his wife had been interned while he was painting in Palestine when war broke out between Britain and Italy in 1940.
26. Leo Glockemann, Interview, 21 November 2023.
27. Andrew McNamara and Ann Stephen, 'Exile, Internment and Hirschfeld-Mack in Geelong', in Goad, Stephen et al. (eds), *Bauhaus Diaspora and Beyond*, Miegunyah Press, Melbourne, 2019, pp. 61-71.
28. Internee Service and Casualty Forms Charlotte Rippert (P36023) and Jakob Rippert (P36022), NAA: MP1103/1, NAA; Gottlieb Ruff's Diary, TSA; Jakob Rippert, Memoir; Garry Stoll, Interview, 1996; Leo Glockemann, Interview. Probably written to assist Jakob in getting work outside the camp after the war, in 1948 the camp references were later attached to his *Lebenslauf*.
29. Frida Zerjal, 'Frida's Story or the Intrepid Internees of Tatura', *The Genealogist*, December 2003, pp. 538-539, TAM; Garry Stoll, Interview (1996 & 2024); Leo Glockemann, Interview; Ted Stoll, 'Childhood Memories'; Sauer, p. 239.
30. 'Ruff, Gottlieb Samuel – Internee', NAA: A367, C71567, NAA. The same intelligence officer wrote this about Gottlieb Ruff: 'Ruff has been Leader here since his arrival in Australia with the Palestinian Germans. He has at all times been completely co-operative with authority, has made an excellent Camp Leader and bears the respect of Internees generally.'
31. Intelligence Reports No. 58 (Feb 1944) and No. 112 (Feb 1945) in 'Franz Joseph Haslinger (personal file and security reports)', NAA: A367, C70614 (NAA); Sauer, p. 239; Christine Winter, 'The Long Arm of the Third Reich', *The Journal of Pacific History*, 38:1, 2003, pp. 94-95, 100, 103.
32. Sauer, p. 245; Intelligence Report No. 72 (May 1944), Intelligence Reports – Tatura, NAA: MP70/1, 37/101/185 Tatura Part 4, NAA.
33. For a longer discussion of this episode, see Samuel Koehne's chapter 'Refusing to leave: perceptions of German national identity during internment in Australia, 1941-45', in Joan Beaumont, Ilma Martinuzzi O'Brien, Mathew Trinca (eds), *Under Suspicion: citizenship and internment in Australia during the Second World War*, National Museum of Australia, Canberra, 2008.
34. Letter, T.S. Hoffman and G. Ruff to J.A. Pietzcker, 15 May 1944, 'Franz Joseph Haslinger', NAA: A367, C70614, NAA; Record of interview with Gottlieb Ruff, 31 January 1946, 'Ruff, Gottlieb Samuel – Internee', NAA: A367, C71567, NAA.
35. Yohanani, p. 259.
36. Intelligence Report No. 72 (May 1944), 'Intelligence Reports – Tatura', NAA: MP70/1, 37/101/185 Tatura Part 4, NAA.

Chapter 8
Peace and Repatriation, 1945 – 1947

On 30 April 1945 the leader of the Nazi Party and Führer of Germany's Third Reich, Adolf Hitler, committed suicide in his Berlin bunker while sheltering from the Soviet Union's final assault on the German capital. Within a few days, German armies began to surrender and on 8 May 1945 the war in Europe came to end when German representatives agreed to Allied terms for unconditional surrender.

News of Hitler's death was reported in Australian newspapers and reached the Tatura camps within a week. On 6 May 1945 a memorial service was conducted by the former Director of Jerusalem's Syrian Orphanage, Pastor Hermann Schneller. According to the historian of the Templers, Paul Sauer, Schneller based his address 'in memory of our Führer Adolf Hitler and his friend Benito Mussolini' as well as the soldiers killed in action, on the Bible passage: 'There is no greater love than this, that a man should lay down his life for his friends (John 15, 13).'

When confirmation of Germany's defeat and surrender quickly followed, Australian authorities insisted on the election of new camp leaders, prohibited parades, use of the 'Heil Hitler' greeting or Nazi literature in the school and called for the handing over of all Nazi-related material such as flags, banners, photographs and literature. This sudden tightening in camp regulations occurred when POWs and internees lost many of their protections under the Geneva Convention once the war had ended.[1]

Rather than hand over the Nazi material, the internees staged a solemn ceremony on 18 May, when they burnt all their Nazi paraphernalia and sang patriotic songs. It was a dramatic gesture that left an impression on all present. A few days later, one of those who had attended the ceremony wrote about his experience in a letter:

> On Friday evening at 6 o'clock we all gathered together in order to put into the fire all the pictures, flags, books and everything pertaining to them [the Nazis]. Mr Ruff made a short, but as always a beautiful speech and committed the most beautiful picture of our beloved führer to the flames, but he goes on living in our hearts.[2]

Grotesquely deluded and defiant, at first glance these responses to Hitler's suicide and Nazi Germany's defeat may appear to be those of fanatical Nazis. Even if there were individuals who fitted this description in Camp 3, however, the extraordinary reaction to the demise of the Third Reich can also be explained by the sudden trauma experienced by a community of Germans who had sustained themselves in internment by maintaining a fierce loyalty to their national government. Given the associated denial and rejection of any news about Nazi atrocities as wartime Allied propaganda, it was going to take some time for most of the internees to process the shock of Germany's defeat and come to terms with the brutal reality of what Nazism had perpetrated in their name.

In July camp authorities attempted to influence this coming-to-terms by requiring internees in all camps to watch the confronting documentary films Allied forces had recorded when they first entered Bergen-Belsen and Buchenwald concentration camps. In Camp 1, Tatura Camp's War Diary recorded, the response to these films was 'very subdued'. In Camp 3, Saur suggests there was an initial resistance to accepting the reality portrayed by these films: 'men and women considered the crimes shown to be so monstrous that they regarded them as infamous enemy propaganda'. Ted Stoll, a child in Camp 3, recalled shock at the revelations of the crimes of the Nazi government and remembered internees finding it 'hard to believe that it could have happened and was true, until the evidence provided (mainly to adults, as it was too graphic for children) could no longer be dismissed as propaganda'. Jakob Rippert's statement, prepared in 1948 for a German denazification tribunal, probably describes the situation of most of the internees and their gradual acceptance of the true nature of the evil ideology they had, to varying degrees, given their allegiance to:

> … most of us had no idea of the true face of National Socialism [Nazism], neither before nor after the war, and certainly not during the internment. Each of us could hardly believe the terrible events that we learned about only in 1946 and 1947.[3]

In her recent study of wartime Germany at a local level, *A Village in the Third Reich*, Julia Boyd argues that it was possible to be 'both a committed Nazi and a decent human being'. The wartime mayor of the village of Oberstdorf, Ludwig Fink, was such an individual. An outwardly devoted Nazi who mouthed the party's rhetoric, in practice he protected local Jewish Germans, interpreted Nazi regulations with humane discretion and was a popular and effective village leader. Some of the Nazi leaders of the small German community in faraway Tatura may be seen in the same light. Despite being one of the prominent Nazi Party members, for example, Gottlieb Ruff was an effective camp leader who was well-regarded by both internees and camp authorities.[4]

In the absence of reflection from Tatura's Nazi Party leaders, there are limitations as to how far we can go in explaining their words and actions in support of Nazism. Just the same, these words and actions should not obscure the fact that there were many Palestine Germans who did not join the Nazi Party, who were concerned about what they had heard from relatives in Germany about Nazism in the pre-war years and who, during internment, struggled to maintain an independent outlook while they attempted to safeguard their families in a nationalistic environment dominated by the Nazi leadership. Ted Stoll remembered his father, Wilhelm, being one of those non-party members who had been alarmed by the pre-war actions of Germany's Nazi government. German historian Heidemarie Wawrzyn has identified Johannes Pross as an 'anti-Nazi' who stood out from the 'silent majority' by expressing his views.[5] Despite Jakob being a nominal party member, the Ripperts were close to the Stoll and Pross families.

In November 1945, as recorded in Gottlieb Ruff's diary, Camp 3 internees met to discuss the Australian government's latest inquiry into their fate, to be conducted by Justice William Simpson (1894-1966). Attendees included moderates such as Johannes Pross and Jakob Rippert. Still, the meeting appeared to maintain a combative tone, with the aim to 'educate comrades about giving evidence' to the investigative commission. The group resolved that Palestine Germans should ask to be 'sent back from where we were dragged away'. The frustration in this language is understandable but as the internees would soon discover, Germans were not welcome in post-war Palestine.[6]

Why were the internees still incarcerated in late 1945, well after the war in Europe had concluded? Why did many internees, including Jakob and Charlotte, remain in the Tatura camp for up to two years after hostilities had ended? This was at a time when the internees were keen to resume their pre-war lives and the Australian government's goal was to rid itself of responsibility for the enemy aliens Britain had burdened it with, close the camps and demobilise their military guards. Unfortunately, in the post-war world there were global obstacles preventing the early repatriation of internees from what, despite their incarceration, were relatively comfortable circumstances in Australia. Firstly, a global shortage of shipping would persist for years. Secondly, in the case of the Palestine Germans, there was great difficulty in their being accepted in either Germany or Palestine. In Germany, the national state of their citizenship and wartime allegiance, post-war Allied occupation governments were struggling to manage a collapsed economy and the influx of refugees from throughout war-devastated Europe. There was no desire to add to this influx when food and accommodation shortages would remain at crisis levels until the late 1940s.

In their Palestinian homeland, the preferred destination for most, the end of the Second World War marked the resumption of conflict between British Mandate authorities, Zionists and Palestinians. This conflict would result in the formation of the state of Israel in 1948. Immediately after the German capitulation, Jewish leaders wrote a letter to the British outlining strong reasons for Jewish opposition to the return of Germans to Palestine. This letter mixed facts with exaggeration, but it made it clear that in the aftermath of full revelations about the Holocaust, there would be no place for Germans in Palestine or any future Jewish state:

> With the advent of Hitler, the vast majority of the Germans of Palestine embraced the Nazi doctrines with enthusiasm and gave every tangible indication of their political and ideological allegiance to the Third Reich. In the disturbances of 1936-1939 their sympathies were avowedly with the terrorist bands ...

> Jews in Palestine feel utterly unable to contemplate the return to their country or the resumption of free residence in it of this community of Jew-haters. It appears to them inconceivable after millions of their brethren were exterminated by the Nazis and their henchmen with the tacit approval of the mass of the German people, that here in the very land of the Jewish National Home, Nazi Germans as fanatical as any of those who perpetrated the horror in Europe, should be allowed to re-establish themselves...[7]

By mid-1945, although still engaged in the war in the Pacific, the Australian government was anxious to turn its attention to implementing plans for post-war reconstruction. Still, the existence of Nazism within internment camps could not yet be left behind as a wartime issue. Apart from anything else, Nazism generated headlines. Even more so if it could be linked with the possibility of former Nazis remaining in Australia to compete with returning Australian servicemen for employment. In October

1945, when the government set up the Simpson Inquiry to investigate security concerns and the suitability of some internees as potential settlers, Adelaide's *News* ran the story under the headline 'Nazism Inquiry Immediately'. The same story quoted the new Minister for Immigration, Arthur Calwell, dismissing stories about Nazi plots in Australia as 'figments of disordered imagination'.[8] This robust response was in keeping with Calwell's long and skilful campaign to establish and promote what in the longer term would prove to be the most important element of the Labor government's reconstruction program, Australia's post-war immigration scheme.

At the end of May 1946, the government appointed Justice Wilfred Hutchins as Commissioner of yet another inquiry, this time focusing on internees 'detained by another Government and sent here for safe custody'. Like Simpson, Hutchins' task was to assess security risks and identify which internees should be deported. As part of this process, in June 1946 the Palestine Germans in Tatura's Camp 3 were given four options to choose from: 1) Did they wish to settle in Australia? 2) Did they wish to be released into the community and decide later? 3) Did they wish to be released into the community while awaiting repatriation? 4) Did they wish to remain in the camp while awaiting repatriation? Most, intent on being repatriated to Palestine, chose option 4. Then, in late June, Hutchins advised camp leaders that the British High Commissioner in Palestine had banned their return to Palestine. At a subsequent meeting, most of the internees changed their choice from waiting on repatriation to either settling in Australia or being released to decide later.[9]

Around the time it became clear that returning to Palestine was not an option, the focus of Hutchins' inquiry effectively shifted from identifying security concerns to recruiting migrants. Not only were most of the Palestine Germans viewed as ideal types, but they were already in Australia and they had assets in Palestine which made them even more attractive as settlers. The Australian government undertook to assist in seeking compensation for these assets and bringing the proceeds to Australia. This would be

8.1 'Getting his Guernsey', a cartoonist's comment on the seeming haste with which the Australian government offered settlement and naturalisation to former internees. The context for this exaggerated view was former Nazi Party internee Arnold von Skerst's application for naturalisation in 1946. The cartoon, by George Aubrey Aria, was published in Sydney's *Sunday Sun* on 26 May 1946.

a complex process and take years to complete. In the meantime, Hutchins was happy to recommend most Palestine Germans as desirable migrants. Not one to miss an opportunity, Immigration Minister Calwell met with some of the camp leaders, gave them a 'warm reception' and offered reassurances about aspects of settlement and employment.[10]

In Paul Sauer's view, Justice Hutchins was a 'discerning, unprejudiced and responsible man as well as a good judge of human character'.[11] Although the records show he could be patronising at times, he brought strong humanitarian instincts to his role. The same was true of his secretary, the public servant Henry Temby (1912-1969), who would go on to act as welfare officer for the Palestine Germans and develop close relationships with a number of them, including the Ripperts. Evidence of Hutchins' sensitivity to the plight of internees as individuals can be seen in an explanation he gave to government ministers for the difficulty some had in leaving their internment camps:

> Many of the internees are ignorant of Australian ways of life, speak poor English, have qualifications only for certain trades,… suffer from diffidence and forms of nervousness due to up to 7 years in internment, have families and assets overseas which they may or may not be able to bring to Australia, and of which they have had no information for years.[12]

Jakob and Charlotte were among the 'diffident' who, faced with no possibility of immediate repatriation, chose to remain in the camp. They were affected by all the factors outlined by Hutchins. In addition, having opted to return to Germany to be reunited with their son and Jakob's mother, they were fearful that leaving the camp and living in the Australian community might cause them to miss out on being notified when a ship became available. In these circumstances, their prison seemed like a familiar haven.

There was yet another cause for anxiety. In the first week of September 1946 Jakob Rippert spent a few days in the army hospital at Camp 1 after developing some alarming stroke-like symptoms — temporarily, his right arm became paralysed and he lost the power of speech. At the time he was working on the camp's lavatories, digging new trench latrines, and had been operating a jack-hammer. Jakob attributed the paralysis and loss of speech to the violent vibrations of the jack-hammer affecting the right parietal bone in his head, where he had sustained a serious injury in 1918 on the Western Front. A record of the doctor's report refers to 'hypertonic cramp' and raised blood pressure. No 'organic disorder' was detected, but Jakob was advised to avoid 'any excess of work, physically or mentally'.[13] Longer term, there is little evidence that Jakob was troubled by this advice, but at the time it was a serious health scare and it underlined how vulnerable Jakob and Charlotte might be 'on the outside' and how well looked after they were in the camp.

In mid-1947 Justice Hutchins began to re-interview those internees who remained in the camps. By this time, it is clear he was becoming impatient with the Ripperts' unwillingness to leave. In one of his interviews with the couple, Hutchins conceded there was still no shipping and that 'Germany cannot handle you at the moment', but then upbraided them: 'Why don't you want to go outside? Now look, you people have been told again, again and again that the fact of being out pending repatriation doesn't affect the position at all.' He was referring to the Ripperts' fear of missing out when a ship became available. Jakob's response was heartfelt: 'We like to go out, for the barbed wire we have had enough.' Even so, he reminded Hutchins, the couple had no funds, their property in Palestine was 'under confiscation and I reckon to see nothing for all my work', and they were aware of others who had left the camp and were struggling to survive on the outside. Charlotte sought reassurance: 'If my husband gets ill again and I have no money and we are out of the camp, are we allowed to come back to the camp?' Hutchins assured her they would be able to return.[14]

The record of Justice Hutchins' interviews with the Ripperts, like his dealings with other internees, makes it clear that his priority was to empty the internment camp and assist them in either returning to Germany or settling in Australia. He also had to assess security risks. It would have been quickly apparent that the Ripperts were not, and never had been, a security risk. In fact, Hutchins gave Jakob a school masterly pat on the back:

> I think if all the internees had acted like you whilst in internment, it would have been far better for the Australian authorities and internees. I want to congratulate you on your general behaviour whilst in internment.[15]

Why, then, had Jakob's name had been placed on an 'obnoxious' list? This peculiar label, attached to many of the internees, referenced a wide range of activities, from espionage and sabotage, to the organisation of pro-Nazi or nationalistic activity, to the maintenance of German national interests or influence. General 'good behaviour' notwithstanding, it would have been easy enough for Jakob to attract the catch-all 'obnoxious' label even though, apart from his Nazi Party membership and association with camp leaders, there is no evidence of his saying or doing anything remotely concerning. But the files relating to the repatriation of internees reveal an interesting complication in the use of the term after the war. In January 1947 there was an exchange of letters between the Department of Army and the Department of Immigration when the Minister for Immigration, Arthur Calwell, queried the appropriateness of so many internees, including women and children, being labelled 'obnoxious'. It was explained that the British government, which was responsible for the Palestine internees, would only prioritise the repatriation of Germans who were deemed a security risk. The 'obnoxious' label may have been kept in place, in some instances, in the belief it would assist an individual's chance of an early repatriation.[16]

In April 1947 Jakob and Charlotte received certificates issued by the Military Government in Germany to advise they had been given permission to return, as long as they stayed with Jakob's mother and undertook not to 'claim additional rooms'. In the following months, on Hutchins' advice, Jakob's name was removed from the obnoxious list. As Jakob later observed, 'my dear wife and I were declared "harmless"'. (While Jakob might note his Australian security assessment with irony, he would be required to prove his harmlessness all over again once he reached Germany.) Finally, Jakob received an offer of employment which, he told Hutchins, would be similar to the 'tropical work' he and Charlotte had done in Egypt and Nubia. The conditions were now in place for the couple to be released from camp while they waited for a ship to take them to Germany.[17]

On 12 August 1947, Jakob and Charlotte left the Tatura internment camp where they had spent the past six years. In Jakob's memoir he describes how they had accepted an offer of work from Pastor August Simpfendorfer, who was Secretary of the Lutheran Church's Finke River Mission. Jakob was engaged to work as a builder at the Church's Hermannsburg Mission in Central Australia while he and Charlotte were waiting to be repatriated. Pastor Simpfendorfer was located at Light Pass, near the town of Nuriootpa in South Australia's Barossa Valley. He had learnt about Jakob, his missionary background and building expertise, from internees who had already been released and found work in and around the Barossa Valley.

Upon their release, Jakob and Charlotte set out on a long journey that would take them through vast areas most Australians at the time had never seen. In the first stage, they travelled by train to reach Light Pass. Here, in the Barossa Valley, they found themselves in a pleasant, fertile wine-growing region which also happened to be the area of Australia with the highest concentration of German ancestry. A large proportion of the local people were descended from Germans who had arrived in South Australia as early as 1838. The Ripperts found a warm welcome from the Simpfendorfers, who had been born in Germany, and the former internees who had arrived in the Barossa Valley ahead of them and, in many cases, would settle there.

The second stage of their journey to Hermannsburg began when, after a few days in the Barossa Valley, Jakob and Charlotte boarded a train known as the Ghan. This name is a reference to camel drivers from British India, known generically as Afghans, whose camels provided essential transport in outback Australia from the 1860s until gradually replaced with motor vehicles by the mid-twentieth century. The 1947 Ghan was very different from the modern Ghan, a luxury train which now takes tourists between Adelaide and Darwin on one of the world's great rail journeys. The Ripperts travelled on the old Ghan, a ramshackle affair drawn by a steam engine. It was slow and subject to frequent breakdowns and delays, including when sections of its track were washed out when the country it traversed experienced rare rainfall. Jakob and Charlotte spent 2 days and 3 nights on the Ghan to reach Alice Springs. Not far into this journey they left behind the fertile land of southeastern Australia and moved into an increasingly dry landscape. They may have caught glimpses of salt lakes, distant purple and red-tinged mountains and wildlife such as kangaroos and emus, and stopped at a few isolated outback towns, but before nearing Alice Springs, they would find themselves spending much of their time travelling slowly across a seemingly endless flat and arid landscape. Late August temperatures gave them a mild introduction to Central Australia but within another month daytime temperatures would begin climbing towards their summer averages in the high thirties.[18]

Alert to his new surroundings, as he had been when he first arrived in Egypt and Nubia, Jakob left the following account of his first impressions of Alice Springs, the town's Finke River Mission precinct and the couple's arrival at Hermannsburg Mission:

> [At Alice Springs] a missionary, Pastor Sam Gross, welcomed us at the terminus of the railroad and took us first to the station of the Finke River Mission, on the outskirts of Alice Springs. This place is situated on a plateau, surrounded by rings of rock faces of the MacDonnell Ranges. The entrance

only opens to the south through a narrow gorge called The Gap. Nearby is the station with the mission houses and a church with a hall. Alice is a freight trans-shipment point. Everything needed in the way of food and building materials, such as timber and cement, is brought up by rail from Adelaide in the south. After a 5-ton truck was fully loaded, we set off in the evening, heading west through the MacDonnell Ranges for about 140 km on a primitive road to Hermannsburg…

We arrived at night, but were warmly welcomed by the whites and natives who lived around the station. The houses were built of rough stones, they looked, with their small windows, like old Odenwald stone houses, except that the roofs, as everywhere in the tropics and subtropical areas where Englishmen have lived, were made of corrugated iron or, as they say here, galvanized corrugated iron. The first missionaries who gave Hermannsburg its name arrived there on a long trek on horseback and partly on foot with sheep, cows, horses and horse-drawn carts in 1877, after having been on the road for two years. Their houses resemble old farmhouses on the Lüneburg Heath. In any case, when we both arrived there in September 1947, there was already an Indigenous Christian community of 500 men, women and children. As the Arrarnta are nomads, they are constantly on the move, alternating between the individual mission stations, which are always located where there is drinking water or water sources. Most of Central Australia is steppe and in many places desert, as we knew it from Nubia and Palestine and Transjordan. In any case, I felt strange in this respect when we first drove from Alice Springs through the mountains and valleys, where there was a lot of red sandstone, like in Nubia, except that we found more greenery, trees and bushes here in Central Australia than in Palestine and Nubia. As I sat on the heavily loaded truck and drove through this wild and romantic area, it was like coming home to Nubia, and my dear wife felt the same way.[19]

After years spent in internment, there was obvious joy in this sense of homecoming. Not only were Jakob and Charlotte returning to their original calling, missionary work, but they were doing it in a location which brought back fond memories of their youthful endeavours in Egypt and Nubia. Hermannsburg Mission had been set up in 1877 as a Lutheran mission to the Aboriginal people of Central Australia on the lands of the Arrarnta. The mission's name derived from its early association with the Hermannsburg Missionary Society, which was based in the north German town of Hermannsburg, located 50 kilometres northeast of Hanover. The area referred to by Jakob as Lüneburg Heath is situated north of the German Hermannsburg.[20]

The missionaries at Central Australia's Hermannsburg were almost all of German descent, with many from the Barossa Valley. According to Jakob, they spoke German 'more or less well'. They gave the Ripperts the same warm welcome they had experienced in the Barossa Valley. At one of their social gatherings, Jakob and Charlotte were asked to talk about their past lives. Jakob told the missionaries about his only prior awareness of Hermannsburg Mission coming from chance encounters with a display featuring Pastor Carl Strehlow's book at Frankfurt's *Völkermuseum* in the 1920s and his meeting with the old missionary Oskar Liebler at the Acre internment camp in 1939. The missionaries informed him that their gathering was taking place in a house built by Oskar Liebler. Jakob was left to reflect on how 'strange and peculiar the ways are that we humans are led by God'.[21]

Jakob began to apply his building skills as soon as he arrived in Hermannsburg, replacing a burnt-out roof and, with the assistance of Arrarnta workers, beginning the repair of one of the mission's

Peace and Repatriation, 1945-1947 85

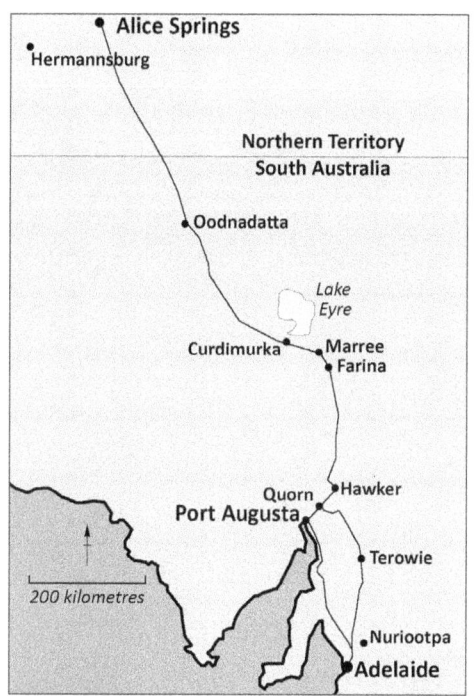

8.2 The Ghan, c. 1950. Photo from the Ripperts' collection. (RPA)

8.3 Map showing the route of the old Ghan (PKI)

8.4. View from the Ghan's engine cabin passing Lake Eyre South, a dry salt lake, c. 1940s (Chris Drymalik Collection)

dilapidated buildings. However, the Ripperts' time at Hermannsburg on this occasion was to be short-lived. At the beginning of November 1947 they received a telegram with the long-awaited news that a ship was available for their repatriation to Germany. They were told to be in Melbourne, ready for departure, by 23 November.[22]

This telegram was a small part of an elaborate logistical operation carried out by the Australian authorities to re-gather all those internees who had been released but were either destined for deportation or had requested repatriation. They were scattered all over Australia and every effort was now made to ensure they did not miss the departure of their ship. Giving Jakob and Charlotte almost a month's notice of their departure date was indicative of the remote nature of their location and limited transport options in 1947. While it is clear from the voluminous files generated by this exercise that Australian officials were anxious to be rid of all those nominated for deportation or repatriation, they also provide evidence of ongoing humanitarian concern. In the midst of the process, for example, it was decided that families with young children should be advised about the likelihood of severe winter conditions in Germany and given the option of postponing their repatriation. It was well informed advice and some families chose to delay their departure.[23]

8.5 Missionary Oskar Liebler and his wife Johanna Maria Luise Liebler, preparing to set out with camels at Hermannsburg, c. 1913 (LAA P06432 12687)

'With God's great help and some Australian help', Jakob later recalled, he and Charlotte arrived in Melbourne in good time. Here, joined by other former internees converging from different parts of Australia, on 24 November they boarded the Australian ship *Kanimbla*, which took them to Fremantle in Western Australia. In Fremantle they were transferred to the *General Stuart Heintzelman*, which departed for Germany on 30 November. The *General Stuart Heintzelman* was an American transport ship with a special place in Australian immigration history. It had arrived in Fremantle a few days earlier with the first group of European refugees or displaced persons to arrive in Australia after the Second World War. It had departed from the German port of Bremerhaven and on its return journey it was used to transport former internees to Germany.[24]

On 31 December 1947 Jakob and Charlotte reached Germany when the *General Stuart Heintzelman* docked at Bremerhaven. Along with other repatriated internees, they were forced to spend a short period in yet another camp, a transit camp near Osnabrück. Here, during what proved to be a bitter German winter, their accommodation was cold and many from Palestine had their first experience of snow. Along with the unwelcoming weather, some of the returnees found resentment from locals who only saw extra mouths to feed at a time when shops were empty and Germans were enduring a long struggle to survive on ration cards. In Doris Frank's account of this difficult homecoming, she describes how one group which was travelling south hired a large truck and trailer to take them to Dortmund. The owner of the truck charged ten cigarettes per head, one cigarette being worth 10 *Reichsmarks* on the black market. Another group, led by Pastor Schneller, travelled south by train. It seems likely that Jakob and Charlotte travelled with this Schneller group. Jakob's memoir records a journey via Hanover, Kassel and Frankfurt to eventually reach Bensheim railway station and his home village of Auerbach.[25]

In a letter written to a former school friend in 1971, Jakob shared his recollection of the end of a long journey:

> … we were happy to finally be home, for me it had been 20 years since I had been home. Unfortunately, I didn't meet my father among the living, he had gone home in 1940, on November 29th. Our [younger brother] Manu hadn't come home either, he was killed in action in Russia in 1941. It was a sad homecoming, because none of us had imagined what Germany looked like back then. But I'm glad that I was able to see it and that I was able to see my mother and brother Wilhelm and family and our boy again in reasonably good health. When we got off the train at Bensheim station, my brother Wilhelm picked me up with my old school friend Fritz Nungesser. Our boy was also there, he had turned 18 in the meantime. When he left me in 1938 and my wife brought him home to Auerbach from Acre in Palestine, he was eight years old.[26]

Endnotes

1. Paul Sauer, *The Holy Land Called: The Story of the Temple Society* (trans. Gunhild Henley), Temple Society of Australia, Melbourne, 1991, pp. 245-246; Tatura Internment Camp 'War Diary, AWM 52 8/7/43/4 May-July 1945, AWM.
2. Sauer, p. 246; Samuel Koehne 'Refusing to leave: perceptions of German national identity during internment in Australia, 1941-45', in Joan Beaumont, Ilma Martinuzzi O'Brien, Mathew Trinca (eds), *Under Suspicion: citizenship and internment in Australia during the Second World War*, National Museum of Australia, Canberra, 2008, p. 77; letter Joh. Kübler to Heinz Kübler, 21 May 1945, in 'RUFF Gottlieb Samuel – Internee', NAA: A367, C71567, p. 43, NAA.

3. 'War Diary, AWM 52 8/7/43/4 May-July 1945, AWM; Sauer, p. 246; Ted Stoll, Childhood Memories – Part 3'; Jakob Rippert, *Lebenslauf*, 1948, HHStAW, Bestand 520/02, Nr. 10797.
4. Julia Boyd and Angelika Patel, *A Village in the Third Reich: How Ordinary Lives were Transformed by the Rise of Fascism*, Elliot and Thompson, London, 2022, pp. 7, 407; 'Tatura Internment Camp – Weekly Intelligence Reports', Report No. 12, February 1945, NAA: A373, 9167, NAA; 'Ruff, Gottlieb Samuel – Internee', NAA: A367, C71567, NAA.
5. Ted Stoll, Childhood Memories – Part 3'; Heidemarie Wawrzyn, *Nazis in the Holy Land 1933 – 1948*, De Gruyter Magnes, Berlin & Jerusalem, 2013, p. 67.
6. Gottlieb Ruff's diary, TSA.
7. Letter, Executive of the Jewish Agency to British High Commissioner for Palestine, Field Marshal John Vereker, Jerusalem, 4 June 1945, Central Zionist Archives, S25/4060, quoted in Wawrzyn, pp. 93-94. This letter referred to a persistent myth that Adolf Eichmann, one of the most notorious perpetrators of the Holocaust, was a Palestine German.
8. 'Nazism Inquiry Immediately', *The News* (Adelaide), 24 October 1945, p. 3.
9. 'Move to Deport Aliens', *The Advocate* (Burnie), 27 July 1946, p. 7; Sauer, pp. 286-289.
10. Sauer, pp. 287-289.
11. Ibid.
12. 'Summary of Proceedings of a Conference Between the Commissioner and the Minister for the Army', Canberra, 28 June 1946, 'Question of Release or Deportation of Overseas Internees…', NAA: A445, 258/1/5, NAA.
13. 'Internee Service and Casualty Form, Jakob Rippert', NAA: MP1103/1, P36022, NAA; Jakob Rippert, Memoir, 1971, HStAD; 'Oral report of the treating MO at Waranga [Camp 1] Hospital', 5 Sept 1946, RPA.
14. Sauer, pp. 292-293; Rippert, Jakob P36022; Charlotte PF36023 – Personal files of internees from Camp 3 Rushworth, NAA: B1356, Camp 3/Rippert J/C, NAA.
15. Rippert, Jakob P36022; Charlotte PF36023 – Personal files of internees from Camp 3 Rushworth, NAA: B1356, Camp 3/Rippert J/C, NAA
16. Letter, Office of the UK High Commissioner, Canberra to Secretary, Department of the Army, 3 December 1946; letter, A. Calwell to C. Chambers, 9 January 1947; letter, C. Chambers to A. Calwell, 6 February 1947; 'Overseas Internees Release', NAA: MT885/1, 255/14/288, NAA.
17. Rippert, Jakob P36022; Charlotte PF36023 – Personal files, NAA: B1356, Camp 3/Rippert J/C, NAA; Jakob Rippert, Memoir.
18. Jakob Rippert, Memoir; letter, Jakob Rippert to Alfred Löther, 22 June 1971, HStAD.
19. Jakob Rippert, Memoir.
20. M. Lohe, F. W. Albrecht, L.H. Leske, *Hermannsburg: A Vision and Mission*, Lutheran Publishing House, Adelaide, 1977, p. 7.
21. Jakob Rippert, Memoir. When one of the authors, Paul Kiem, visited Hermannsburg with his wife in 2024, he was informed that the building they were staying in was the first to have been repaired by Jakob Rippert.
22. Jakob Rippert, Memoir.
23. 'List of Internees in Qld', NAA: BP242/1, Q33797, pp. 74/75, 144-145, 181, 184-189, NAA.
24. Jakob Rippert, Memoir; 'Rippert, Jakob P36022', 'Charlotte PF36023 – Personal Files', Camp 3 Rushworth NAA: B1356, Camp 3/Rippert J/C, NAA; Doris Frank, 'Repatriation trip of the ex-internees on the *General Stuart Heintzelman* in November 1947', unpublished MS, 2024, TSA; Jayne Persian, *Beautiful Balts*, New South, Sydney, 2017, pp. 6, 9-10.
25. Jakob Rippert, Memoir; Frank, 'Repatriation trip of the ex-internees'.
26. Letter, Jakob Rippert to Alfred Löther, 22 June 1971.

Chapter 9
Germany, 1948 – 1950

After Jakob and Charlotte returned to Germany at the beginning of 1948, they lived at Auerbach with Jakob's mother for the next six months. At Auerbach they experienced the great happiness of being reunited with their son Reinhart after an enforced separation of ten years and catching up with other family members, including Jakob's mother, whom he had not seen for twenty years. On the other hand, they had to cope with serious challenges beyond the family. They found themselves sharing with all Germans the severe economic hardships of a country devastated by war and overwhelmed by millions of refugees swelling the population in the years after the war. To add to Jakob's difficulties, part of his homecoming experience included submitting to Germany's post-war denazification process and giving an explanation for his membership of the Nazi Party. In mid-1948 he was offered work with the Schneller Orphanage's German headquarters in Cologne. The family still struggled with the hardships of everyday life, but accepting this work gave Jakob the satisfaction of moving back into missionary-related work with the Schneller family. By the end of 1949, the Ripperts were faced with a decision. Would they accept an invitation to help the Schnellers re-establish their institution in the Middle East or would they return to Hermannsburg Mission in Central Australia?

When Jakob and Charlotte arrived at his mother's house, according to an account he wrote in a letter to a friend in 1971, she did not recognise him. Not only had he been 'long and thin' when she had last seen him in 1928, but he had been 'so well fed' in Australia and on the voyage to Germany that his mother, 'who was lying in bed, weak and miserable', at first refused to believe that the healthy-looking new arrival was her son. In the event, it would not be long before Jakob lost weight and took on more the appearance of a calorie-deprived German. Apart from these comments, there is surprisingly little in Jakob's written accounts about what it was like to resume family relations after such long separations. He did note that 'our boy' Reinhart had been an eight-year-old when he last saw him and 'had turned 18 in the meantime'. During the war, Jakob summarised, 'we only heard from each other through the Red Cross, very rarely; it was a difficult time for all of us'. We are left to imagine just how difficult it must have been for Reinhart and his parents and how they dealt with the lost years during which the little boy had become a young man.[1]

Jakob and Charlotte tried to make contact with friends and colleagues from the 1920s and 1930s to clarify their fates. Even before they left Australia, Charlotte received a long letter from a former SPM colleague dealing with her own family and acquaintances such as a Mr Höpfner, Jakob's successor in Egypt:

> Our Mr. Höpfner has finally returned home after five years. He was in various camps – America, England, Germany. He has become an inwardly mature man. How he would love to go to Egypt. When will that be allowed to happen! And when, dear Lotte, will you finally be able to see your boy. How your hearts must long for him. It is a hard road. Today, torn families are the order of the

day. All our nephews and great-nephews are now back, the last one came from Stalingrad. None of our six brothers are still alive. Minna and I are the last of the real family.[2]

Letters like this gave Jakob and Charlotte a forewarning of what they would face in Germany. As soon as they arrived in Auerbach they experienced the reality of survival in a society where even the most basic foodstuffs were strictly rationed or had to be bartered for. Luckily, Jakob and Charlotte had brought with them coffee beans, which had been sent to them from New Guinea by missionaries they had met at Hermannsburg. They exchanged these coffee beans for potatoes.[3]

In his recent book, *Out of the Darkness*, historian Frank Trentmann describes Germany after 1945 as the site of a prolonged 'humanitarian catastrophe'. The existence of a primitive barter economy was just one manifestation of this. Six million German soldiers had been killed or were missing. One third of all homes had been destroyed and large sections of major cities had been reduced to rubble, leaving millions homeless. Infrastructure had been destroyed. Food was in short supply and shortages would remain severe until near the end of the decade. The bitter winter of 1946-1947 was referred to as the 'hunger winter'. With the economy in a state of collapse, only the black market flourished. Millions of former camp inmates, forced labourers and refugees — Europe's new category of 'displaced persons'

9.1 Charlotte Rippert's painting of Auerbach's Evangelische Bergkirche (RPA)

9.2 Reinhart with his grandparents soon after arriving in Auerbach in 1938 (RPA)

— were in transit across the country. On top of this, between 1944 and 1950, in Europe's largest population transfer, western Germany was forced to absorb an estimated 12 million ethnic Germans who fled or were expelled from Eastern Europe. In these circumstances, the setting up of international programs to accept displaced persons and deliver aid to Germany was critical. Between 1945 and 1955, up to 115 million kilograms of foreign aid reached western Germany, peaking in 1948.[4]

American CARE packages were the major source of aid to Germany during the immediate post-war crisis, but sending relief packages was also a significant activity of the Australian Lutheran Church and its individual members. Bethany Pietsch, archivist at the Lutheran Archives of Australia, has examined a collection of letters sent from northeast Germany by individuals who received relief packages from Australia during the period 1947-1949. The letters express gratitude for the aid, sometimes describe the contents of the packages and add detail to our understanding of conditions in Germany at the time. In a letter sent from Hamburg in November 1947, Dorothea Riecken wrote:

> In July 1943 we lost our home and all our belongings. We ended up on the street with two suitcases, then we moved into our son's apartment — and there we were completely bombed out

9.3 Reinhart, his grandmother and Charlotte after they were reunited in 1948. The photo is taken outside the Rippert family home at Auerbach Ludwigstraße 12. The building is little changed today. (RPA)

> a second time. Now, through the death of my mother, we've acquired a bed — one table and two stools is all our wealth. But our faithful God has kept us healthy thus far, and we are thankful to Him from the bottom of our hearts.
>
> We are very much concerned that we haven't received any news from our son (and only child) out of Russia since February 1945. May our faithful Lord grant to us, that we will yet hear from him someday…[5]

The last prisoners of war to survive captivity in Russia did not return to Germany until the mid-1950s.

In a letter of thanks for a parcel received for Christmas 1947, Magdalena Binnewies listed the contents of the package. They included biscuits, sugar, Milo Nestle's 'fortified tonic food', soap, slippers, wool, powdered milk, beef dripping, flour, cotton and hair pins. Milo, still a household brand name in Australia, was a chocolate malt drinking powder created in 1934 as a nutritional supplement for children during the Great Depression. It seems like an ideal inclusion. Magdalena Binnewies concluded:

> Your choice of gifts was so all-encompassing, you thought even of hairpins. I wonder if you realise quite how poor we are in Germany. I simply could not say which was the loveliest or most valuable item in the parcel.[6]

In September 1947 Emily Weber described the rationing situation in Germany:

> The food situation here is indeed truly catastrophic. The current weekly rations are the following: 35 grams fat, 100 grams meat or sausage, 125 grams sugar or jam, 25 grams cereal and 30 grams cheese. There were hardly any vegetables this season because of the drought… This is why I am so overjoyed with your lovely gifts… here there is nothing to buy. Not even sewing needles or ties, the most basic things are not to be had. For the last few weeks, we have not even received our piece of soap.[7]

Sometimes letters were received requesting assistance. In January 1948, Heinz Roeseler of Gummersbach wrote to Betty Miller in Australia in polite desperation:

> I received your treasured address from my friends in Baven, whom you some time ago helped out of the greatest distress. I beg your leave to make a polite inquiry, as to whether it would perhaps be possible for you to one day send such a parcel to me and my family.[8]

The Ripperts were among those Germans who sent similar requests to friends or acquaintances in Australia. On one occasion, in early 1948, Charlotte wrote a letter to M. A. Suter, a nursing sister she had met at Hermannsburg Mission the previous year. In a subsequent letter Suter wrote to Hermannsburg's superintendent, Pastor Albrecht, she mentioned the Ripperts and told him: 'I have had one very pathetic letter from her [Charlotte] altho in spite of everything she sounded glad to be with her dear ones. I have sent her a parcel…'.[9]

The economic and humanitarian situation in Germany only began to improve when currency reform and the Marshall Plan, the massive American aid program for Europe, were initiated in 1948 and started to have an impact ahead of West Germany's economic recovery in the following decade. Looking back from the 1970s, Jakob retained a strong impression of the period: 'none of us who experienced this difficult time after the Second World War will ever forget it. Those of us who got away thanked our God from the bottom of our hearts for all the help and protection we received.'[10]

Following Germany's defeat in 1945, it had been divided into four occupation zones by the victorious Allied powers. The USSR occupied and administered the east, the British the northwest, the French the southwest and the Americans the south. One of the goals in each of the occupation zones was de-nazification — the elimination of Nazi ideology and the identification and, depending upon their level of involvement, punishment of former Nazis. The village of Auerbach, which had been incorporated with neighbouring Bensheim in 1939, was in the American zone.

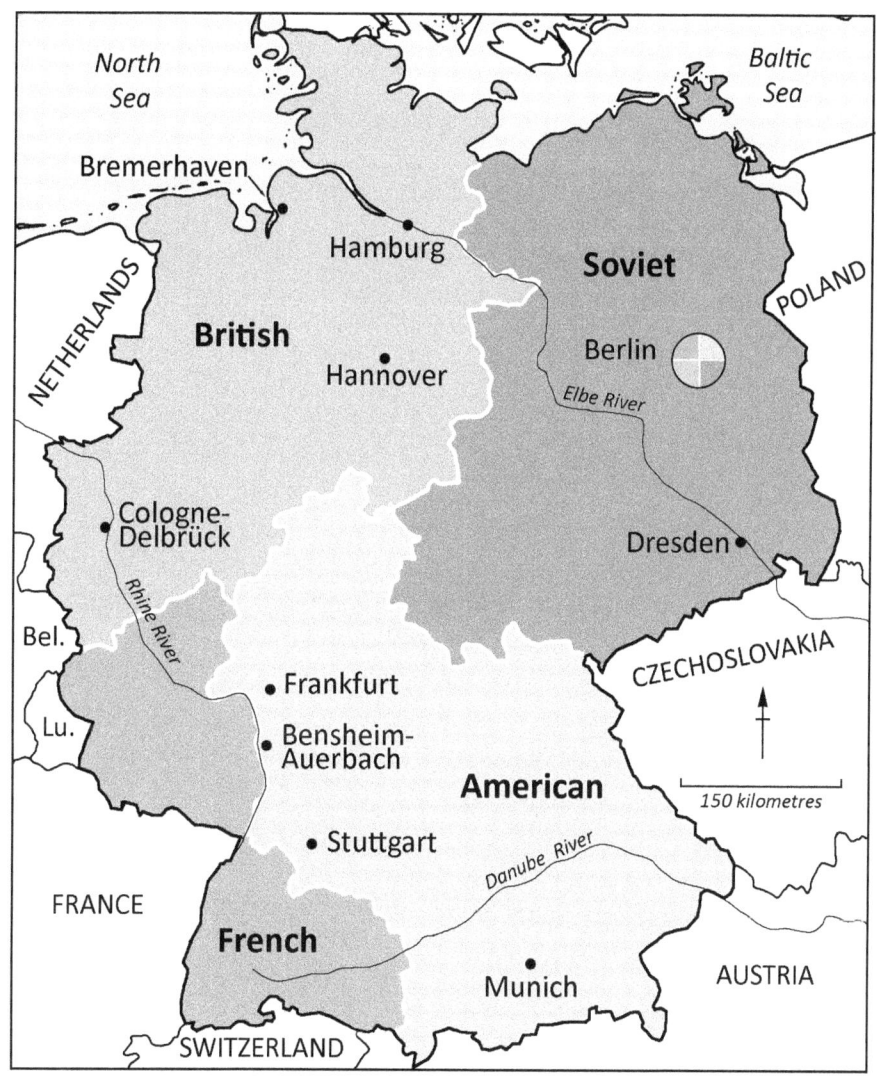

9.4 Germany in 1945, showing British, French, American and Soviet/Russian Occupation Zones (PKI)

Initially, the Americans pursued denazification with zeal, requiring every adult in their zone to complete a questionnaire about their past.[11] At the individual level, within the Rippert family a story has been passed down about Reinhart being interviewed by Henry Kissinger, the future American Secretary of State. Kissinger served in the American army during the Second World War and in 1945-1946 he was based at Bensheim, where he worked in intelligence and denazification. Reinhart may have attracted interest because he had been forced to join the Hitler Youth during the war, but he would have been only fifteen or sixteen at the time Kissinger was in Bensheim.[12]

Dealing with a small number of major war criminals, at the Nuremberg International Military Tribunal (1945-1946) and later trials, aroused some controversy but had been accomplished in the early years of occupation. Beyond this, extending denazification to deal with lower-level Nazis was a complex challenge, as outlined by historian Ian Kershaw:

> Who were these people, how great was their guilt, how were they to be singled out? How were the occupying powers to distinguish not just between the guilty and the innocent, in their eyes, but between degrees of guilt, when over 8 million Germans — about 10 percent of the population — had been Nazi Party members and tens of millions more had been members of one or other party affiliation?[13]

The American questionnaire required Germans to provide a detailed account of their lives and reveal any Nazi involvement. By the end of 1945, 1.6 million questionnaires had been processed in the American zone but around 3.5 million former Nazis still awaited classification. Overwhelmed by the numbers, the realisation that Nazi affiliation was only a crude measure of commitment to Nazism and the desperate need to focus on rebuilding the German economy, in 1946 the Americans handed denazification over to local German authorities. The Germans continued to use a modified version of the questionnaire and anyone suspected of a Nazi past was required to submit it, a *Lebenslauf* (curriculum vitae) and accompanying testimonials to a local tribunal. The intention was to assess guilt according to categories ranging from 'principally guilty' down to 'uncompromised'. Around 90% of those processed were judged minor offenders and the process generated both resentment and cynicism among Germans. The testimonials, invariably attesting to a person's good character and non-Nazi credentials, were widely referred to as *Persilscheine* (Persil certificates). Persil was a popular laundry detergent which, according to its advertising slogan, 'washed whiter than white'.[14]

By the time Jakob Rippert arrived in Auerbach at the start of 1948, the denazification process had lost its momentum and was moving towards a general amnesty. Nevertheless, as a former member of the Nazi Party he was required to complete a questionnaire and submit it, with his *Lebenslauf* and testimonials, to a tribunal. As a nominal party member at worst, and someone who had lived outside of Germany for the past twenty years, Jakob was only ever going to be assessed in the lowest 'uncompromised' category. In fact, his case was dealt with by a general amnesty issued at the start of 1948. Preparing his submission, an onerous and ultimately unnecessary chore, was one more challenge the Ripperts had to overcome. It would not have made a difficult homecoming any easier. Thankfully, though, the contents of this submission have been a great source of information on

9.5 First page of the questionnaire Jakob Rippert submitted during the German denazification process. It deals with his membership of NSDAP (Nazi Party) organisations (HHStAW).

Jakob's life. With one exception, the information he provided can be corroborated with other sources. The exception is that Jakob gave the year he applied to join the Nazi Party as 1937, even though a membership card exists which shows he joined in 1934.[15] With early membership of the party being regarded as indicative of more serious commitment to Nazism, at first glance this is a worrying discrepancy. It will be discussed below.

These are the institutions or individuals who provided the testimonials Jakob included with his submission to the denazification tribunal:

1. German Mission (former Sudan Pionier Mission), Wiesbaden, 30 May 1933
2. Dr O. Rubitschung, medical doctor interned with the Ripperts, Tatura (Rushworth), 12 January 1947
3. Major C. Chapman, Camp Commandant, Australian Army, Tatura (Rushworth), 17 March 1947
4. Staff Sergeant Archibald Blackwood, Australian Army, Tatura (Rushworth), 11 August 1947
5. Pastor Hermann Schneller, former Director of Palestine's Syrian Orphanage, interned with the Ripperts, Tatura (Rushworth), 12 August 1947
6. Pastor F. W. Albrecht, Superintendent, Hermannsburg Mission, 25 November 1947
7. Pastor Werner Schmitt, Catholic priest interned with the Ripperts, Kloster Frauenberg Fulda, 15 January 1948
8. Albert Kahn, Bensheim-Auerbach, 5 February 1948

This is not a list of *Persilscheine*. Most are statements of service or character references, dating from 1933, collected from superiors or colleagues to assist with ongoing employment. They are consistent in attesting to Jakob's good character, expertise and conscientiousness and are convincingly authentic. Why he chose to submit the testimonial from Schneller, a man who surely had his own questions to answer about Nazism, is puzzling but it may suggest Jakob had a blind spot when it came to the man who had been his employer in Palestine and pastor in the Tatura camp. Only the last two testimonials appear to have been solicited specifically for the denazification process. The final one, from Albert Kahn, is of particular interest.

As outlined earlier, Albert Kahn (1887-1959) was a Jewish German who, together with his wife Marie Clara (1890-1976) and son Harry Kahn (1919-2016), fled from Germany to Palestine after Hitler came to power in 1933. Within the Kahn family a story has been passed down about the Kahns being advised to flee by a relative who was in a relationship with a local Nazi. In Palestine, the family was helped by the Ripperts, initially by being given accommodation on the Ripperts' farm and then by Jakob helping Albert to find work in Haifa. In Germany, the Kahns had lived in Auerbach, where they ran a transportation business. In 1947, Albert and Marie Clara returned to Germany and resettled in Auerbach, where they are celebrated as being among the first of a small minority of Jewish Germans who returned to Germany in the 1940s.[16] The Ripperts and Kahns had almost certainly been acquaintances in their home village and managed to stay in contact. When the Ripperts returned to Auerbach in 1948, they found the Kahns already there and Albert appears to have been only too happy

> **Albert Kahn's Testimonial for Jakob Rippert**
>
> I am aware of the consequences of making a false affidavit.
> I declare on oath:
>
> When I had to flee Germany as a Jew with my family in 1933 and emigrate to Palestine, it was Mr. Jakob Rippert in Acre/Palestine who lovingly took us into his house on his farm, accommodated us for a few weeks and thus gave us the opportunity to gain a foothold in Palestine. Mr. Rippert and his wife went to great lengths to make it easier for my family and I to settle into our new surroundings. Mr. Rippert has become a trusted friend who has never disappointed me throughout the years of our association. I had the opportunity to observe Mr. Rippert and his behaviour for years and can testify with a clear conscience that he was free of any Nazi ties. For him, whose entire commitment was to the flourishing of his farm and the adjoining settlement and who also lived out his original profession as a missionary builder in his practical work with and among Arabs, it was completely out of the question for him to ever appear as a propagandist or activist in the sense of the Nazi movement.
>
> As I was able to observe, Mr. Rippert's behaviour towards Europeans, Jews and Arabs was always equally friendly and helpful. English officers and government officials also frequented his house. Mr. Rippert's farm was located about 4 km from Acre and about 28 km from Haifa, away from the traffic. His farm, which he built up from fallow land, was regarded as a model farm in northern Palestine. I also know that Mr. Rippert worked as a master builder for the Syrian Orphanage (a Protestant missionary organisation) in Jerusalem, carrying out construction work alongside his farming profession.
>
> In conclusion, I note that Mr. Rippert has always remained first and foremost a Christian and a helper and is one of the few who has lived out his Christianity to everyone through action. He is a truth-loving character at the core of his being, whose statements and explanations are to be believed at all costs.
>
> I myself returned to Germany from Palestine with my wife last year.
>
> Albert Kahn

to provide Jakob with a very supportive testimonial. Subsequently, the Kahns' son, Harry, maintained contact with the Ripperts until near the end of their lives.

Two questions remain. Firstly, why did Jakob Rippert join the Nazi Party? In the *Lebenslauf* he submitted to the denazification tribunal, he gave this explanation: 'We Germans were told openly there that it would be impossible for our children to attend school in Germany unless their parents joined the foreign organization of the NSDAP [Nazi Party] or one of its subdivisions.' Thus, he joined the party so that Reinhart could be sent to Germany in 1938. This was similar to large numbers of Germans who joined the Nazi Party for largely pragmatic reasons, including to keep their jobs or seek advancement. Jakob, in his words, 'let myself be recruited for the foreign organisation in 1937' because it appeared, from Palestine, that the Nazis were providing Germany with good government. In any case, as a socially conservative, patriotic war veteran who was apolitical, he is unlikely to have given the Nazi ideology much scrutiny: 'I lacked time and interest in politics. As an expatriate German, I always strove to lead a quiet, orderly life without offense and not to bring dishonour to my homeland.'[17]

According to Jakob, he never became an active party member and was distrusted by those who were:

> I never received a membership card, so I was an aspirant until the outbreak of the war. I attribute the fact that I did not receive a membership card to the fact that I was not considered irreproachable by the leading party men among the Germans in Palestine because of my evangelical-missionary attitude and my ongoing intercourse with Englishmen, Jews and Arabs. This view of mine was confirmed during my later internment by my efforts to found an evangelical camp congregation.[18]

This explanation is supported by everything we have learnt about Jakob from numerous records covering most of his life. His 'evangelical-missionary attitude' is always evident. Anything to do with Nazism, or even politics in general, is absent.

This brings us to the second question. Why did Jakob claim to have joined the Nazi Party in 1937 when a membership card can be found in Germany's Bundesarchiv for Jakob Rippert, 'farmer engineer of German Farm Acre', dated 1 June 1934? There are reasons why he may have joined in 1934. Firstly, he may have been influenced by the director of the Syrian Orphanage and his employer, Hermann Schneller. Jakob was a lifelong admirer of the Schnellers for their evangelical-missionary work, but both Hermann and his brother Ernst applied to join the Nazi Party in 1933. Hermann Schneller later delivered the deeply disturbing eulogy for Hitler in the Tatura camp in 1945. Secondly, at this time Jakob and Charlotte were borrowing money from members of the Palestine German community to purchase land. Conceivably, party membership could have helped with this. Regardless of this speculation, why did Jakob not reveal the 1934 date in his submission to the 1948 denazification tribunal? He had no incentive to lie. On the one hand, giving false information was regarded seriously. On the other hand, as someone in the lowest category of party involvement, he had nothing to hide. The likelihood is that as an apolitical, non-active member who may not have received his copy of the original membership card, he genuinely forgot about the 1934 membership when he responded to the denazification tribunal's questions fourteen years later. Indeed, the fact that he recalled applying to join in 1937 suggests that any earlier application may have lapsed or been overlooked at that time, when a second application was made. There is support for this explanation in Heidemarie Wawrzyn's book *Nazis in the Holy Land*. In an appendix where she lists Palestine Germans who joined Nazi organisations, Jakob's 1934 membership is recorded, with the details matching those on his membership card. But there is another entry for H. Rippert, a 'missionary-builder' living at Acre. This entry has no date for the membership but, assuming the H. initial is a transcription error and that a 'missionary-builder' living at Acre can only have been Jakob, this almost certainly refers to Jakob's 1937 application, which is the one he remembered in 1948.[19]

In mid-1948 Jakob accepted an offer to work for the Evangelical Association for the Syrian Orphanage at Cologne. This was the German headquarters of the Schneller family's Syrian Orphanage Jakob had worked for in Palestine. It is clear from references in his writings that Jakob had a special attachment to the Schneller brothers, chiefly Hermann who he had worked for in Palestine and been interned with at Tatura, but also Ernst who took over the running of the Cologne headquarters from his uncle, Ludwig Schneller, in the late 1940s. The Schnellers' missionary activity was inspired by their Christian faith but leaned towards the provision of practical vocational training and social services. Their ambitions seemed to require constant building work. All of this appealed to Jakob, who had enjoyed his work as a builder/engineer in Palestine and he seems to have formed an immediate bond with Ernst Schneller, a qualified engineer.[20]

Jakob gladly accepted the Schneller family's offer to build a new Schneller orphanage for German war orphans at Cologne-Dellbrück, but the task was to be very different from the work he had carried out in Palestine. His co-workers were often refugees from the east who had undergone horrific experiences. While the occupation authorities were happy to see accommodation being built, both building materials and funding were difficult to obtain. And the work took place alongside ongoing food shortages. Jakob has left this account of a time when he had little to fall back on but his Christian faith and some help from Australia:

> We often didn't have the money for wages, but at the right time it was there. When I started a year ago on an empty field of 20 acres, first alone and then with an East Prussian refugee of the same age, whose wife and 2 sons were torn to pieces in front of his eyes during the flight, I was often desperate and thought nothing would come of our efforts. We cried out to God and he helped, he also helped me physically when I was dizzy with hunger and the earth was spinning around me, because what food was available on [ration] cards was not enough for a strong, hard-working person to live and not enough to die. Then the parcels from Australia often came and helped us... I heard the believers over land and sea, and this was a strength to us.[21]

When they had been given permission to return to Germany, the Ripperts had agreed to only use the accommodation provided by Jakob's mother at Auerbach. When he accepted the work offer from the Schnellers at Cologne-Dellbrück, Jakob would be moving from the American occupation zone to the British zone. Presumably, this was acceptable because Jakob was engaged to build new accommodation and when he started work in mid-1948 he lived alone on the building site. (By this time the two occupation zones had been economically merged but movement between them was still restricted.) He was joined a little later by Reinhart, who helped with the building work. It was not until Christmas 1948 when 'brave Lotte arrived' to live in a builder's hut Jakob had erected on the site. The family lived in this hut until the first of the orphanage's buildings was complete at the end of the 1949, when they moved into an apartment on the upper floor. While they were living at Cologne-Dellbrück, Reinhart attended a nearby science high school and graduated in the spring of 1950. His matriculation would have some bearing on the family's next move later in the year. While studying, Reinhart continued to work as a labourer on the building site, along with several classmates.[22]

The building Jakob constructed over eighteen months between 1948 and 1949 was built under the most difficult conditions, with challenges at every step, from funding, to sourcing materials to carrying out the day-to-day work on a building site with a workforce made up of malnourished and sometimes recently traumatised men. Despite these difficulties, it was well built. In 2025, in the final stages of the research for this book, we were surprised to discover that this building is still in use. Located at Dellbrücker Mauspfad 131, it is now the administration building for Fuchs Grabmalkunst, a long-standing stone masonry business. Purchased from the Schneller Orphanage in 1961, the building has undergone minor changes and refurbishment but it is still clearly recognisable as the building seen in a photograph taken during construction in 1949.[23]

Even though Jakob took pride in the work he did to assist the Schnellers in providing accommodation for war orphans at Cologne-Dellbrück, he and Charlotte never intended to stay in Germany. Correspondence shows that they were making arrangements for their next move as early as 1948. They were torn between two options. Firstly, the Schnellers had asked Jakob to assist them in re-establishing their institution in the Middle East. When he was unable to re-open the Syrian Orphanage in Jerusalem, Hermann Schneller developed a plan to open a new school in Lebanon. This led to the founding of the Johann Ludwig Schneller School in Lebanon's Bekaa Valley in 1952. This was followed, at the end of

9.6 The first building of the Schneller Orphanage built by Jakob Rippert at Cologne-Dellbrück. The photograph was taken during construction in 1949. The small building on the right is likely to have been the builder's hut where Jakob and his family lived in 1949. (RPA)

9.7 The Schneller Orphanage building, located at Dellbrücker Mauspfad 131, is now used as the administration building for a stone masonry business, Fuchs Grabmalkunst. (Fuchs Family)

the decade, with the founding of the Theodor Schneller School in Amman, Jordan. Both schools are still in operation under the auspices of the Syrian Orphanage's successor organisation, the Evangelical Association for Schneller Schools, which is based in Stuttgart.[24]

Working with Herman Schneller in Lebanon was Jakob and Charlotte's preferred option. They had been trained to work in the Middle East, they spoke Arabic and had a fondness for the region and its people. In addition, Jakob was an admirer of the Schnellers and their work and was attracted to the construction activity their new projects would require. At the same time, he and Charlotte were pursuing a second option — returning to Australia to work at Hermannsburg Mission. They had both enjoyed the short time they had spent there in 1947, they maintained contact with the mission's superintendent, Pastor Albrecht, another figure Jakob admired, and they were conscious of the support and encouragement they had received from different individuals and groups in Australia.

Germany's economic situation, and the lack of opportunity for Jakob and Reinhart, provided an additional incentive to migrate. However, the overriding factor motivating Jakob and Charlotte was their determination to return to the front line of missionary work. As Jakob wrote to Pastor Albrecht in 1949: 'The old homeland does not hold us, for we had long since broken away when we were sent out as young people to serve on the mission field.' Thus, throughout their time in Germany, Jakob and Charlotte kept both options for returning to missionary work open. When they did make a decision about the next stage of their lives, it was probably as much an outcome of practical considerations as anything else — they had requested entry permits for both Lebanon and Australia and the Australian permit was the first to be granted.[25]

Endnotes

1. Letter, Jakob Rippert to Alfred Löther, 22 June 1971, HStAD.
2. Letter, Gustel? to Charlotte Rippert, 6 November 1947, HStAD.
3. Letter, Jakob Rippert to Alfred Löther, 22 June 1971.
4. Frank Trentmann, *Out of the Darkness: The Germans 1942-2022*, Allen Lane, London, 2023, pp. 88, 327, 329.
5. Bethany Pietsch, '"Dear Sisters in the Faith": Letters of Thanks from Post-War Germany', *Journal of Friends of Lutheran Archives*, No. 33, 2023, pp. 58-59.
6. Ibid., pp. 59-60.
7. Ibid., pp. 60-61.
8. Ibid., p. 64.
9. Letter, M. A. Suter to Pastor and Mrs Albrecht, 19 October 1948, FRM.
10. Dietrich Orlow, *A History of Modern Germany: 1871 to Present*, (8th ed.), Routledge, New York, 2018, p. 248; letter, Jakob Rippert to Alfred Löther, 22 June 1971.
11. Orlow, p. 252.
12. *Bensheimer Anzeiger*, 20 July, 1994.
13. Ian Kershaw, *To Hell and Back: Europe 1914-1949*, Penguin, London, 2016, p. 483.
14. Kershaw, pp. 483-485; Orlow, pp. 252-253; Trentmann, pp. 121-124.
15. Jakob Rippert, Spruchkammer Bergstraße File, HHStAW, A: 520/02, N: 10797; Jakob Rippert, NSDAP (Nazi Party) Membership Card, No. 3455038, Das Bundesarchiv.
16. Klaus Rippert and Paul Kiem, 'Jakob Rippert und Albert Kahn, zwei ungewöhnliche Auerbacher und ihre Schicksale', *Museumsverein Bensheim Mitteilungen*, 89, February 2024, pp. 64-73; Trentmann, p. 187.
17. Jakob Rippert, *Lebenslauf*, 1948, HHStAW, Bestand 520/02, Nr. 10797.

18. Jakob Rippert, *Lebenslauf*.
19. Jakob Rippert, NSDAP (Nazi Party) Membership Card; Heidemarie Wawrzyn, *Nazis in the Holy Land 1933-1948*, De Gruyter Magnes, Berlin & Jerusalem, 2013, pp. 186-187, 182-185.
20. Letter, Jakob Rippert to Alfred Löther, 22 June 1971.
21. Letter, Jakob Rippert (Cologne-Dellbrück) to F. W. Albrecht (Hermannsburg), 4 September 1949, HStAD.
22. Letter, Jakob Rippert to Alfred Löther, 22 June 1971.
23. Details of the site's recent history were provided by the current owners, the Fuchs family.
24. Gil Gordon, 'Die Schneller Dynastie – Drei Generationen protestantischer Missionsarbeit im Orient', H. Goren and J. Eisler (eds), *Deutschland und Deutsche in Jerusalem, Eine Konferenz in Mishkenot Sha'ananim, März 2007*, Mishkenot Sha'ananim, Jerusalem, 2011, pp. 117-136; Marcel Serr, 'Was ist bildsamer, was ist verheißungsvoller als ein Kind?' (Schneller-Familie), 7 February 2018, www.israelnetz.com (1 April 2025).
25. Letter, Jakob Rippert to Pastor F. W. Albrecht, 4 November 1949, RPA; Jakob Rippert, Memoir, 1971, HstAD.

Chapter 10
Migration and Compensation

On 25 May 1949 the SS *Oxfordshire* berthed in Adelaide, South Australia. It was one of many ships, beginning with the arrival of the *General Stuart Heintzelman* in 1947, to bring post-war displaced persons from Europe to Australia. On its return journey to Europe, we saw in a previous chapter, the *General Stuart Heintzelman* had taken Jakob and Charlotte Rippert to Germany. Since then, Australia had received tens of thousands of displaced persons from Europe. Those who had arrived on the *General Stuart Heintzelman* had been almost exclusively from the Baltic states of Latvia, Lithuania and Estonia and were promoted as the attractive north European face of Australia's ambitious post-war immigration program. The new arrivals on the *Oxfordshire*, gathered together at the Bagnoli camp in Italy, were a more diverse mix, but those from the Baltic states were still prominent. Among them, from Estonia, were Eugen and Valentina Sacharias-Saarelinn and their children, Nina and Paul. Within two years of their arrival, Nina would enrol in Medicine at the University of Adelaide. Following her graduation in 1957, she married a classmate, Jakob and Charlotte's son Reinhart Rippert.[1]

Australia's wartime Labor government had begun planning for a major post-war immigration scheme as early as 1943. In July 1945 it set up a new Department of Immigration under an energetic minister, Arthur Calwell, to put its plans into operation. In the post-war world, nonetheless, there were challenges to be overcome. These included the global shipping shortage, the need to fund the migration scheme and Australia's housing shortage. Just as important as these practical hurdles, the Australian electorate needed to be persuaded of the government's vision for a more populous future. Most immediately, would migrants compete for employment with returning service men and women? Longer term and even more importantly, would prospective migrants come from the traditional source of the nation's immigrants, the British Isles, and would there be any undermining of the race-based White Australia policy which envisaged Australia as a permanently white, effectively British, haven? A problem with this last concern, it soon became apparent, was that while many Britons would migrate to Australia after the war, the British Isles could not supply anywhere near the number of new settlers the Australian government anticipated. The White Australia policy continued sacrosanct for a few more decades, but these circumstances helped to undermine it.[2]

Arthur Calwell found an opportunity to cut through some of the obstacles to his vision when, in July 1947, he signed an agreement with the International Refugee Organisation (IRO) for Australia to accept some of Europe's millions of displaced persons. At one level, it was a genuine humanitarian contribution to assisting the IRO deal with a crisis in post-war Europe. At another level, the agreement with the IRO came with generous funding to bring migrants to Australia in American-supplied shipping. And it came at a time when anxiety about post-war employment was easing. Indeed, in an expanding post-war economy and often regardless of their qualifications and experience, displaced

Europeans were relied upon to fill low-skilled gaps in the Australian workforce. By 1953-54, more than 170,000 displaced persons, including those from the *General Stuart Heintzelman* and the *Oxfordshire*, had arrived in Australia under this scheme. It is credited with getting Australia's post-war migration program off to a successful start, it complemented existing migration pathways and it prepared the way for Australia to make migration agreements with a range of European countries, including Germany, in the 1950s. An average of at least a million migrants arrived in each of the decades to follow.[3]

Australia's ongoing post-World War Two immigration program has been one of the most important elements in its modern nation building. In their 1990 study of the country's German migration, *Australia, Willkommen: A history of the Germans in Australia*, Jürgen Tampke and Colin Doxford attached great significance to Calwell's acceptance of European displaced persons in 1947: 'This decision was to change Australia from a staunchly British society to one of the most tolerant multicultural societies of our time.'[4] This observation draws a long line between Calwell's acceptance of displaced Europeans in 1947 and the successful multicultural society that was to emerge decades later, but the diversification in Australia's migrant intake adopted partly for pragmatic reasons in the late 1940s developed its own momentum. By the late 1960s, in a rapidly decolonising and globalising world, the White Australia policy had become an embarrassing anachronism and soon crumbled.

Australian historians are largely in agreement about the 'visionary and, ultimately, successful' immigration scheme put in place by Australia's postwar Labor government as a key component of its bold reconstruction plans. While Prime Ministers Curtin and Chifley ensured cabinet support for his plans, the driving force behind the goal to dramatically increase migration and build Australia's population was Immigration Minister Calwell. The long-term significance of his work has been underlined by Frank Bongiorno: 'among those politicians who never achieved the office of prime minister, none have greater claim than him to a hand in the making of modern Australia.'[5]

An important part of his role, Calwell realised, was to break down prejudices against non-British migrants. In historian Stuart Macintyre's assessment, this was 'a task that Calwell tackled with vigour and not a little artifice'. The artifice was evident in Calwell's promotion of the 'beautiful Balts' who arrived on the *General Stuart Heintzelman* in 1947. Young, north European in appearance and carefully selected by Australia's immigration officers, Calwell presented this first wave of displaced persons to the Australian press as the attractive prototype of the nation's new migrants: 'The men are handsome and the women are beautiful.' He introduced the term 'New Australian' and encouraged its use to describe new arrivals. It was thought to be welcoming and preferable to 'Balt', 'reffo' or a range of more pejorative terms in common use. It also implied reassuringly rapid assimilation.[6] Soon, the migration intake changed and began to include more eastern and southern Europeans. In some contexts, the term 'New Australian' acquired negative connotations and could be used interchangeably with the old pejorative labels. The New Australians themselves were not always happy with their experiences. And the wisdom and feasibility of rapid assimilation would later be questioned. Nevertheless, by the time he left office as Minister for Immigration in December 1949, Calwell had successfully established Australia's postwar immigration scheme. His legacy has become entrenched and, arguably, has given Australia its most distinguishing national feature.

Although the 1947 decision to accept European displaced persons is regarded as seminal in the implementation of Australia's post-war immigration scheme, it might be argued that the wartime internment camps were really the first recruiting grounds for Calwell's New Australians. Even while the nature of their wartime Nazi allegiance was being scrutinised immediately after the war, Templers and other Palestine Germans were being targeted as potential migrants. Faced with no possibility of returning to their homes in Palestine and with Germany in desperate circumstances, Australia became an attractive option. After all, in Australia the Palestine Germans had generally been well-treated, even in internment. For both the Australian government and opposition, once any security concerns were quickly put behind, the Palestine Germans appeared to be ideal migrants. They were viewed as decent and hard-working people. Earlier German migrants, the largest non-British minority in Australia prior to 1945, had a reputation for easy assimilation. Additionally, the Palestine Germans were already in the country, would require minimal support and had significant assets which were expected to be recovered from Palestine.[7]

In a move that made settlement in Australia even more attractive for both sides, the Australian government undertook to assist the Templers in receiving compensation for their Palestine assets and transferring the funds to Australia. In 1949, when he spoke in Parliament in support of the Temple Society Trust Fund Bill, which would establish a fund to administer this compensation, Calwell gave this reassurance:

> I have personal knowledge of the migrants affected by this measure, and I believe that they will be a distinct asset to Australia…
>
> Not one penny of Commonwealth funds has been expended in bringing them to this country, and, under this measure, no Commonwealth funds will be expended in administering their assets or in settling them in Australia.[8]

Calwell pointed out that the Temple Society Trust Fund would collect and disburse funds not just to Templers but to other residents such as 'German or former German nationals who were transported to Australia with the Templars (sic) in 1941 and were similarly permitted to settle here'.[9] This included the Ripperts who, despite not settling in Australia until 1950, played a role in developing the Templer claim and would eventually be beneficiaries.

In the end, 450 of the 536 Templers interned in Australia chose to settle in the country after the war. They were joined by non-Templer Palestine Germans, along with many of the Germans who had remained in Palestine or been transferred to Germany during the war. Together, the settlement of this small but distinctive group of New Australians was part of a first phase of Australia's post-war immigration scheme. Large numbers of these Palestine Germans settled in Melbourne suburbs; smaller groups went to South Australia's Barossa Valley, Sydney or rural areas.[10]

In the 1970s, Jakob Rippert recalled, 'we Palestinian-Germans could not have imagined in 1939 that we, most of us, would one day end up at the end of the world, in Australia'. By this time, he wrote, 'some have already built up nice livelihoods'. There was one significant difference between their lives in Australia and their previous lives in Palestine. A condition of their settlement in Australia had been that they were not to form separate 'German colonies'. Even without this condition, assimilation in Australia would prove to be irresistible. As Werner Struve observed in a letter to his sister only two months after his arrival in 1949: 'I am very content here and already feel quite at home. However, there is one thing one has to be clear about: that one gradually becomes an Australian and loses one's German identity.' Garry (Gerhard) Stoll has related an amusing example of this assimilation being fast-tracked when, after his family left their Tatura internment camp and settled in South Australia, he and his brothers were enrolled in their first Australian school. Their teacher promptly re-christened Garry and his brother: Gerhard became Garry and Siegfried became Fred. Not something that would be approved of in a later multicultural society, in the 1940s it was accepted not just as a convenience for Australians unwilling to grapple with foreign names, but as a kindly gesture from a teacher concerned about the names being too obviously German at a time when there was still anti-German sentiment in the community. The two men would retain their new names for the rest of their lives.[11]

No sooner had the Ripperts arrived back in Germany at the end of 1947 than Jakob began to make inquiries about returning to Australia. In May 1948 he wrote a letter to the Australian Department of Army's Henry Temby requesting information about immigration and the government's proposal to seek compensation for the German properties in Palestine. Temby had been secretary to Justice Hutchins during his 1946 inquiry which, while set up to investigate the Palestine Germans as security risks, laid the foundations for most to settle in Australia. Temby subsequently assumed the role of welfare officer for the Palestine Germans and played a major part in helping them to settle in Australia and pursue the compensation claim for their property. He was late in responding to Jakob's May 1948 letter because, having accompanied the Ripperts and other repatriated internees on the *General Stuart Heintzelman*, he had remained in Europe to make inquiries about compensation and investigate the possibility of bringing to Australia those Palestine Germans who had remained in Palestine or gone to Germany. The Ripperts were on friendly terms with Temby and in later years sent correspondence to his home address.[12]

When Temby did respond to Jakob's inquiries in September 1948, it was to advise that 'landing permits' were not currently being granted to German nationals living in Germany unless sponsored by close relations already living in Australia. Temby also reported that, to the best of his knowledge, German property in Palestine 'remained unsold' at the close of the British Mandate on 15 May 1948. While the Australian government intended to help with the disposal of these assets and the transfer of funds to Australia, this could not be done for residents of another country. For the time being, Temby noted, the Australian government first needed to recognise 'whatever Government succeeds the British Government in Palestine'.[13]

Thus, having declined the opportunity to settle in Australia in 1947, the Ripperts now faced difficulty in returning. They did not fit into the category of displaced persons, they had no relatives in Australia to sponsor them, they had no funds to cover the cost of travel and they had to secure employment for Jakob and make arrangements for Reinhart. Moreover, if they were not resident in Australia, they would not receive assistance from the Australian government to recover their assets in Palestine.

Fortunately, the Ripperts had friends and supporters in Australia. These ranged from individuals who had known them at Tatura or Hermannsburg, to influential figures such as Temby and senior members of the Lutheran Church. By the time he replied to Jakob, Temby had already been in contact with the President of the United Evangelical Lutheran Church of Australia (UELCA) in Adelaide, Dr Johannes Stolz. 'Knowing the Rippert family well and having a high opinion of them', Temby undertook to support Stolz if he wrote to the Department of Immigration requesting special consideration for the Ripperts.[14]

At the time, Lutherans in Australia were already responding to the desperate situation in Europe. As we have already seen, in response to appeals in Lutheran publications or letters from individuals in Germany, Australian Lutherans sent relief packages to Germany in the period up to 1949, when the food crisis in Europe eased. More significant was the assistance provided for immigration, particularly after the Lutheran World Federation drew attention to the plight of Europe's 10-20 million displaced persons, many of them Lutheran. In Australia, the two synods of the Lutheran Church, the UELCA and the Evangelical Lutheran Church of Australia (ELCA), developed special programs to support immigration from Europe. The UELCA set up a Board of Immigration which was bombarded with requests for assistance. The Ripperts were among numerous families and individuals assisted under the UELCA's program. In his correspondence with Dr Stolz on behalf of the Ripperts, for example, Henry Temby appealed for the Church to fund the immigration of other former internees who had been repatriated to Germany but now wanted to return to Australia. These people, he emphasised, were Lutherans and 'deserving cases of good character' who were under mental and material stress in Germany. While they had family sponsors in Australia, he explained, those family members had already expended their funds by sending food parcels to Germany.[15]

From the time Henry Temby and Dr Stolz began to correspond about applying to the Department of Immigration for special consideration for the Ripperts, the process took more than twelve months. During this time, the Church's Immigration Board agreed to fund the Ripperts' travel costs and Finke River Mission confirmed that Jakob would be welcomed back as a builder at Hermannsburg Mission, a position which came with accommodation. Individuals also offered help. Pastor August Simpfendorfer, who had provided the Ripperts with accommodation at his Light Pass manse in 1947, began to make arrangements for Reinhart to enrol in Medicine at the University of Adelaide when he arrived. Frances Murton, who had been a Senior Warden in charge of women and children at Tatura, wrote a letter to Immigration Minister Calwell in support of the Ripperts. 'They are both very fine people, peace loving, educated and hard working with a sincere Christian outlook', she assured him. Finally, in October 1949 Dr Stolz was notified that Calwell had given approval for the Ripperts to come to Australia.[16]

In November 1949, Jakob wrote to Pastor F. W. Albrecht (1894-1984), Superintendent of Hermannsburg Mission, to let him know that Minister Calwell had approved his return to Australia. Charlotte and Jakob had 'rejoiced like children' on hearing this wonderful news, Jakob told Albrecht. The opportunity to return to Australia was an answer to their prayers because, despite being dedicated to his work at Cologne-Dellbrück, Hermannsburg had always remained in Jakob's 'heart, mind and soul'. They had been sustained by Albrecht's desire to have them back:

> The knowledge that you all wanted us to come back from the bottom of your hearts, which spoke to us from many a letter from there, did us so much good and we longed more and more to unite our forces with yours, to be allowed to help you in your difficult but blessed work.[17]

No doubt sincere in the enthusiasm and commitment to missionary work it seeks to convey, this letter to Albrecht was not completely transparent about the Ripperts' motivations. They had been trying to gain entry to Australia and Lebanon simultaneously. Australia only emerged as the preferred destination for the Ripperts when its entry permit arrived first. And there were practical considerations, including the difficult situation in Germany, the generous support provided by the Australian Lutheran Church and the desirability of being included in the Australian government's action to recover assets in the new state of Israel. Another factor influencing the family decision-making was Reinhart's plans. In a subsequent letter to Albrecht, Jakob told him about Reinhart's ambition to become a 'missionary doctor', with the prospects for study perceived as being better in Australia than post-war Germany.[18]

10.1 Details and photos submitted to the Lutheran Church's (UELCA) Immigration Board (LAA)

In 1950, the three members of the Rippert family became participants in Australia's great migration story. Their journey began after a short break with Jakob's mother in Auerbach, which had been Reinhart's home for most of the previous twelve years. Jakob, Charlotte and Reinhart then left Germany in early July. They travelled by train from Heidelberg to Genoa where, on 12 July, they boarded the *Toscana*, an Italian ship operating a regular service via Naples, the Suez Canal and Colombo to Australia. Travelling 3rd class, the Ripperts arrived in Melbourne on 21 September.

They spent a few days at Pastor Philipp Scherer's Lutheran manse in the Melbourne suburb of Doncaster. In the UELCA archives there is a single page document, an expenses claim from Pastor Scherer, which offers a glimpse into the workings of the Lutheran Church's immigration scheme. Firstly, it is clear, Scherer was part of the Church's migrant support network, meeting those who arrived in Melbourne, providing accommodation and organising onward travel. Secondly, even seemingly minor expenses added up. They ranged from more than 8 shillings for a telegram to Hermannsburg to over £17 in medical fees for a migrant who had needed to consult a ship's doctor. (Today, the value of 8 shillings is about A$15 and £17 over A$500.) Understandably, with 'Christmas approaching' and having 'been mostly on the paying out end on Immigration during the past weeks', Pastor Scherer appealed for a speedy settlement from the UELCA and Finke River Mission treasurers. Thirdly, at considerable cost, we learn that the Ripperts arrived with 14 cases of freight. Included would have been Jakob's tools but we can also assume that many of the cases were devoted to the large collection of books and all manner of family documents and artefacts they managed to transport around the world.[19]

10.2 The first page of a multi-page inventory of the books Jakob and Charlotte brought with them to Australia (RPA)

From Melbourne, the Ripperts were passed on to the next stage in the Church's support network, Pastor Simpfendorfer's manse at Light Pass, South Australia. For Jakob and Charlotte, it was a return to where they had first experienced freedom after their release from Tatura in 1947. The family spent more than three weeks at Light Pass, probably while Simpfendorfer helped Reinhart get established. Then, on 18 October, Jakob and Charlotte set out for remote Hermannsburg and left Reinhart to begin his new life in Adelaide.[20] It must have been a difficult moment for Jakob and Charlotte to separate from their son once again after the family had been reunited for the past few years.

In December 1950, Adelaide's Lutheran Immanuel College published the Christmas edition of its *Immanuel College Weekly*. Included was an article written by Reinhart entitled 'Impressions of a Voyage from Europe to Australia'. At the end of the article, he refers to the school having been his home for the past two months. Apparently, Reinhart had enrolled temporarily at Immanuel College after his arrival in Australia to improve his English language skills. As the article demonstrates, this appears to have been very successful. Along with diligent description of his recent journey, much of which duplicated his parents' earlier journeys, his writing hints at past trauma and conveys a young man's eagerness to make the best of an opportunity to restart a life that had been on hold. At the end, showing a grasp of colloquial Australian English and sensitivity to a cherished aspect of the national self-image, there is an acknowledgement of being given 'a real fair go'. Following are some extracts from the article:

> On whizzed the express [train] to Genoa. The fact that I was on my way again, the prospect of seeing foreign countries, of meeting people, the opportunities to listen to the heartbeats of the world made me forget my tiredness…
>
> On we went on the blue and pellucid sea to Naples. There we trod on historic ground: Pompeii and Herculaneum. Ruins and excavations nearly 2,000 years old, in the glaring sun, with the fuming Vesuvius brooding in the background…

10.3 This unlabelled photo is possibly Reinhart's class when he attended Immanuel College, Adelaide in 1950. He is 4th from the left at the rear. (RPA)

We arrived in Port Said in the twilight of sunset. Bumboat-pedlars swarmed around the ship … Ashore we at once were enchanted by the atmosphere of this country of 'the Arabian nights', and since it is the land I was born in I even felt at home in a way.

I think the Red Sea is one of the most effective Turkish Baths in the world. It worked so well (assisted by the unbelievable bad hygienic conditions on board), people not only lost superfluous weight but sometimes their consciousness…

Well, I am here now, and life is going on like a ship sailing from port to port towards her destination. From time to time she stops, giving us moments of joy in which we meet people we like; moments which make us forget the past; then on she goes to the next harbour.

And since I am leaving Immanuel College now which has been a home to me for nearly two months I cannot but thank you all, teachers and fellow-students, for your patience, for your willingness to help, and for the real fair go you have given me.[21]

From 1951 until 1956, Reinhart was enrolled in Medicine at the University of Adelaide. He was accepted into the course based on his matriculation in Germany and passing an English test. In his first year, with the help of Jakob and Charlotte, he needed to pay course fees and cover his own living costs. In 1952 he was awarded one of the recently announced Commonwealth Scholarships, created by the new Menzies Liberal government to support capable students in their tertiary studies. As a recently arrived migrant and an older student, Reinhart was fortunate to receive this award. Conditional on satisfactory progress, it covered course fees and provided a living allowance until he graduated in 1957. The University of Adelaide's records show Reinhart's address as the Lutheran Seminary in North Adelaide.[22] In fact, for most of the period he was at university, he boarded with his future wife's parents, the Sacharias-Saarelinns.

Throughout his life, Reinhart retained a photograph of the University of Adelaide's 1953 class of Third Year Medical students. It is a magnificent photograph, with the students all splendidly attired as one might expect of the period, but showing a surprising diversity of names and faces for 1950s Adelaide. This was a consequence of

10.4 Reinhart, Charlotte and Jakob heading for Australia on the *Toscana*, 1950 (RPA)

some of the students being among the earliest beneficiaries of the Colombo Plan, a development scheme which allowed Asian students to train in Australia during the 1950s and 1960s. Others, like Reinhart and Nina Sacharias-Saarelinn, were recently arrived New Australians. After matriculating in her first year in Australia, Nina had enrolled in Dentistry before transferring to Medicine during 1951. Like Reinhart, she was awarded a Commonwealth Scholarship in 1952.[23]

10.5 University of Adelaide's 1953 Third Year Medicine class.
Nina is 4th from right in the 1st row; Reinhart is 2nd from left in the 2nd row. (RPA)

Nina's father, Eugen Sacharias-Saarelinn (1906-2002), had been born in Germany, the family was German speaking and they had lived in Germany during the war. Prior to this, Eugen had been a successful architect in the Estonian capital, Tallinn, where his legacy is still highly regarded. Though listed as a labourer when selected to come to Australia as a displaced person, he soon found work as an architect in Adelaide and the family settled in the suburb of Prospect.[24] According to a story passed down within the family, Nina and Reinhart became acquainted when, during a laboratory class, Reinhart dropped a test tube and exclaimed 'Scheiße'. 'I see you are a German speaker', Nina responded.

The couple married in 1957, the year they graduated together as doctors. Eventually moving to Melbourne, where they found more opportunity for training and practice, they both became eminent medical specialists and recognised pioneers in their different fields, Nina as a radiologist and Reinhart as an anaesthetist. In 2016 Nina would receive an Order of Australia award for 'service to medicine in the field of radiology'.[25] For Reinhart, it was a different career trajectory than his parents might have envisaged when they supported him in what they believed were his first steps to becoming a 'missionary doctor'. What seems evident is that after experiencing adolescence in wartime and post-

10.6 The unveiling in 1956 of an Adelaide memorial to commemorate the visit of Queen Elizabeth II in 1954. The memorial was funded by recent arrivals from Europe and designed by Nina's father, Eugen Sacharias-Saarelinn. Left to right: Harold Holt, former Minister for Immigration and future Prime Minister; L. Trett, representing the Good Neighbour Council of South Australia and Eugen Sacharias-Saarelinn. (NAA: A12111 1/1956/17/32)

war Europe, Reinhart and Nina grasped every opportunity they were given in their new country to build lives that would become showcase migrant success stories.

Even though Jakob and Charlotte had work and accommodation at Hermannsburg, they had to support Reinhart in his first year at university and, as an older couple, they had no savings. Eleven years after being forced off their farm in Palestine, they were desperate to access their assets and thankful to be included in the process being developed by the Australian government to seek compensation for these assets. A first step in this process was for Australian Templers, who acted on behalf of Templers and other Palestine Germans such as the Rippers, to gather evidence for their property claims. This proved to be an enormous task, generating large volumes of paperwork.[26]

As well as providing details and photographs of his own farm, Jakob was the main source for maps created to show the extent of German settlement north of Acre. He would have been relying on memory to do this in the early 1950s, but Jakob was uniquely placed to provide this information. He had always been a keen observer of landscape, he had technical drafting skills and he had worked throughout the area on German, Arab and Jewish properties. Jakob's contribution in helping to record the extent of this German settlement north of Acre is historically valuable because it is otherwise poorly documented and largely forgotten.[27]

While the Templers organised the paperwork to support a collective claim, the Australian government found the new government of Israel resistant to any agreement on compensation. Following the proclamation of the State of Israel on 14 May 1948, German properties had been transferred to the Israeli Custodian of Enemy Property. Subsequently, 31 July 1949 was set as a deadline to settle any claims. The Australian government appealed for a delay but found the Israeli government hostile to any suggestion that a Jewish state would compensate Germans. Protracted negotiations remained in deadlock until the new West German government became involved. In 1952 the West Germans agreed to make substantial compensation payments to support the settlement of displaced European Jews in Israel. At the same time, the West Germans were persuaded by the Australian government to link these payments to compensation for Palestine Germans. Reluctantly, the Israeli government agreed in principle to the Palestine Germans having a right to compensation.[28]

It took another ten years for the value of the compensation to be settled. In 1955 Professor Karl Brandt, an agricultural economist who had left Nazi Germany for the United States and worked at Stanford University, was accepted as an independent expert and engaged to assess the value of the German properties. In late 1955 he visited Israel on two occasions to carry out site visits and confer with Israeli officials. He also came to Australia to examine documents and meet the claimants' advocate, Henry Temby. In August 1957 Brandt produced a detailed report which estimated the total value of all German property at UK£11,245,745.[29]

Brandt's valuation was rejected by the Israelis, new experts were engaged and negotiations continued until 1962, when an agreement was finally reached to value the German properties at UK£6,057,885. With interim payments having already been made, Israel completed payment of the balance of this sum to West Germany by 1963. The German government divided these payments between Templers in Germany and Australia's Temple Society Trust Fund, which managed the complex disbursement of funds to individuals in Australia. After several interim payments, beginning in 1957, the Ripperts received their last substantial payment in 1966 and a final payment in 1971. Reflecting the sum the Trust Fund was given to distribute, the Ripperts' total compensation was around 60% of the value they had given to their property. By Jakob's own estimate, they received 37% of Professor Brandt's valuation for their property.[30]

Even though Professor Brandt's valuation was rejected, his extensive report is a fascinating historical document. It discusses a wide range of issues, from fluctuations in the price of oranges, to the difficulty in establishing a fair date for the valuation of properties last seen by their owners fifteen years ago, to the quality of Templer buildings, some of them being the 'finest buildings in Israel'. This last observation is reflected in modern Israel's conservation of German precincts in cities such as Haifa and Jerusalem. Brandt was at pains to establish his objectivity. He made a point of rejecting an Israeli official's claim that the Templers were 'ardent Nazis'. He also claimed to ignore dispassionately the valuations of owners whose estimate might be based on the fact that 'his property spelled "home" to himself and his family'.[31]

The report is strong in identifying and describing the German properties north of Acre. The Ripperts' farm is singled out, along with two others, for comment: 'The three most valuable and high-income-yielding properties were the horticultural enterprises of Richard Beilharz, Jakob Rippert and Christian Stoll.' This assessment was supported by a detailed description of the Ripperts' farm, its infrastructure and abundant produce. No doubt, Jakob and Charlotte would have been heartened to read this. Even so, it is interesting to speculate on how Brandt could have based his description and assessment on his 1955 visit. Sincere efforts at objectivity notwithstanding, it is possible that when he visited Australia he was influenced by material Jakob had given to the Templer committee and was describing the area and farm much as Jakob and Charlotte had known it in the late 1930s. Some of Jakob's photographs, taken in 1938, were included in Brandt's report.[32]

In the unfinished memoir he wrote in 1971, Jakob reflected on the loss of the family's possessions in Palestine and the extended compensation process that had only recently come to an end. In doing so he disavowed any bitterness; as always, he and Charlotte were prepared to submit to what they saw as God's will. Nonetheless, a lot of feeling is conveyed in this simple statement: 'We loved our home near Acre very much, the country and the people.' Clearly, Jakob and Charlotte were among those identified by Professor Brandt as having an emotional as well as financial investment in their property. Bitter or not, there was enormous regret about their loss. This regret about personal loss was accompanied by regard for the far worse plight of Arab neighbours who, unlike the handful of Germans, received no compensation for their dispossession. Today, reading Jakob's thoughts on the long legacy of this dispossession, written at the height of the Cold War, one is struck by the thoughtfulness and ongoing relevance of his observations. His reflection begins with some detail about the fate of the German Evangelical Community Cooperative which, in 1939, was being developed northeast of his farm:

> In the meantime, the settlement cooperative of the German Evangelical Community Co-op had been formed in Haifa, and I was elected to its board. The aim was to buy land for about 16 young German

sons from Haifa and Waldheim families and to create a German settlement for a mixed economy. Three times a land purchase failed because each time the Zionists offered the Arab landowners larger sums than we Germans did. But finally an Arab village sold us 1400 dunam [dunam ~ 1000 square metres] about 4 km from our farm to the northeast. It was good land and could be irrigated to plant gardens and green fodder for cattle. We had also bought a piece of land there, a so-called half lot, for our Manu, where we wanted to build a farm for him. The Second World War made all this impossible and all our work and planning went to the Jews, they got all the German property in Palestine.

With the help of the German and Australian governments, after years of negotiations, we received compensation, i.e. 37% of a valuation that Professor Brandt, an American, made with the Jews. The money came mainly from German Reich compensation to Israel, without which we would have received nothing for all our work and investments. After each of the Akko [Acre] settlers had been deducted the amounts that almost all of us owed to the settlement cooperative, each of us was left with a small sum that we needed because the old age pension in Australia is not very large and we have mostly all become too old to be able to work and earn money ourselves. In any case, we thank God that we didn't lose everything and are very grateful to the German and Australian governments for supporting us in our claims.

We loved our home near Acre very much, the country and the people. Many of our former Arab friends now live in Lebanon and Transjordan, often under difficult circumstances. We are also in written contact with some of them. Most of the Arabs fled in 1948 and lost everything, just like us.

Thank God we are not bitter about our fate, it was almost foreseeable even before the war that the Jews would get Palestine. After all, no one among the Arabs today talks about the fact that their large landowners had already sold most of the good Palestinian land to the Zionists before the war. All this land used to be leased by the poor Arab farmers or fellahs, as they are called there. We witnessed all this and saw how the light gradually dawned on the rich Arabs, but by then it was decidedly too late, the best land in Palestine was legally bought by the Jews from the large Arab estates and the war threw the other land into their laps for almost nothing. There's a lot more that could be said, but it's all worthless, fate will take its course and Israel will no longer hand over anything it owns. And the refugee issue can only be solved internationally. Everything would be easy to solve if the two superpowers wanted to use some of the vast sums they are shooting to the moon and Mars to solve the refugee question. Of course, the bitterness among the Palestinian Arabs today is so great that they are no longer open to a solution to the question of, say, resettlement in Iraq, for example, where there is still a lot of good land that could be irrigated. Nobody who knows the situation in the Orient [Middle East] today sees a way out of the more than confused situation with regard to the Palestinian-Arabs.[33]

Endnotes

1. Nominal Roll SS *Oxfordshire*, Naples 24 April 1949 – Adelaide 25 May 1949, NAA: D2002, *Oxfordshire* 24/4/1949, NAA.
2. Frank Bongiorno, *Dreamers and Schemers: A Political History of Australia*, La Trobe University Press, Melbourne, 2022, pp. 208-209; Jayne Persian, *Beautiful Balts*, NewSouth, Sydney, 2017, pp. 6, 52.
3. R. T. Appleyard, 'Post-War British Immigration', and Ann-Mari Jordens, 'Post-War Non-British Migration', in James Jupp, ed., *The Australian People: An Encyclopedia of the Nation, Its People and Their Origins*, Cambridge University Press,

Cambridge, 2001, pp. 62-65 & 65-70; Persian, pp. 9-10, 74, 183-184; Victoria Mence, Simone Gangell and Ryan Tebb, *A History of the Department of Immigration*, Department of Immigration and Border Protection, Canberra, 2017, p. 85.
4. Jürgen Tampke and Colin Doxford, *Australia, Willkommen: A history of the Germans in Australia*, NSW University Press, Sydney, 1990, p. 243.
5. Persian, p. 201; Bongiorno, pp. 208-209.
6. Stuart Macintyre, *Australia's Boldest Experiment: War and Reconstruction in the 1940s*, NewSouth,Sydney, 2015, pp. 405, 401-405; 'Minister Dislikes Use of Word "Migrant"', *Sydney Morning Herald*, 16 December 1947, p. 9; Persian, pp. 6, 50, 63-64.
7. Christine Winter, 'The Long Arm of the Third Reich', *The Journal of Pacific History*, 38:1, 2003, p. 105; Anne Seitz & Lois Foster, 'German Nationals in Australia 1939–1947: Internment, forced migration and/or social control?', *Journal of Intercultural Studies*, 10:1, 1989, pp. 26-27; S.P. Koehne, '"You have to be pleasing & co-operative": Australia's vision splendid for post-World War II migrants', Traffic (Parkville), no. 5, July 2004, pp. 3-7.
8. Calwell's speech, Parliament of Australia: House of Representatives, 23 September 1949, Hansard, p. 552.
9. Ibid., p. 551.
10. Deitrich Ruff and Rolf Beilharz, 'Templers', in Jupp (ed.), *The Australian People*, pp. 375-377; Paul Sauer, *The Holy Land Called: the story of the Temple Society*, (trans. Gunhild Henley), Temple Society of Australia, Melbourne, 1991, pp. 286-297.
11. Jakob Rippert, Memoir, 1971, HStAD; Werner Struve, quoted in Sauer, p. 318; Garry Stoll, Interview, 1996, FRM, p. 11.
12. Letter, Henry Temby (Department of Army) to Jakob Rippert, 28 September 1948, RPA; Sauer, pp. 294, 308; letter, Jakob Rippert to Henry Temby, 24 April 1955, RPA.
13. Letter, Henry Temby (Department of Army) to Jakob Rippert, 28 September 1948.
14. Letter, Henry Temby (Department of Army) to Dr J. Stolz, 17 September 1948, UELCA Immigration, Box 19, F2, LAA.
15. The *Australian Lutheran*, 13 November 1946, pp. 374-375; Bethany Pietsch, '"Dear Sisters in the Faith": Letters of Thanks from Post-War Germany', *Journal of Friends of Lutheran Archives*, No. 33, 2023, pp. 50-51; Adam Kauschke, 'Discovering the stories of our post Second World War migrants', *Journal of Friends of Lutheran Archives*, No. 29, 2019, pp. 30–44; letter, Henry Temby (Department of the Army) to Dr J. Stolz, 17 September 1948.
16. Certification of funding, Dr J. Stolz, President, United Evangelical Lutheran Church of Australia, 8 December 1949, RPA; letter, Jakob Rippert to Pastor F. W. Albrecht, 15 March 1950, RPA; letter, Frances Murton, of Melbourne's Elizabeth Fry Retreat, to Minister Calwell, 7 March 1949, UELCA Immigration, Box 19, F2, LAA; letter, Dr J. Stolz to H. Temby, 27 October 1949, UELCA Immigration, Box 19, F2, LAA.
17. Letter, Jakob Rippert to Pastor F. W. Albrecht, 4 November 1949, RPA.
18. Letter, Jakob Rippert to Alfred Löther, 22 June 1971, HStAD; Gil Gordon, 'The Schneller Family: the Longest Protestant Missionary Dynasty in the Orient', MS: http://www.gordonarc.co.il/Academic-research.html , p. 13; letter, Jakob Rippert to Pastor F. W. Albrecht, 15 March 1950.
19. Letter, Jakob Rippert to Alfred Löther, 22 June 1971; Temporary Travel Document, Jakob Rippert, RPA; letter, P. Scherer to UELCA and FRM treasurers, 1 December 1950, UELCA Immigration, Box 18, F2, LAA.
20. Letter, Jakob Rippert to Alfred Löther, 22 June 1971.
21. Reinhart Rippert, 'Impressions of a Voyage from Europe to Australia', *Immanuel College Weekly*, 9 December 1950, pp. 8-10, RPA.
22. University of Adelaide Special Collections, Archives Series 1117, Index cards to students: 1900-1985, Rippert, Reinhart.
23. Ibid., Sacharias-Saarelinn, Nina.
24. *Meie Kodu, Australian Estonian Weekly*, 26 April 1956, p. 3.
25. C. Ball and M. Buckland, 'Obituary: Reinhart Rippert', *Anaesthesia and Intensive Care,* Vol. 39, Supplement 1, July 2011, pp. 30-32; 'Dr Nina Sacharias, Radiologist, Educator, Innovator', www.radiologybeyondatextbook.com/biography/index.html (13 January 2025); 2016 Queen's Birthday Honours List, honours.pmc.gov.au/honours/search (26 September 2025).

26. See, for example, 'Templar (sic) Property in Israel', NAA: B1374, 4 and 'Basic Palestine Documents regarding Templar (sic) Property…', NAA B1312, 9, NAA.
27. See, for example, the map 'Deutscher Besitz 1939 Sub-District Akko, Palästina', drawn by H. Ruff, based on information from J. Rippert, 1953, TSA.
28. Sauer, pp. 296, 299-302; Suzanne D. Rutland, '"Buying out of the Matter": Australia's Role in Restitution for Templer Property in Israel', *Journal of Israeli History*, 24:1, 2005, pp. 140-149.
29. Sauer, p. 304; Rutland, p. 148.
30. Sauer, pp. 305, 308; Rutland, p. 149; letter, Department of Immigration, Melbourne to Jakob Rippert, (Final Account for Temple Society Trust Fund), 24 July 1971, RPA; Jakob Rippert, Memoir.
31. Karl Brandt, *Report on the Value of Secular Real Estate in Israel Owned by Former Residents of German Nationality or Extraction* (*Report*), 1957, NAA: B1365, 1, pp. 1, 8, 22, 52-53, 98, NAA.
32. Brandt, *Report*, pp. 130-132.
33. Jakob Rippert, Memoir. The Ottoman dunam was standardised to 1000 square metres (¼ acre) in 1928.

Chapter 11
Hermannsburg, 1950 – 1955

Hermannsburg Mission was the most significant and longest lasting Lutheran mission in Australia. It was established in 1877 on the Finke River, on the lands of the Western Arrarnta, about 130 kilometres west of modern Alice Springs. The site is just south of the MacDonnell ranges, which help to give the area a higher rainfall within an otherwise extremely arid zone. The Finke River is normally a dry riverbed with separated water holes surviving the long periods between rain. On the rare occasions when the Finke fills after rain over its catchment in the MacDonnell Ranges, the water flows south until it is lost in the Simpson Desert.

The site had been recommended to the Lutheran Church after members of its mission committee had applied to the South Australian Surveyor General, George Goyder, about the possibility of establishing a mission to Aborigines in Central Australia. After the government granted the Church a mission/pastoral lease on the Finke River site, arrangements were made with the Hermannsburg Institute in Germany to supply the mission with its first missionary leaders, Pastors A. H. Kempe and W. F. Schwarz. Following their arrival in South Australia in 1875, Kempe and Schwarz set out for Central Australia with a small party and livestock. It was the start of an epic journey which took more than eighteen months. Much of this time was spent waiting for rain at Dalhousie Springs before they could proceed any further into the dry interior. After the exhausted party finally arrived at the lease site on 8 June 1877, a location was chosen for the mission on the north-east side of the Finke River where they found a source of underground water.[1]

In 1878, Kempe and Schwarz were joined by a third missionary, Pastor L. G. Schulze, who led a small group sent out from Germany. This group included Dorothea Queckenstedt and Wilhelmine Charlotte Schulz, the fiancées of Kempe and Schwarz respectively. These two were among the earliest European women to settle in Central Australia. Dorothea was a twenty-four-year-old farm servant from the village of Knesebeck, Germany. Her family's story is indicative of the enormous hardships the first missionaries endured. She and Pastor Kempe had seven children at Hermannsburg. One of the sons, Ludwig, died at the age of six. Kempe experienced

11.1 Central Australia and Hermannsburg (PKI)

11.2 Looking across the Finke River towards Mount Sonder, north of the MacDonnell Ranges (PKI)

11.3 Former missionary homes in Hermannsburg's historic precinct (PKI)

two bouts of serious illness, including typhoid fever. Dorothea died on 13 November 1891, a few weeks after the birth of her last child. Kempe left the mission a few weeks later. Dorothea and her son Ludwig are buried in Hermannsburg's historic cemetery.[2]

In spite of the enormous challenges these pioneer missionaries faced, with the acceptance and help of the Arrarnta people, they were able to establish the mission and it survived difficult periods until its position was consolidated under two outstanding leaders, Pastor Carl Strehlow and Pastor Friedrich Wilhelm (F. W.) Albrecht. Strehlow was mission superintendent at Hermannsburg from 1894 until his tragic death in 1922 and Albrecht from 1926 until 1952. Scholars, linguists and social justice advocates ahead of their time, as well as dedicated Christian missionaries, Strehlow and Albrecht gave Hermannsburg a long period of continuity. During this time, the mission developed into a unique institution which ministered to the spiritual and material needs of Western Arrarnta and their neighbours. When the Ripperts arrived at the mission in 1950, despite the physical hardships missionaries still faced at this time, they were fortunate to be able to experience Hermannsburg at its peak, before social change and an array of outside influences began to impinge on the small enclave and herald the end of the mission era.

Today, the Hermannsburg Mission site and its beautiful old buildings are preserved as a historic precinct within the Aboriginal community of Ntaria. The site is on the checklist for tourists driving the popular circuit out of Alice Springs and around the spectacular western MacDonnell Ranges. Although the traditional missionary era ended with the closure of Hermannsburg Mission in 1983, the work of its governing body, the Finke River Mission, continues in Alice Springs and throughout Central Australia. The mission's legacy is evident in the strong relationships that continue to exist between the Lutheran Church and many Aboriginal people.

The Ripperts arrived at Hermannsburg on 25 October 1950 and Jakob began working on its new school building on the following morning. He and Charlotte were accommodated in one of the mission's old buildings which, though picturesque and solid looking, Jakob spent a lot of time repairing. The couple was to remain at Hermannsburg for the next five years, during which time they had at least one long break in Adelaide. We are able to glimpse some aspects of their lives during this time from photographs they retained and from personal letters or documents preserved in the archives of the Lutheran Church and Finke River Mission.

11.4 Crosses on the graves of Dorothea and Ludwig Kempke in Hermannsburg's historic cemetery (PKI)

During 1952 the mission superintendent, Pastor Albrecht, visited Germany with his wife for the first time in decades. In July Jakob wrote a long letter to Albrecht from Hermannsburg. It was a familiar letter, full of news about the mission and family. Jakob welcomed news that the Albrechts intended to visit his mother and brother in Auerbach, encouraged them also to visit Ernst Schneller at the Schneller Orphanage and warned they would 'both be shocked by the enormous changes that have taken place in the old world'. He reported on the progress of the school building and told Albrecht that government builders from Darwin had commended it as among the 'finest in the Northern Territory', with the building's cost being about one third of a government school. 'I am quite sure', Jakob suggested, 'that the money the church spent on my trip was worth it for this one building project.'

There were struggles with the work. Firstly, Jakob was distracted by other tasks, such as planning to build a home in Alice Springs for the mission's stockman, Arthur Latz, and repairing white ant damage on mission buildings at Hermannsburg and Alice Springs. Secondly, Jakob confided, he had had to adjust patiently to the work habits and attitudes of his Aboriginal workers. He passed on various details about events in the lives of these men, all of whom were obviously personally known to Albrecht. Among the workers singled out for their helpfulness were Manasse Armstrong, Keith Namatjira and Benjamin Landara. All were assisting with construction work as one of their many roles at Hermannsburg and in surrounding communities. Manasse Armstrong was a skilled craftsman and leather worker. Keith Namatjira was the son and Benjamin Landara the son-in-law of the celebrated artist Albert Namatjira. Both Keith and Benjamin became acclaimed artists themselves.

Despite the building challenges and enduring a 'very hot and sandstorm filled summer, with no rain for months', Jakob assured Albrecht, he and Charlotte thanked 'the faithful God who has led us here'. Even if everything was not easy, they were ready to 'continue on our path in faith as long as we are needed here'. He told Albrecht about Reinhart visiting for six days in June. He had not been able to stay longer because of the need to stay on top of his studies to ensure he kept the scholarship he had

11.5 Jakob and his work team at Hermannsburg in 1951. Left to right, according to the caption on the back: Eric, Bruno Tapani, Manasse Armstrong, Benjamin Landara (foreman), Mac, Jakob Rippert. (RPA)

been awarded, 'as a gift from God and a generous gesture from the Australian government'. It was planned for Reinhart to visit again for 3-4 weeks at Christmas. 'It's not good for us', Jakob reflected, 'to be separated for that long and the boy needs to know he has a home here with us.'[3]

During 1952, Jakob was also corresponding with the Finke River Mission Board about his plans to build the mission's new hospital. There is an interesting passage in a letter from the board's Chairman, Pastor R. B. Reuther, where the latter comments on their agreement about Jakob writing in German and Reuther writing in English. Reuther appears to have been mindful of the need for clear communication, primarily with regard to the board's concern about the project not being 'too extravagant'. This is a reminder that Jakob had to quickly gain proficiency in English, not only to ensure clear communication with the board, but to produce building plans and order materials from suppliers. There is evidence in the board's files, in the form of a detailed plan in English, that he was able to achieve this by the end of the year.[4]

In 1953, it is evident that at least some members of the board remained anxious about the cost of the hospital proposal, along with some aspects of Jakob's role. This contributed to a serious misunderstanding at Hermannsburg. In the middle of the year there was an exchange of letters between F. W. Albrecht, who was back in Australia, and Adelaide businessman and board member Lou Borgelt, where they discussed the fallout from a recent board meeting which dealt with concerns about the Hermannsburg building projects, including how long it had taken to complete the school building. Someone had conveyed a version of this board discussion to the Ripperts and Charlotte had reacted strongly against what she perceived as unfair criticism of her husband. Lou Borgelt urged Pastor Albrecht to reassure the Ripperts that, while the board had closely scrutinised the building projects, there had been no criticism of Jakob or his work.[5]

Despite this reassurance, it is evident that concerns had developed about the scope, cost and building

11.6 Jakob and Charlotte with Reinhart, who helped with the work at Hermannsburg during university holidays (RPA)

11.7 Hermannsburg's old Church, with the faint arrow at the bottom of the photo indicating the house at the rear, where the Ripperts lived during the 1950s (RPA)

11.8 The same scene in 2024 (PKI)

time of Jakob's major projects. And there was a shift in Pastor Albrecht's views. In late 1950, soon after Jakob's arrival, Albrecht had told artist Rex Battarbee 'Mr Rippert is a great builder and I am beginning to wonder what would have happened if he hadn't arrived in time'. By mid-1953, he was telling Lou Borgelt that while Jakob was a tremendous worker, he was 'far too particular in his work for our requirements'. Completion of the school had given Jakob something to show for his efforts but, Albrecht asked, 'if we want to continue at this rate, when shall we finish, and where is the money to come from?'[6]

At the end of 1954, the Lutheran Church (UELCA) and Finke River Mission Treasurer Bert Doering visited Hermannsburg for a month and produced a report. It recognised great improvements since his last visit. One of the improvements he pointed to was the athel pine trees which provided shade around the mission. These trees had been planted in their hundreds by Jakob. He referred to them as 'fast-growing cypresses' and their planting recalls his extensive planting of cypresses on his Palestine farm. Natives of North Africa and other arid zones, the athel pines thrived at Hermannsburg and they are prominent in photographs from the 1960s. Unfortunately, while attractive as a shade tree and widely planted in the Northern Territory, the athel pine is an invasive species in Australia. The trees at Hermannsburg have been removed and are being eradicated or controlled elsewhere, including where they spread along the Finke River.[7]

Doering's report provides evidence of the ongoing concerns about the mission's building projects. Defects were already evident in the recently completed school building and the hospital project was slow to begin, with workers often diverted to other jobs. 'On the whole,' he pointed out, 'our big projects are not systematically planned…'. Doering went on to make a number of observations about the Ripperts. 'We all know his fine work', he wrote of Jakob, 'his planning and his fine work are an asset to our Mission; some maintain that he is a little too methodical and too exact. His mission spirit is to be admired.' Charlotte, he reported, was not in good health and there had been misunderstandings about the mission's coverage of the cost of medical fees and medicines. The Ripperts, he noted, were going to Adelaide for a holiday at the end of the year and the mission had agreed to cover the cost of one leg of a flight.[8] In 1954, flying would have been an expensive novelty for any of Hermannsburg's missionaries. It may have been the Ripperts' first flight.

It is significant that only one leg of the flight from Alice Springs to Adelaide could be funded. Similarly, when Jakob recommended steel framed doors for the new hospital as a precaution against white ants, the mission's board baulked at the additional cost of £10 per door. The board needed to manage carefully its limited resources and this dictated frugality. The missionaries themselves were frugal. This was exemplified, in a minor way but redolent of the world they inhabited, when in one of Pastor Albrecht's letters to Bert Doering, he asked for the return of his razor strop: 'I am enclosing a stamp and would thank you if you would kindly send me my razor strop which I left in your bathroom.'[9]

The mission's frugality, both a necessity and consistent with the personal ethos of the missionaries, was clearly a source of some tension with the Ripperts. Of course, the Ripperts were themselves frugal missionaries. But Jakob was not a bush carpenter. He was a designer and builder/engineer who worked methodically and meticulously, perhaps beyond the expectations of those who were accustomed to making do with less ambitious structures that could be constructed quickly within tighter budgets. Even so, while there were differing views around aspects of the mission's building program, there was never any questioning of Jakob's commitment or work ethic.

The two major projects Jakob worked on were Hermannsburg Mission's new school and the Carl Strehlow Memorial Hospital. After a lengthy build time, the school opened on 9 August 1953. The *Lutheran Herald* celebrated the event with a detailed report and front-page photographs of the school and opening ceremony. It paid tribute to the building's architect, Dick Drogemuller, and its builder, Jakob Rippert: 'The Mission certainly owes a debt of gratitude to him for the tremendous amount of work he has done so conscientiously and faithfully.' Jakob's hard work and expertise, it was recognised, had helped to keep the total cost below £6000. So too, had the contributions of others such as Dick Drogemuller, who provided his services free of charge, and Vic Modra, a South Australian farmer who had sown a special 100 acres of barley and donated the proceeds to the school. The opening ceremony was attended by distinguished visitors, including Church and government officials. Pastor Albrecht and Evangelist Konrad addressed the assembly in Arrarnta. After Mr Rippert handed over the key of the new school to Board Chairman Pastor Reuther, separate afternoon teas were provided for children, for the Hermannsburg community and for distinguished guests. The event was reported in Alice Springs' *Centralian Advocate* and as far afield as Melbourne, where the *Age* explained how the school was built by 'native labour' under the direction of Mr Rippert, who was erroneously described as 'formerly a civil construction engineer on the great Aswan dam in Anglo-Egyptian Sudan'.[10]

Photographs of the school building show what was, in contrast to the mission's earlier buildings, a strikingly modern structure. It had been designed, by architect Dick Drogemuller, to run in an

11.9 Hermannsburg School, opened in 1953 and later demolished (LAA P03551 07349)

east-west direction, so that the summer sun travelled directly overhead, with the building's interior protected by wide awnings. In winter, the sun fell on north-facing louvre windows, providing efficient heat for the interior during the cold desert winters. The roof sloped towards the centre, from where it collected rainwater to be stored in an underground tank. Sadly, despite these visionary features, serious defects in the school's design became apparent soon after it was opened. In 1954, Bert Doering's report referred to a sagging roof and a collapsing water tank, which affected the foundations.[11] The building, which had been greeted with so much excitement when it was opened, later had to be demolished.

Jakob drew up plans for the Carl Strehlow Memorial Hospital in 1952. These plans were revised in February 1954, following advice from health authorities. Preparation of the site commenced in January 1955 and Jakob spent the remainder of the year supervising construction of the main building. Major components of the construction were 41,000 concrete bricks, a building material Jakob would have been familiar with from Palestine. Overseen by Mr Roy Burton, these bricks were manufactured on site using purchased cement and Finke River sand. The main building was ready to receive its first patients at the end of the 1957 and smaller outlying buildings were finished a year later.[12]

The building of the Carl Strehlow Memorial Hospital was a significant achievement for the mission. This was marked by a dedication ceremony and publication of a souvenir history in July 1960. As this history proclaimed, the hospital gave physical expression to an important element of Lutheran mission tradition: 'the ministry of physical healing has been the handmaiden of the spiritual ministry of the Gospel'. Building and equipping the hospital came at a total cost of £28,756. Almost half of this substantial sum came from government grants but the remainder was raised from donations and the building was only made possible through considerable effort on the part of mission staff and Aboriginal workers. The souvenir history acknowledged the key role of Mr Jakob Rippert, 'builder-architect and civil construction engineer', in providing the mission with a building which impressed officials with the quality of its design and workmanship. The mission's Visitor Book records a range of

11.10 The Carl Strehlow Memorial Hospital, opened in 1957 and currently serving as a cultural centre for the Ntaria community (PKI)

visitors who came to Hermannsburg for the dedication or in the weeks before and after. They included the artist Rex Battarbee and his wife Bernice, Carl Strehlow's son Ted Strehlow, the artist Judy Cassab and the German Ambassador, Hans Mühlenfeld, and Frau Mühlenfeld.[13]

The Carl Strehlow Memorial building remains in place as a substantial resource for the Ntaria Aboriginal community. Although no longer used as a hospital, the features of Jakob's design and quality of the workmanship are still evident. It is a large, solidly constructed building, with wide verandahs providing protection from the sun for separate internal wards and specialist rooms, all connected by corridors. Underneath is a cellar which provided the hospital with a much-needed cool storage area.

The building projects of the 1950s and 1960s, which included construction of a new church, were an investment in Hermannsburg's future and a sign of confidence in the mission's future. Change, nonetheless, was on the horizon. It would soon have a dramatic impact on what anthropologist Diane Austin-Broos has referred to as a unique local world 'on the periphery of the state' which, 'in their unequal positions', the missionaries and Arrarnta had struggled to create and preserve. In coming decades, the paternal authority of the missionaries would be gradually overturned by Aboriginal demands for self-determination and the encroachment of the modern welfare state, with its insistence on land rights, wage equality and the provision of social welfare. As Austin-Broos describes the transformation, the mission era was overtaken by the Western Arrarnta's 'growing rights in citizenship and their inclusion in the market society, albeit as marginalised participants'.[14] While the work of the Lutheran Church and Finke River Mission would continue in Central Australia in other forms, in 1983 the Hermannsburg mission and pastoral lease was handed back to its Aboriginal owners and the community adopted a new name, Ntaria, the traditional name for the nearby Finke River waterhole.

At one extreme, the end of the mission era was welcomed by those who associated it with paternalism, forced assimilation, the imposition of Christianity and the destruction of Aboriginal culture. Such assessments ignore the complex nature of the mission experience, including the critical role played by missions such as Hermannsburg in helping Aboriginal people withstand the threat posed by the rapid intrusion of a European society with little restraint on its rapaciousness. Mission leaders such as Carl Strehlow and F. W. Albrecht were truly impressive figures. Rather than riding rough shod over Aboriginal culture, they took the trouble to learn local languages, developed a deep understanding of the cultures these languages gave access to, and formed close relationships with people they lived with and to whom they committed their lives. Certainly, they were paternalistic in their attitudes and primary expectation of guiding Aboriginal people towards Christian enlightenment. And yet, there were always practical secular goals associated with Christian evangelising — hence the building of a school and a hospital. For Albrecht, above all, preparation for work was important.

Alongside firm views about the need to understand and respect Aboriginal cultures, Albrecht believed European culture had imposed irreversible changes that required adaptation in Aboriginal culture and economy. He placed great faith in education, training and employment as essential to empowering Aboriginal people to succeed in the larger economy. At Hermannsburg, this was given practical expression with the provision of traditional schooling but also in workplace training on the mission's cattle station and in a range of local enterprises, including the operation of an extensive leather working and tanning operation.

In the longer term, the most successful of these enterprises was the development of the Hermannsburg water colour school. Although encouraged and supported by Albrecht, this was the initiative of Albert Namatjira. Described by Albrecht as 'Hermannsburg's most famous son from a secular viewpoint', in 1934 Namatjira had been inspired by the work of visiting artists, including Rex Battarbee. Captivated by their depiction of his Country, Namatjira felt that he could produce similar paintings and began to expand his existing interest in art and craft. Two years later, he accompanied Battarbee on a painting expedition into the surrounding area. Namatjira worked as Battarbee's camel driver while Battarbee tutored him in watercolour techniques. Namatjira soon developed exceptional skill in capturing the extraordinary landscapes and vivid colours of the MacDonnell Ranges. When his paintings were exhibited in southern cities they quickly sold and Namatjira went on to become a household name. In 1954 he was taken to Canberra and presented to Queen Elizabeth II during her first tour of Australia. Even though he painted in his own distinctive version of a European style, Namatjira's success as an Aboriginal artist in the wider community prepared the way for the popular acceptance of more traditional Aboriginal art.[15]

Rex Battarbee took a keen interest in Namatjira's career, moved to Alice Springs and was a regular visitor to Hermannsburg. He almost certainly met the Rippers, who kept a photograph of him. This prompts speculation about a historical coincidence — did Jakob Rippert, Rex Battarbee and F. W. Albrecht discuss their shared experience of the First World War? Jakob and Rex Battarbee had served on opposite sides on the Western Front, where they had both been severely wounded. F. W. Albrecht had served in the German Army's medical corps on the Eastern Front, where he had been awarded an Iron Cross for assisting wounded men under fire. Battarbee's wartime injuries had prompted the career change which resulted in him becoming an artist.[16]

In 2024 Barry Judd and Katherine Ellinghaus published a book, *Enlightened Aboriginal Futures*, which takes a fresh look at the work of Hermannsburg Mission and F. W. Albrecht. Barry Judd, Deputy Vice Chancellor Indigenous at the University of Melbourne, is of Pitjantjatjara, Afghan and British descent. He and Ellinghaus adopt a measured approach which challenges recent interpretations that focus only on the missionary era's perceived shortcomings. Thus, Judd and Ellinghaus suggest, despite the mission's basic objectives appearing to place Christianity and the European Enlightenment into opposition with Aboriginal concepts around kinship, obligation and spirituality, missionaries like Albrecht were not 'oppressive and assimilationist' in the way they worked. On the contrary, like his predecessor Strehlow, Albrecht was respectful of Aboriginal culture and immersed himself in it, there was inter-cultural dialogue rather than one-way proselytising and the mission created a community where there could be 'greater Indigenous freedom, choice and autonomy, often in opposition to the settler-colonial state and public opinion'. Albrecht was an evangelist, motivated by a deep Christian faith, but he also prioritised the secular task of securing a sound social and economic future for Aboriginal people 'in a contemporary settler Anglo-Australia hostile to their very existence'. This priority was channelled into the provision of schooling, workplace training and initiatives to support a variety of Aboriginal enterprises, from a tannery to arts and crafts. This support for education and training for participation in the European economy did imply acceptance of some degree of assimilation as a longer-term outcome. For Albrecht, such assimilation was not based on a desire to obliterate Aboriginal culture but on a recognition that the old Aboriginal economy was simply no longer viable.[17]

Contrasting F. W. Albrecht's ideals with what has been achieved under the auspices of the welfare state in the fifty years since Hermannsburg Mission's closure, Judd and Ellinghaus make a strong statement:

> Whereas Albrecht never deviated from the idea that paid work would provide a pathway to secure Aboriginal futures, Australian governments at national and territory levels have seemingly condemned Aboriginal people to a present charactered by endless welfare dependency, poverty, ill health and social disfunction.[18]

Always the thoughtful observer, how did Jakob Rippert reflect on his experience of working with Aboriginal people? He was asked this question in 1959 in a letter from Pastor C. J. Pfitzner of Hahndorf, South Australia. Jakob's immediate response was to advise Pfitzner to consult F. W. Albrecht, whom he clearly held in enormous regard for his intimate knowledge of Aboriginal culture. He went on to observe how complex the Aboriginal world was and how much knowledge was required to understand it — 'every mission worker should learn the native language thoroughly'. Goodwill and anthropological interest were not enough to bridge the gap between cultures, Jakob explained; what was needed was 'abundant love, patience, and real mission mindedness'. Overlooking some jarringly paternalistic language used in association with the 'gap between cultures', this letter conveys both the genuineness of Jakob's respect for Aboriginal culture and the depth of his religious faith.[19]

What is less obvious in the 1959 letter, but which comes through strongly in a report he wrote for the mission board at the end of 1951, is Jakob's alignment with Albrecht in his belief in the importance of education and training. In his own missionary career, Jakob had always been a practical doer of the word rather than a preacher. The influence of his own training in manual and technical skills was always evident. He was disappointed to find that Aboriginal workers were poorly equipped to engage in the complex construction work he was carrying out. It was demanding work and required more commitment, he realised, than quickly putting up 'a hut made of bush timber and corrugated iron'. Nevertheless, Jakob believed it was vital for the young men to be trained to work expertly with tools in the way he had been. Like Albrecht, he saw the success of Hermannsburg's art movement as an encouraging sign of what could be achieved with training and commitment.[20]

How did Aboriginal workers at Hermannsburg reflect on their experience of working with Jakob? All that we have on record is an amusing anecdote from Garry Stoll, who arrived to take up a position at Hermannsburg soon after the Ripperts had left. It appears Jakob had made a very positive impression on the Aboriginal men who had worked with him and they were fond of retelling stories about him. One of those stories, related to Garry with appropriate accents and gestures, told of how Jakob had asked some of the men to collect buckets of rocks to use in a foundation. He was perplexed when they

Hermannsburg, 1950-1955 131

11.11 Albert Namatjira, at the front, painting with his sons near Hermannsburg, 1952 (RPA)

11.12 One of Albert Namatjira's earlier paintings, *Hermannsburg Mission with Mount Hermannsburg*, 1937 (Araluen Art Collection, AC 2007:019, Namatjira Legacy Trust)

returned with their pockets full of rocks, just as they had been when they heard his German accented English and mistook 'buckets' for 'pockets'.[21]

On 14 April 1954 Jakob and Charlotte placed a notice in Alice Springs' *Centralian Advocate* to announce their intention to apply for Australian naturalisation. They gave their length of residence as nine years. This included the long period they had spent in internment. They became Australian citizens on 29 March 1955. Coincidentally, two months before the Ripperts were naturalised in Alice Springs Court House, Reinhart's future father-in-law, Eugen Sacharias-Saarelinn, was naturalised in Adelaide. All three naturalisations were recorded on the same page of a July 1955 issue of the *Commonwealth of Australia Gazette*.[22]

Two days before he and Charlotte received their naturalisation certificates, on 27 March 1955, Jakob wrote a letter of resignation to the Chairman of the Finke River Mission Board, Pastor R. B. Reuther. Jakob advised that he was forced to resign as the mission's builder because of Charlotte's health issues, which included a liver complaint and a heart 'too worn out for longer stay in the hot climate of Central Australia'. He undertook to remain at Hermannsburg until the end of 1955 to complete work on the main hospital building. After this, he explained:

> I see it as my duty to my wife and also to our son, to go to a healthier climate [in] South Australia to look there for a job, and there try to make a home for my small family, so that we 3 are again united before it is too late for it…

> This is in no way easy for me, since we could not save up much money here, and had to help our son to be able to get through his studies. I am sure to find a building job, but to find a home and to furnish it will be not so easy. There is little hope for us in the near future, to get repayment of our

11.13 Opposition Leader Arthur Calwell about to speak at the unveiling of Hermannsburg's Namatjira Memorial in 1962. From row: artist Rex Battarbee, Minister for Territories Paul Hasluck, Pastor F. W. Albrecht. Second row: Namatjira's sons, Enos, Oscar, Ewald, Keith and Maurice. Calwell, as Immigration Minister in 1949, had approved the Ripperts' entry into Australia. (RPA)

property in Palestine, and should it once be done, it will perhaps be too late for us older people. But, we know, that the Lord, to whom we dedicated all our life for the service on the mission field, will also not forsake us in this new situation.[23]

Reuther responded, on behalf of the board, to express deep regret at the news of Jakob's resignation, to acknowledge all his hard work and to thank him for committing to finishing the main hospital building. There was no reference to Jakob's outline of the difficult situation his resignation would leave his family in.[24]

A few weeks after advising the Finke River Mission Board of his resignation, Jakob wrote a long letter to Henry Temby, the Australian official who was assisting Australia's Palestine Germans with their compensation claim in Israel. Addressing Temby almost as a family friend, Jakob told him about his and Charlotte's recent naturalisation, reported on Reinhart's successful studies and attached a copy of his resignation letter. He again emphasised, for Temby, the financial challenges ahead, especially when he and Charlotte could no longer rely on the Church or mission board for financial support:

> In our former home country the mission board would have offered us other work in the many branches of home mission and also a home after resigning from mission service in a foreign country. This is not so here. The Lutheran Church here is only a small Church, and so when a mission worker is no longer capable to do his special work, or other circumstances hinder him, he has to resign and to find himself another job and home…
> Not being born Australians we shall have to live here for 20 years, before having the benefit [of an] old age pension…
> You will understand how much it would mean for us, in our new situation, to have some money from a compensation of our properties, it would be a God send.[25]

At the end of 1955, the Ripperts were confronted with a situation similar to when they had left the relative security of their internment camp in 1947. Once again, Jakob would need to find work, they

11.14 The Ripperts being farewelled from Hermannsburg in December 1955. Left to right: Essie Simpfendorfer (teacher), Charlotte Rippert, Lorna Petering (teacher), unknown, Jakob Rippert. (Photo, Ralph Kernich, FRM)

had to find a home and they had very little money. Moreover, this time they were heading for a strange city. Hermannsburg may have had a harsh climate, but it was the sort of small, secluded community Jakob and Charlotte had been used to and mission work in similar locations had been their loved vocation. For them, even provincial Adelaide was a daunting prospect — an unfamiliar metropolis, busy with commercial activity. On top of all these factors, Jakob and Charlotte were now conscious of their age and the onset of serious health issues.

Endnotes

1. M. Lohe, F. W. Albrecht and L. H. Leske, *Hermannsburg: A Vision and a Mission*, Lutheran Publishing House, Adelaide, 1977, pp. 7-13; Barry Judd and Katherine Ellinghaus, *Enlightened Aboriginal Futures*, Routledge, London, 2024, pp. 22-23.
2. Lohe et al., pp. 14, 20-21; Dorothea Queckenstedt, Naturalisation Certificate, South Australia, 5 November 1877.
3. Letter Jakob Rippert in Hermannsburg, Australia, to F. W. Albrecht in Germany, 27 July 1952, HStAD.
4. Letter, FRM Chairman Pastor R. B. Reuther to Jakob Rippert, 18 June 1952; Hospital Proposal (undated), UELCA Box 11, LAA.
5. Letter, F. W. Albrecht to Lou Borgelt, 10 June 1953; letter Lou Borgelt to F. W. Albrecht, 16 June 1953, FRM.
6. Letters, F. W. Albrecht to Lou Borgelt, 10 June 1953, 19 August 1953; letter F. W. Albrecht to Rex Battarbee, 25 November 1950, FRM.
7. Bert Doering, 'Report on Hermannsburg Trip, 14 October 1954 – 10 November 1954', FRM; letter, Jakob Rippert to Alfred Löther, 22 June 1971, HStAD; 'Weed Management for Athel Pine 2017-2027', NT Department of Environment, Parks and Water Security, Darwin, 2021.
8. Doering, 'Report on Hermannsburg Trip'.
9. Doering, 'Report on Hermannsburg Trip'; letter F. W. Albrecht to Bert Doering, 4 December 1948, FRM.
10. *Lutheran Herald* (Australia), 10 October 1953, pp. 299-301; *Centralian Advocate* (Alice Springs), 14 August 1953, p. 1; *Age* (Melbourne), 15 August 1953, p. 16.
11. *Lutheran Herald* (Australia), 10 October 1953, p. 300; Bert Doering, 'Report on Hermannsburg Trip'.
12. 'Opening and Dedication of the Carl Strehlow Memorial Hospital, Hermannsburg, N.T., Sunday, 31st July, 1960: A Souvenir History', UELCA Pamphlet Folder, LAA; History Plaque – Carl Strehlow Memorial Hospital (Draft), FRM.
13. 'Souvenir History'; Hermannsburg Mission Visitor Book, July-August 1960, FRM.
14. Diane Austin-Broos, *Arrernte Present, Arrernte Past: Invasion, violence, and imagination in Indigenous Central Australia*, University of Chicago Press, Chicago, 2009, pp. 34, 78.
15. Lohe et al., pp. 70-73; Judd and Ellinghaus, pp. 56-57.
16. 'Rex Battarbee' and 'F. W. Albrecht', *Australian Dictionary of Biography*, https://adb.anu.edu.au
17. Judd and Ellinghaus, pp. 4-5, 16-17, 25-26, 38, 58.
18. Ibid., p. 106.
19. Letter, Jakob Rippert to Rev. C. J. Pfitzner, 15 June 1959, RPA.
20. Jakob Rippert, 'Work report on the construction of the new school in Hermannsburg, October 26, 1950 – December 31, 1951', RPA.
21. Garry Stoll, Interview, June 2024.
22. *Centralian Advocate* (Alice Springs), 14 April 1954, p. 4; *Commonwealth of Australia Gazette*, No. 33, 14 July 1955, p. 2130.
23. Letter, Jakob Rippert to Pastor R. B. Reuther, 27 March 1955, UELCA Box 11, LAA.
24. Letter, Pastor R. B. Reuther to Jakob Rippert, 12 May 1955, UELCA Box 11, LAA.
25. Letter, Jakob Rippert to Henry Temby, 24 April 1955, RPA.

Chapter 12
Nuriootpa, 1956 – 1975

The last chapter in Jakob and Charlotte Rippert's story begins with yet another attempt to restart their lives, this time in Adelaide. It was a difficult but brief period, before they moved north to Nuriootpa in South Australia's Barossa Valley. Here, they found a place in a supportive rural community which had become home to other Palestine Germans. The distinctive German character of the Barossa Valley, along with the role played by Lutheran Church groups within its towns and villages, were important elements of this support for the Ripperts. Increasingly beset by health problems, in financial hardship for much of the time and always struggling to come to terms with both the loss of the life they had had in Palestine and their inability to work any longer in the missionary field, the final years of their lives were not easy. On the other hand, sustained by their Christian faith and received as respected elders within their new community, Jakob and Charlotte found a degree of contentment at the end of their tumultuous lives in a part of the world they could never have imagined when, as young missionaries, they set out for Egypt and Nubia.

We know about the Ripperts' difficult time in Adelaide because in June 1956 Jakob described it in a long letter to Wilhelm, his brother in Germany. The letter reads like it was Jakob's way of working through the trauma of the recent experience. He asked Wilhelm not to reveal the distressing contents to their mother. Jakob wrote the letter, he told his brother, from his sick-bed, where he had been confined because his knee had been giving him trouble with 'war memories' from 1918. He then went on to describe the ordeal he and Charlotte had endured in their first months after leaving Hermannsburg at the end of 1955. They had gone to Adelaide with the aim of Jakob entering a partnership with someone who had invested in land and wanted to build quickly on the site. Jakob does not name the partner or give much detail about him in the letter, but it sounds like he hoped to use Jakob's skills as a project manager and builder to complement his own entrepreneurial vision.

For Jakob, it quickly became apparent, the partnership could not work. He did not have the funds for speculative investment and he could only work in his customary methodical and meticulous way. Jakob withdrew from the partnership when he could no longer cope with what he saw as the partner's hasty and haphazard way of working. From the partner's perspective, Jakob surmised, he probably came across as 'too precise, in short, perhaps too German'. While Jakob chose to associate this 'precision' with a German stereotype, in his case it appears to have been a strong personal characteristic, observed by others, including other Germans at Hermannsburg.

The business partnership failed at a time when Jakob and Charlotte were struggling to manage living in Adelaide. They had been able to stay in a mission holiday house for a short time, but it was out of the city and Jakob found it costly to travel for work. They could not afford to pay rent and found temporary accommodation with a missionary family, the Trudingers. The cost of living, the need to find permanent accommodation and getting around Adelaide, all while trying to find work, were overwhelming at a time when Jakob and Charlotte found that 'life in the big city is already restless enough'. On top of all these difficulties, Jakob began to exhibit signs of ill health. Reinhart, who was by now a final year medical student, was concerned by the symptoms and took his father to a heart specialist. The doctor diagnosed arteriosclerosis. Medication improved the condition, but it was made clear that Jakob would need to slow down and would no longer be capable of hard physical work.[1]

Jakob and Charlotte's unhappy existence in Adelaide lasted only a few months. By April 1956 they had moved to Tanunda, where they were able to stay on a friend's farm while Jakob looked for work. Tanunda is a small town in the Barossa Valley. Only seventy kilometres north of Adelaide, in the 1950s the Barossa Valley was a world away from South Australia's state capital. In an article published in 1950, Adelaide's *Advertiser* newspaper described this small regional area which was to become a refuge for the Ripperts:

> Set in rolling downs and pleasant plains, green with close-ranked vineyards and orchards, the towns of the Barossa Valley have a character all their own, the heritage of the Lutheran German colonists who thought to found a little Germany there, and created instead a unique corner of Australia.[2]

The German character of the Barossa Valley was the result of a large wave of German immigration into South Australia from the mid to late nineteenth century. From November 1838 until January 1839 ships carrying 500 Old Lutherans arrived in the colony. Led by Pastor August Kavel, this group originated from Klemzig in the then German state of Prussia. Kavel and his congregation had opposed Prussian King Frederick William III's religious decrees and came to South Australia seeking the freedom to maintain their own traditional practices. Following the successful settlement of Kavel's group, Germans continued to arrive in South Australia and by the late 1850s there were up to 10,000 German speakers in the colony. No longer fleeing religious persecution, the later migrants came in search of a better life, drawn by the good reports they received from relatives and friends who had already settled in South Australia. Arriving in the British colony so soon after its establishment in 1836, the Germans formed an unusually large non-British group within the founding European population. Unlike in any other Australian colony, they managed to establish a distinct non-British enclave within the settler population which was to have outstanding longevity.[3]

Kavel's congregation established a first settlement at Klemzig. Now an Adelaide suburb, its name was changed to Gaza during the First World War amidst the nation-wide fervour to erase German place names and replace them with patriotic British names which, like Gaza, were often associated with Australian military actions. In 1935, in response to public calls for German place names to be restored as a recognition of South Australia's German heritage, Klemzig was reinstated. In contrast, the original Klemzig is now a Polish city, Klępsk. Other early German settlements in South Australia were Hahndorf and Lobethal. Located in the hills to the east of Adelaide, these towns also had their German names restored in 1935.[4]

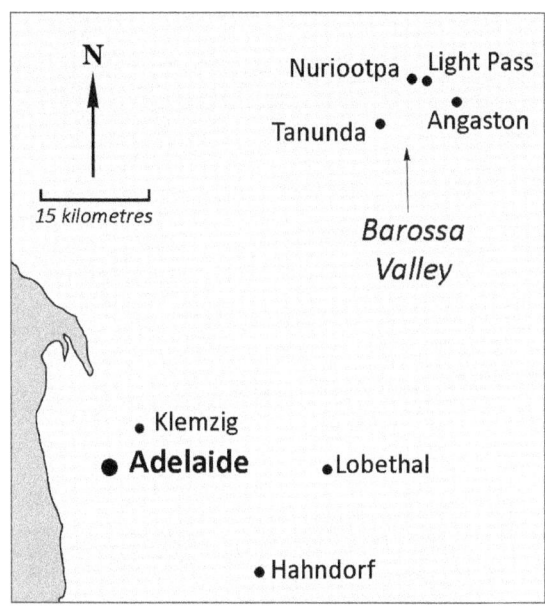

12.1 Adelaide and the Barossa Valley (PKI)

12.2 One of many vineyards surrounding Barossa Valley towns like Nuriootpa and Tanunda (PKI)

As early as 1842, Germans began to move north of Adelaide to settle in what became known as the Barossa Valley. By the start of the 1850s, when the German adventurer and popular author Friedrich Gerstäcker passed through the area, the Germans were well-established. Gerstäcker wrote this impression of early Tanunda, now one of the Barossa Valley's major centres:

> Tanunda … is a small town of a few hundred inhabitants, with buildings that are somewhat English in style, but the population, with the possible exception of a few isolated cases, is entirely German. It was a strange feeling for me, in a foreign country and part of the world, as well as in an English colony, to suddenly find myself surrounded by Germans and, in fact, a purely German way of life and work. Sometimes I really had to think carefully, especially when I saw small groups standing in the streets everywhere and heard *everyone* speaking German, whether I was really in Australia.[5]

An astute observer, Gerstäcker saw the exceptional quality of the grapes and wine being produced in the surrounding areas and predicted that 'wine-growing will one day become a very important branch of industry for the country'. Although the industry was in the earliest stages of its development when Gerstäcker visited, the Barossa Valley would become Australia's best-known wine-growing region.[6]

For several reasons, the Germans in the Barossa Valley were able to preserve their *Deutschtum*, or 'Germanness'. The critical factor was their adherence to Lutheranism. Germans who came to South Australia in the nineteenth century were predominantly from Lutheran areas of Germany and in Australia they maintained both their religious faith and the social cohesion this gave them. By contrast, in other areas of Australia, such as the Hunter Valley in New South Wales, there was rapid assimilation when a sizeable group of German Catholics blended quickly with the wider population. Church services in German, the publication of German language newspapers, the popularity of German clubs and cultural groups and the development of German language schools, all helped to maintain *Deutschtum* in the Barossa Valley's rural communities where Germans were plentiful and had the status of pioneers within the European settler population. Intermarriage between early German descendants, as high as 78% in the late 1860s, played a self-sustaining role and appears to have continued at high levels well into the twentieth century.[7]

Deutschtum was preserved to a notable extent in the Barossa Valley, but its society was never static and assimilation, albeit incremental, was impossible to resist. After Melbourne University Professor of German, Augustin Lodewyckx, toured Australia's areas of German settlement in the 1920s, he regretted that the German language had largely been lost. In his 1932 book, *Die Deutschen in Australien*, he wrote: 'the history of the Germans in Australia is the history of their anglicisation'. True of Australia as a whole, this observation was also relevant to the Barossa Valley, where the end of significant migration from Germany by the start of the twentieth century, generational change, the First World War and the closure of German languages school during that war, had all contributed to an erosion of *Deutschtum*. In 1953, only a few years after celebrating the unique German character of the Barossa Valley, Adelaide's *Advertiser* raised concern about the decline in its German speakers. Under the headline 'German Dying Out in Barossa Valley', it revealed only older people still spoke German.[8] There was an interesting reaction to this report in South Australia's

Catholic newspaper, *Southern Cross*. At a time when New Australians were expected to assimilate rapidly, this article proposed the Barossa Valley as a model of how Australia might benefit from accepting gradual assimilation:

> German migrants in considerable numbers settled on the land. Over a span of three generations their industrious work has established a highly productive rural industry and a thriving, vital type of community life.
>
> The main lesson to be drawn from the Barossa Valley, however, is that assimilation is a gradual process. It is something that cannot be forced. Time alone breaks down the old differences.
>
> At the end of three generations a closely-knit, well-defined national grouping has merged into the Australian community at large, absorbed by it, enriching it by its own contributions.[9]

It is hardly surprising that the Barossa Valley's special German character would evolve since the 1840s. Ongoing assimilation and modernising influences affecting the whole of Australian society have only hastened the erosion of remnant elements of German heritage in the decades since the 1950s. And yet the German legacy is still evident, nowhere better illustrated than in responses to Australian census questions, which show both decline and continuity in the Germanness of Barossa Valley towns relative to the rest of Australia — see Table 12.1.

	2021			2016			2001		
	Tanunda	Nuriootpa	Australia	Tanunda	Nuriootpa	Australia	Tanunda	Nuriootpa	Australia
German Ancestry	28.56	25.9	4.0	21.2	19.6	3.1	-	-	-
Lutherans	26.8	21.1	0.6	30.8	27.4	0.7	44.4	40.1	1.3
German Speakers	0.7	0.7	0.3	0.9	0.8	0.3	2.0	1.2	0.4

Table 12.1 Australian census statistics comparing percentage responses in Barossa Valley towns Tanunda and Nuriootpa with the responses for the whole Australian population. Based on Australian Bureau of Statistics Quick Stats, www.abs.gov.au

In the late 1940s and 1950s, Germans from Palestine, including the Ripperts, were responsible for a small revival in German immigration to the Barossa Valley. Their experiences are interesting not only for their own stories but for the 1950s snapshot they provide of the region's German heritage. The German newcomers found a welcoming community with strong German influences and their responses offer a glimpse of this community at a time when those influences were still readily discernible. The story of one of the extended Palestine German families has been well documented in Herb Meinel's history, *Nothing Can Make Them Stumble: The Story of the Stoll/Meinel Family*. In telling the story of how the children of Jakob and Anna Maria Stoll's children came to the Barossa Valley, it illustrates the three different routes by which Palestine Germans arrived in Australia: via Tatura internment camp, via Germany after the Second World War or via Cyprus after 1948.

Jakob (1865-1940) and Anna Maria Stoll (1868-1945), who had moved from Germany to the Templer colony in Haifa in the late 1880s, were married in 1893 while Jakob was establishing what would become the family's bakery business in Haifa. The couple had five children, Wilhelm (1894-1976), Hulda (1897-1989), Anna (1900-1901), Maria (1902-1988) and Christian (1904-1982). Anna died in infancy. The other four children and their families would all end up in the Barossa Valley.[10]

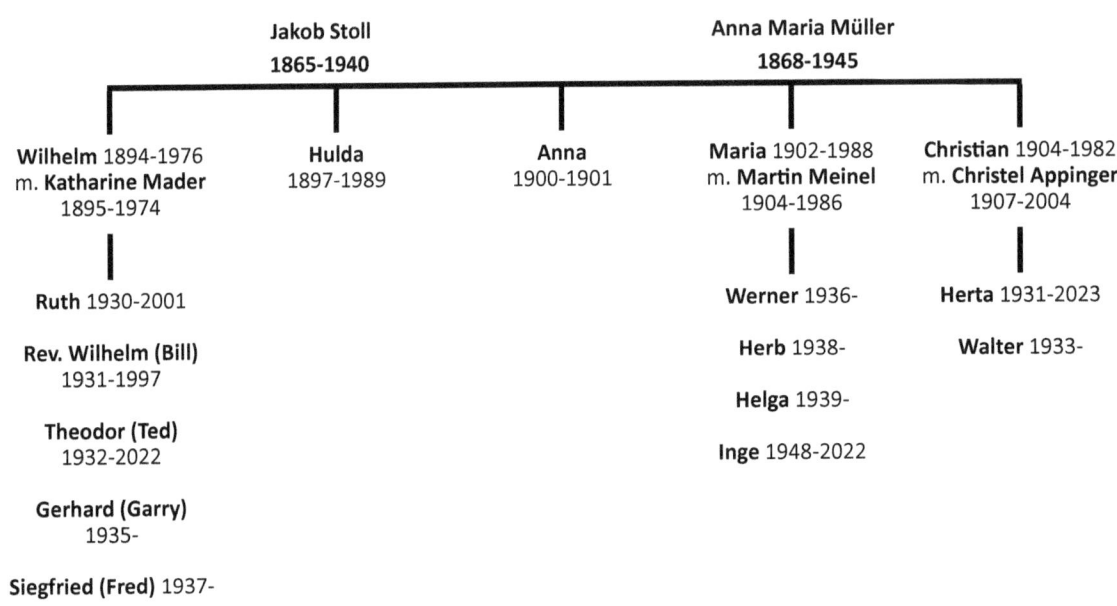

Table 12.2 The Stoll and Meinel Families

The coming of the Second World War affected Stoll family members in different ways. Christian Stoll, who operated his flower nursery next to the Ripperts' farm, and his sister Maria's husband, Martin Meinel, were conscripted into the German army and, along with other young German men, left Palestine before the war broke out. Because they both spoke Arabic, Christian and Martin served with Rommel's Afrika Korps in North Africa. Taken prisoner by the Americans, they spent years in the United States as prisoners of war. In the meantime, their wives and families were interned, along with the elderly Jakob and Anna Maria Stoll and their daughter Hulda, in the Lutheran settlement at Waldheim, near Haifa. The eldest son, Wilhelm, was not conscripted but, being considered of military age by the British, was interned with Jakob Rippert in the men's camp north of Acre.[11]

In 1941 Wilhelm Stoll, his wife Katharine and children Ruth, Wilhelm (Bill), Theodor (Ted), Gerhard (Garry) and Siegfried (Fred) were deported to Australia on the *Queen Elizabeth*. Along with the Ripperts, Wilhelm's family spent the war in the Tatura internment camp. After the war, they chose to remain in Australia and established new lives in the Barossa Valley.

Christian Stoll and Martin Meinel's families were participants in one of the more unusual and little-known episodes of the Second World War. Especially where husbands were serving in the German army, it was proposed that German families interned in Palestine be allowed to go to Germany in exchange for internees held there. The so-called internees in Germany were Jews being held in concentration camps. After agreement was reached, trainloads of Jews from Germany and Germans from Palestine were exchanged at Istanbul. In this way, up to 500 Jewish lives were saved and many German families from Palestine spent the remainder of the war in Germany. Martin Meinel and Christian Stoll were reunited with their families in Germany after the war. In the early 1950s, encouraged by Wilhelm Stoll's reports of life in Australia, they took advantage of Australia's willingness to accept family-sponsored Palestine Germans from Germany to bring their families to the Barossa Valley. Martin's family comprised his wife Maria and children Werner, Herb, Helga and Inge. Christian's family comprised his wife Christel and children Herta and Walter.[12]

Jakob Stoll died at Waldheim in 1940. Rather than be exchanged to Germany, Hulda Stoll chose to remain in internment with her elderly mother, who died in 1945. Hulda was still at Waldheim when, in April 1948, the settlement was attacked by the Jewish paramilitary group Haganah. She was fortunate to survive a confrontation with the gunmen who shot some of the German residents. After this attack, the British evacuated those Germans who remained at Waldheim, including Hulda, to a refugee camp in Cyprus. In January 1949, sponsored by her brother Wilhelm, she came to Australia and settled in the Barossa Valley.[13]

The Meinels arrived in the Barossa Valley in 1952. According to Herb Meinel, they were able to affirm Wilhelm Stoll's glowing reports of his family's experience. By the early 1950s, he recalls, the Stolls were enjoying their new lives in the Barossa Valley:

> Things were looking up for them. There was plenty of work and a good education system for the children. So much of their new country reminded them of their homeland of Palestine. There was the Mediterranean climate, the diverse mix of arid and fertile landscape, and the large plantations of oranges, apricots and vineyards. Even the eucalyptus tree was common to both countries.[14]

There was also the German heritage of the area, with its many Lutheran churches and large numbers of people still speaking German, or at least Barossa *Deutsch*: 'The Stolls began to feel at home in this beautiful land, among these kind and generous people who had such a strong and vibrant faith, and a rich German heritage.'[15]

When he first arrived, Herb Meinel describes feeling awkwardly German when his first day at Nuriootpa High School began with the singing of Australia's then national anthem, *God Save the Queen*, and declarations of allegiance to the nation's new monarch, Queen Elizabeth II of England. His spirits immediately lifted when the roll was called and he 'listened in amazement' to all the German names of his classmates. Later, in the school yard, these students did their best to welcome him in their Barossa *Deutsch*.[16] Ironically, while the Palestine Germans coming to Australia had not been permitted to form German enclaves, as they had in Palestine, those who came to the Barossa Valley found a large group of German descendants who had managed to preserve some aspects of German culture for more than a century.

When the Ripperts arrived in the Barossa Valley in 1956 they were at a low ebb. Jakob made this clear when writing to his brother:

> ... building a new life at the age of 57 was and is not easy, because my previous life and work ... was so completely different and under different circumstances. I am not complaining, on the contrary, I thank my God that he has led me through depths that I did not yet know. That he took away my last securities in a foreign country, homeless, so that I only had to depend on his help. He has not abandoned me and my loved ones, he has set us on a new, albeit strange, path and with him we will continue to fight with confidence...[17]

Happily, they could not have come to a better place. Sustained by their faith in God, along with support from 'old friends', the Palestine Germans, and 'new friends' in the Barossa community, Jakob and Charlotte were soon able to get back on their feet. An important first step in their recovery was Jakob being offered work at the large building company C. O. Juncken, located at Nuriootpa. Here, his work as a quantity surveyor and draughtsman kept him away from the site work he loved, but it made good use of his expertise and was an ideal transition for someone experiencing ill-health.[18]

In 1995, the Juncken company marked the one hundredth year since its foundation with the publication of a booklet, *C. O. Juncken Builders – 100 Years*. This publication includes an outline history written by the then managing director, Ted Stoll, who had joined the company as a young man soon after his family had settled in the Barossa Valley. As Stoll records, Junckens had been established at Nuriootpa in 1895 by Hermann Julius Juncken, the son of Otto Johannes Wilhelm Juncken, who had emigrated to Australia from the Danish province of Schleswig Holstein in the 1850s, and Irish woman Margaret Fitzgerald. The business remained in the family until it was bought by employees, including Ted Stoll, in 1985. The centenary publication's list of long-serving employees shows the role the company played in providing employment for Palestine Germans and the significant contribution they made to the company. Ted Stoll was with Junckens for more than forty years. Theodor Wieland, a former Haifa architect, served for more than twenty years and was manager of the firm before the staff buy-out. Christian Stoll, the former nurseryman and florist, served for more than twenty years. Johannes Pross, the former Haifa hotel proprietor, served for ten years and ran the company's store. Theodor Wieland employed Jakob Rippert in April 1956, on the recommendation of Johannes Pross. Jakob worked at Junckens for more than ten years.[19]

At Junckens, Jakob told his brother soon after he began work, his closest colleagues were 'all Lutherans and nice people who have welcomed me kindly'. Charlotte began to feel better about their 'calmer life' as they settled into the small town of Nuriootpa. They still had to find their own home but were offered temporary accommodation with a Mr and Mrs Warnest, an older couple who spoke German and who had connections with Hermannsburg. Both Jakob and Charlotte found comfort in the presence of old friends such as the Stolls and Meinels.[20]

In the 1960s the Meinel family moved into a new home in Tanunda. Martin Meinel worked in local bakeries but also operated a commercial bakery from his home kitchen. From early in the morning, he cooked a range of breads, pastries and specialist cakes. These were stored in a large pantry, from where they were sold or distributed to friends throughout the day. One of Martin's speciality German products, *Bienenstich*, gained legendary status and is mentioned in a popular publication, *Barossa Food*:

> People who came from Germany or visited there from the 1890s onwards perhaps knew of *Bienenstich* but anyone who lived in Tanunda in the 1960s can tell you how the cake really came to be known there. It was because of a baker called Martin Meinel… A recent immigrant from Germany, in 1964 Mr Meinel introduced to his customers some of the recipes he knew from living in Europe but the one that immediately became popular was *Bienenstich*.[21]

Bienenstich may have been a German product but Martin Meinel developed his recipes in Haifa. Further, the home bakery operation was made possible because, Herb Meinel relates in his family history, the large pantry in the Meinel home had been built by their family friend from Palestine, Jakob Rippert.[22]

With limited memory of their earliest years in Palestine, the recently arrived Stoll and Meinel children encountered the Ripperts in the Barossa Valley as respected elders. Both Herb Meinel and Walter Stoll recall Onkel Jac and Tante Lotte as significant figures within family and church circles. Garry Stoll, who lived with the Ripperts at Tatura, has referred to them as 'like second parents'. Charlotte took a keen interest in the lives of young people such as Walter Stoll, whom she had known from infancy in Palestine. Walter still has Charlotte's violin, which she gave him before she died.[23] This much travelled violin had been given to Charlotte by her father in Germany, was taken to Egypt and Palestine, was used in the orchestra and to give music lessons in the Tatura camp and had been backwards and forwards between Hermannsburg and Germany.

12.3 Walter Stoll in 2024 with the violin given to him by Charlotte Rippert (PKI)

Jakob and Charlotte rented accommodation in Nuriootpa until they were able to purchase a house in the early 1960s in Third Street. This was a central location, near where Junckens was then located, around the corner from St Petri's Lutheran Church and within easy walking distance of friends such as the Stolls. Incredibly, Christian Stoll's family, who had owned the neighbouring farm in Palestine, lived a few doors down in Third Street. Jakob renovated their new home and he and Charlotte took pride in a large garden they developed around the house. Sadly, they were not able to enjoy this home for long due to deteriorating health. Charlotte was confined to bed for long periods, suffering from sciatica and heart problems, but was looked after by neighbours when Jakob went to work. Eventually, Jakob's own health problems forced him to work part-time from a drawing office in the house before reluctantly giving up work. They sold their home in 1969 and moved to a small retirement village and then a nursing home.[24]

Jakob and Charlotte could afford to purchase a home when they did only because they were lent money by friends. The sums involved were substantial, ranging from £400 to £1000. Some of these debts were forgiven but most, presumably, were repaid from the compensation received from Israel for the Ripperts' Palestine properties. The first instalment of this compensation was not received until 1957 and Jakob and Charlotte did not receive their final payment until 1971. Their total compensation amounted to £9747 (A$19,494). This was not an insignificant sum at the time, but the drawn-out process had kept the Ripperts in relative poverty and anxious about their retirement for many years. The lowering of the residency qualifying period for an Australian pension to 10 years in 1962, in response to the needs of large numbers of post-war migrants, and receipt of the final compensation payment in 1971, gave them a degree of financial security only at the end of their lives.[25]

12.4 Charlotte and Jakob at Nuriootpa, 1961 (RPA)

12.5 Kalleske grave, Nuriootpa (PKI)

12.6 Wieland grave, Nuriootpa (PKI)

12.5-12.7 Nuriootpa cemetery shows evidence of the waves of German migrants who came to the Barossa Valley.

Eduard Kalleske (12.5) arrived in South Australia with Pastor Kavel and the historic first wave of Lutheran settlers in 1838. The Kalleske family settled in the Barossa Valley and descendants today operate Kalleske Wines, one of the region's prominent wineries.

Nuriootpa cemetery also contains graves of Palestine Germans who arrived in the 1940s and 1950s, including Theodor and Kaethe Wieland (12.6) and Wilhelm and Katherine Stoll (12.7). Their headstones record their birthplaces in locations such as Jerusalem and Haifa. Like the pioneer Eduard Kalleske, these Palestine Germans or their families made a point of honouring their origins.

12.7 Stoll grave, Nuriootpa (PKI)

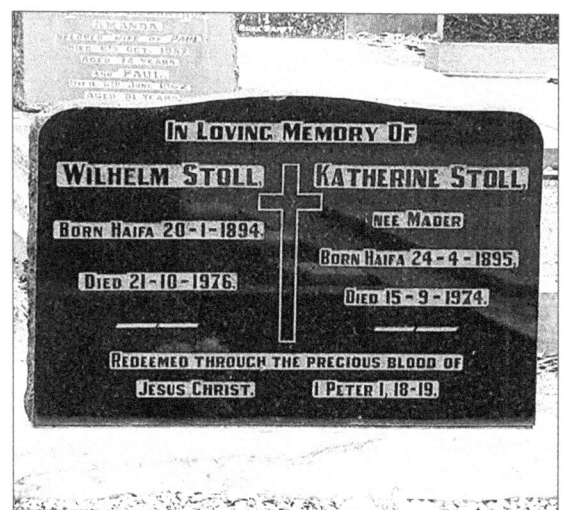

Among the thousands of documents and books kept by Jakob and Charlotte is a little red booklet, the *Decimal Currency Conversion Ready Reckoner*, purchased for two shillings and sixpence or twenty-five cents (both prices are on the cover). It was used to calculate currency conversions when decimal currency, or dollars and cents, replaced pounds, shillings and pence on 14 February 1966. The conversion was not terribly complex, £1 converting to $2, but older Australians often struggled with the change and for years afterwards were forever reminding themselves what something was worth 'in the old money'. Now a forgotten artefact of Australian social history, the *Ready Reckoner* would have had a particular use for the Ripperts beyond everyday shopping. Their compensation payments originated in Israel, were calculated in British pounds and German marks and were paid to them in Australian pounds. For the last instalments, the introduction of decimal currency introduced yet another conversion to be closely monitored.

Ill-health and frugality meant that Jakob and Charlotte led increasingly constrained lives in their last decade, largely confined to the small world of Nuriootpa. Fortunately, it was an actively close-knit community which, even in their adopted country, offered much that was familiar. They also kept in touch with people around the world by letter, were sent postcards when members of local families travelled and received visitors.

On at least one occasion, we know from a photograph taken in 1964, they were visited by Harry Kahn and his family. Harry was the son of Albert and Marie Clara Kahn who, it will be recalled, were the Jewish couple who fled Germany after Hitler came to power and found refuge with the Ripperts on their farm when they reached Palestine. After the war, when Albert and Marie Clara returned to Germany, their son Harry remained in Israel. He qualified as a chef, worked in locations around Europe and, in 1956, arrived in Melbourne as a chef with the German Olympic team. After the Olympics, Harry remained in Melbourne with his family and, well before the era of celebrity chefs in Australia, made a name for himself at some of the city's most prestigious hotels. During the 1970s the *Australian Jewish News* published several articles about Harry, outlining his life and showcasing his achievements. These included being chosen to cater for a Royal Banquet at Parliament House Canberra and being the only chef in Australia to have won five gold medals at the international Culinary Olympics.[26]

Why did Harry Kahn visit the Ripperts at Nuriootpa thirty years after they had sheltered his family on their farm in Palestine? It seems the two German families from Auerbach, one Jewish and one Christian, had a close relationship and had maintained contact. We have limited written evidence for this, but it would explain Albert Kahn supplying a testimonial for Jakob's denazification hearing in 1948 and his son's trek to out of the way Nuriootpa to visit the elderly Ripperts in the 1960s.

Jakob had always been a prolific writer and his output was diverse: the marvellously observant articles for *Der Sudan Pionier*, hundreds of letters to family and friends, long reports on his building work and an extensive correspondence on German landholdings in Palestine. His writing, in German or English, was always lucid and interesting, whether describing his own life or offering insights into the different places he and Charlotte had lived.

Jakob's life-long zeal for missionary work was always evident in his writing. So, too, was his Christian faith and acceptance of God's will in the face of life's trials. No doubt, this was a strength in allowing him and Charlotte to deal with the inevitable challenges of old age and declining health. Nevertheless, towards the end of their lives Jakob and Charlotte had disappointments to contemplate. War and internment had robbed them, not just of ten years of their lives, but of the opportunity to see their only son grow up. In some of his letters from Hermannsburg, Jakob wrote of his ambition to have his small family back together again as a family unit. It was an unrealistic ambition that seemed not to have taken account of the irrecoverable years between when Reinhart was sent to Germany as an eight-year-old boy and when he arrived in Australia as a young man with his own aspirations. Reinhart's busy professional life took him and his family to Melbourne. In the 1960s, well before plane travel was commonplace, this meant there would be limited contact between Reinhart and his parents. Where once they had spoken of Reinhart becoming a 'missionary doctor', Jakob's later letters began to focus on his achievements as an eminent specialist doctor. At the same time, Jakob and Charlotte might have reflected, Reinhart's separation from them in pursuit of his career may not have been so different from the way their pursuit of their own vocations had separated them from their own parents in Germany from an early age.

There is surprisingly little resentment expressed in Jakob's writing about the time he and Charlotte spent 'behind barbed wire' at Tatura. On the other hand, no amount of submission to God's will can disguise the deep regret he and Charlotte harboured about the loss of their farm in Palestine. This loss, and the inadequate compensation belatedly received, was a topic Jakob returned to often in his letters. He had put an enormous amount of work into establishing the farm and it was taken away from him just as it was about to deliver a return on investment. Equally important, the farm was the one place where the family had lived together for an extended period. The only tangible things left for Jakob and Charlotte from this happy time were their cherished photos showing the farm buildings and Reinhart, at different stages of childhood, with his proud parents.

Both Jakob and Charlotte were avid readers. As Jakob told an old school friend in 1971, retirement had allowed him to indulge his hobby of 'reading and studying'. By this time, the couple had accumulated 1200 books.[27] Many, including Charlotte's Arabic, Turkish and Japanese language books, had travelled around the world with them. Others were purchased with their meagre funds during their time at Nuriootpa. Regular mail orders, for example, were placed with Adelaide's well-known Mary Martin Bookshop. The result was an incredibly eclectic collection of non-fiction and fiction, suggesting an intellectually curious and broad-minded approach to what was good reading. The novels range from classics and important literature of the period to popular science fiction. The non-fiction reflects a search for understanding of the locations and cultures the Ripperts had experienced. These are some of the titles in the collection: Oscar Wilde's *The Picture of Dorian Gray*, Australian novelist Morris West's *The Tower of Babel*, Ernest Hemingway's *For Whom the Bell Tolls*, Leon Uris' *Exodus*, Ray Bradbury's *Something Wicked This Way Comes*, Heinrich Gerlach's *The Forsaken Army* (about Stalingrad), Yuri Suhl's *They Fought Back: The Story of the Jewish Resistance in Nazi Europe*, Leo Reinisch's 1879 *Die Nuba-Sprache* (on Nubian languages), archaeologist Leonard Woolley's *Dead Towns and Living Men*, Charles Mountford's *Brown Men and Red Sand: Journeyings in Wild Australia*, and Geoffrey Ashe's *The Land and the Book: Israel – The Perennial Nation*.

Books were only one of the things Jakob and Charlotte collected. They were hoarders who hung on to everything — artefacts from Nubia, copies of the letters they wrote, postcards, photographs, receipts for even minor purchases and numerous documents from all stages of their lives. This may not be atypical for older people who often leave their families with a bewildering mixture of valuables and ephemera to be sifted and culled. Unlike similar hoards, however, it is difficult to imagine the trouble Jakob and Charlotte must have gone to in order to preserve their collection as they moved around the world, sometimes under duress, or lived in often primitive circumstances. Fortunately, much of the earlier material appears to have survived long storage in Palestine. Beyond the normal urge to hoard, it is tempting to see their careful preservation of these artefacts and documents as recognition of the unusual nature and significance of their lives. They appear to have had some appreciation of how varied, eventful and interesting their lives were and of how they were enmeshed with some of the larger historical events and developments of their time. Humble and sincerely God-fearing though they were, their hoarding may have been influenced by a consciousness of posterity. They certainly left a treasure trove for researchers.

Charlotte Rippert died at Nuriootpa on 12 January 1975. Her devoted husband Jakob lived on by himself for only a few more weeks, before passing away on 23 February. Their lives were celebrated in two long tributes published in the local newspaper, *The Barossa and Light Herald*. An outline of Charlotte's life detailed her training in nursing and tropical medicine, her study of languages, including Arabic, her nursing work at Aswan and with German soldiers during the First World War, her contribution to the Karmel Mission in Palestine and work for the welfare of Arab families and her work for Aboriginal health at Hermannsburg. Selected aspects of Jakob's eventful life were highlighted, including his building and water-boring work with the Sudan Pioneer Mission, his

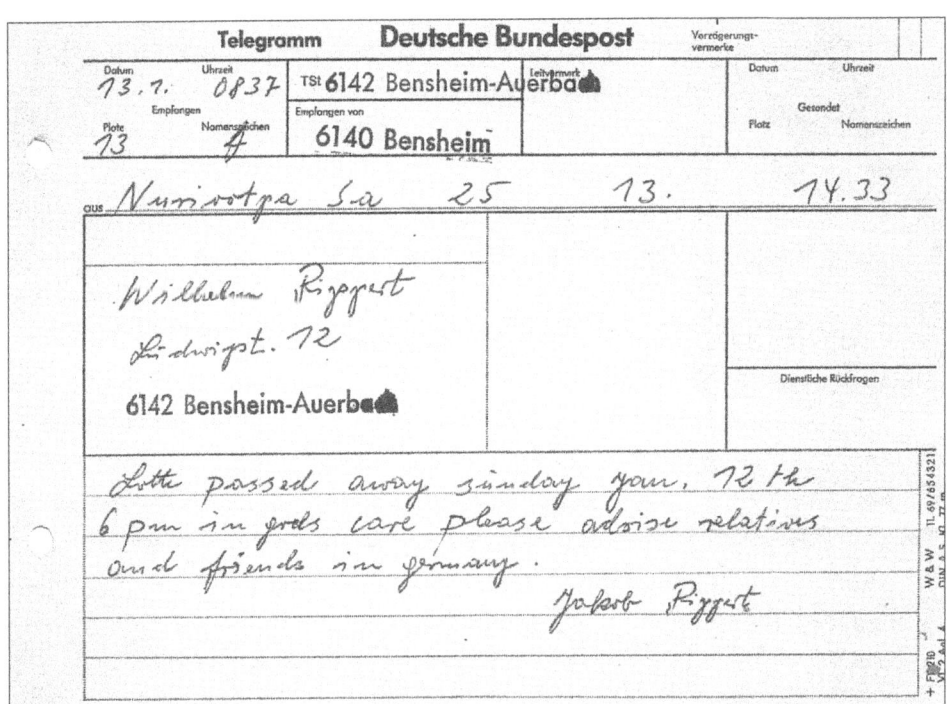

12.8 Telegram sent by Jakob to his brother Wilhelm to advise him of Charlotte's death (HStAD)

similar work with the Syrian Orphanage in Palestine and later in Germany, the development of the couple's farm in Palestine, their internment and contribution to the Hermannsburg Mission. It was noted that Charlotte and Jakob had many friends among the Templers. At Nuriootpa, the 'work of the couple, and their faith in their declining years, gained admiration, love and friendship from many people'. Charlotte and Jakob's funerals were conducted by Pastor Siegfried Held at St Petri's Lutheran Church, Nuriootpa. Among their pall bearers were Ted Stoll, his brother Pastor Bill Stoll and their uncle, Martin Meinel. Ted had worked with Jakob at Junckens, as children Ted and Bill had been interned with the couple at Tatura and all three had known the Ripperts since Palestine.[28]

Endnotes

1. Letter, Jakob Rippert in Nuriootpa to Wilhelm Rippert in Germany, 17 June 1956, HStAD.
2. 'Close-Knit Community of Barossa Towns', *Advertiser* (Adelaide), 8 April 1950, p. 10.
3. Jürgen Tampke, *The Germans in Australia*, Cambridge University Press, Melbourne, 2006, pp. 25, 31-32; Andrew Caillard, *The Australian Ark: The Story of Australian Wine* (Vol. 1), Longueville Media & The Vintage Journal, Sydney, 2023, pp. 161-163.
4. Tampke, pp. 25, 31-32; Lyall Kupke, 'The Restoration of German Place-Names in South Australia', *Journal of Friends of Lutheran Archives*, No. 27, 2017, pp. 51-62.
5. Friedrich Gerstäcker, *Australia*, JG Gotta'scher Verlag, 1853 (Projekt Gutenberg-DE).
6. Ibid.
7. Paul Kiem, 'Overlooked German Catholics of the Hunter Valley', *Journal of the Australian Catholic Historical Society*, Vol 46, 2025; Charles Meyer, *A History of the Germans in Australia*, 1839-1945, Monash University, Melbourne, 1990, pp. 53, 101, 128-133.
8. Meyer, pp. 126, 133, 142; *Advertiser* (Adelaide), 25 August 1953, p. 5.
9. *Southern Cross* (Adelaide), 18 September 1953, p. 6.
10. Herb Meinel, *Nothing Can Make Them Stumble: The Story of the Stoll/Meinel Family*, Adelaide, 2016, pp. 53-57.
11. Ibid., pp. 125-126, 197-201. Like Jakob Rippert, Wilhelm Stoll had served with the German Army during the First World War, when he had been seriously wounded.
12. Ibid., pp. 135-140. The exchange involving Maria Meinel and her children occurred in late 1942. While the details are uncertain, some Australian civilians interned in Germany may have been included with the Jews exchanged for Palestine Germans on this occasion — see the *Argus* (Melbourne) 2 January 1943, p. 8.
13. Meinel, pp. 141-143.
14. Ibid., p. 229.
15. Ibid., p. 230.
16. Ibid., pp. 243-244.
17. Letter, Jakob Rippert in Nuriootpa to Wilhelm Rippert in Germany, 17 June 1956.
18. Letter, Jakob Rippert to Henry Temby, 4 June 1956, RPA.
19. *C.O. Juncken Builders – 100 Years*, 1995, pp. 1-3, 5; letter, Jakob Rippert to Henry Temby, 4 June 1956.
20. Letter, Jakob Rippert in Nuriootpa to Wilhelm Rippert in Germany, 17 June 1956.
21. Angela Heuzenroeder, *Barossa Food*, Wakefield Press, Adelaide, 2020, p. 296.
22. Meinel, pp. 262, 264.
23. Garry Stoll, Herb Meinel and Walter Stoll, interviews, 2024.
24. Letter, Jakob Rippert to Alfred Löther, 22 June 1971, HStAD.
25. Letter, Vic Modrow to Jakob Rippert, 2 June 1953, RPA; letter, Jakob Rippert to Henry Temby, 4 June 1956;

letter, from the Australian Department of Immigration to Jakob Rippert regarding a final account for the Temple Society Trust Fund, 24 July 1971, RPA; Diana Warren, 'Towards higher retirement incomes for Australians', Melbourne Institute, 2008, p. 69.
26. *Australian Jewish News* (Melbourne), 16 July 1976 p. 3 and 27 June 1980 p. 3; Klaus Rippert and Paul Kiem, 'Jakob Rippert und Albert Kahn, zwei ungewöhnliche Auerbacher und ihre Schicksale', *Museumsverein Bensheim Mitteilungen*, 89, February 2024, pp. 64 – 73.
27. Letter, Jakob Rippert to Alfred Löther, 22 June 1971.
28. *The Barossa and Light Herald*, 16 January 1975, p. 7 and 6 March 1975, p. 3.

Epilogue

In early 1970, Jakob and Charlotte Rippert received an unexpected letter from Bournemouth, England, written by a former British policeman in Palestine, William (Bill) J. Covell (1906-1973). Exquisitely nostalgic about Palestine in the 1930s, we can imagine it being a bitter-sweet source of joy and sadness as it was read, perhaps many times, by Jakob and Charlotte.

During the 1930s Sergeant Bill Covell had been the mess caterer at the Mazra'a British police camp, located on the Mediterranean coast a few kilometres north of Acre, just west of the Ripperts' farm. Covell had not seen the Ripperts for thirty years but had been given their address by one of their contacts, a Miss Nasser in Beirut, Lebanon. In the 'happy days' before 1939, Covell reminded Jakob and Charlotte, he had purchased vegetables and bananas from their farm. When the Second World War broke out, Jakob was then interned along with other enemy aliens at the Mazra'a camp. This had been an 'embarrassing situation', Covell recalled, because the British guards 'knew most of the internees in everyday life'. Confirming Jakob's own recollection of his good relations with the British and his role as camp quartermaster, Covell also remembered Jakob's helpfulness during his internment: 'You were indeed a great help to us in many ways, so I know that you will not mind if I say "Thank You" once again after thirty years have elapsed.'

Covell had only recently visited Israel with his wife and reported on many of the changes he had noticed. He was amazed to see 'double roads with Palm trees' heading out of Haifa, the 'tall blocks of flats' and the extent of the built-up area around the former German settlement at Sarona. Coming from Tel Aviv, he found the 'first sight of Jerusalem has been spoilt as you now see the big blocks of flats instead of the quaint skyline of Jerusalem that we had known so long'. He spent time at Acre, observed the redevelopment of the former internment camp and informed the Ripperts that there were 'still one or two old buildings amongst the trees where you used to live'.

Living in retirement at Bournemouth, the former servant of the British Empire had very fond memories of Palestine and the people he had known there. He had felt compelled to convey this to the Ripperts:

> It was very nice to know you in Acre, but I most sincerely wish it had been under better circumstances. If you have any of our old friends near to you, please give them my regards. Tell them that I often think of them.

Covell's wistful account of his recent departure by sea from Israel, following his description of the sad state of their former farm, would surely have struck a chord with Jakob and Charlotte:

> When we left Haifa, I stayed on deck and with deep regret watched Haifa go out of sight and wondered if I would ever be able to visit this wonderful country again, which held so many memories for me.[1]

It seems appropriate that Covell shared his reflections, written only a few years before his own death in 1973, with Jakob and Charlotte near the end of their lives. It is also significant that this former policeman took the trouble to track them down in far off Australia and compose a heartfelt, carefully typewritten letter they would have cherished. It is just one indication of the impression Jakob and Charlotte made on the many people they encountered in their eventful lives.

Something that was confirmed many times during the research for this book was that Jakob and Charlotte were fondly remembered, more than fifty years after their deaths, by those who had known them. Their names were also familiar to those who had not known them at first hand but had read of their exploits in *Der Sudan Pionier* or other records of the Sudan Pionier Mission. They were remembered as good people who had made a contribution in whatever circumstances they found themselves. What also became evident during our research was that memories of the Rippperts were compartmentalised, with people typically being aware of only one or two episodes in their lives and being astonished to learn of the full trajectory. Revealing the full story appears to have been timely.

Although they always saw themselves as humble missionaries, Jakob and Charlotte were closely involved with major events of the twentieth century. Their stories help to illustrate these events from the perspective of individuals at the periphery of the headlines that summarise history. The fact that they were rarely agents of their own destiny but jostled along by the events, including two world wars, makes their story even more fascinating and helps to reveal the fate of so many others in similar situations.

The First World War was the first of the major events to intervene in Jakob and Charlotte's lives. For Jakob, the horror of the Western Front reinforced his Christian faith and confidence in God's guidance through whatever adversity was to come. For Charlotte, the outbreak of war interrupted her career as a young missionary, ensured she experienced the hardships of the German home front and resulted in her introduction to Palestine. In Egypt and Nubia in the late 1920s they both found fulfilment in their missionary roles and interactions with local people, particularly in the Nubian villages that would soon disappear under the waters of the Nile. During the 1930s they shared an idyllic lifestyle with a unique community in Palestine before the brief golden era was destroyed by conflict over Jewish settlement, the rise of Nazism in Germany and the outbreak of the Second World War. They spent most of the 1940s 'behind barbed wire', firstly in Palestine and then in Australia, before returning briefly to Germany, where they had to confront both the material and the moral consequences of Nazism. In the 1950s Jakob and Charlotte returned to Australia with the first wave of post-war migration and worked in remote Hermannsburg before settling in Nuriootpa, where they lived relatively conventional lives for the first time.

What has been the legacy of these remarkable lives?

As noted in the last chapter, the obituaries published in *The Barossa and Light Herald* paid tribute to the way in which the 'work of the couple, and their faith in their declining years, gained admiration, love and friendship from many people'. Perhaps unsurprising words in an obituary, but the esteem in which Jakob and Charlotte were held at the end of their lives is consistent with the views expressed by Sergeant Bill Covell from the 1930s. Jakob and Charlotte were good people who, true to their Christian ideals, lived good lives, often in very challenging circumstances.

There is also a more tangible legacy. As a builder Jakob was very much focused on providing material improvement in the often remote locations where he worked. In some of those locations his work has been obliterated. Along with prehistoric artwork and many ancient Egyptian monuments, the mission station he built at Koshtamne is now beneath Lake Nasser. The site of Tatura internment camp, where Jakob built a recreation hall and supervised many other improvements for its wartime community, is once again a bare paddock. The school he built at Hermannsburg has been demolished and the athel pines he planted around it have been uprooted. On the other hand, the former Carl Strehlow Memorial Hospital building at Hermannsburg remains as a memorial to Strehlow and a testament to Jakob's building skills. The house he built at the Finke River Mission's Alice Springs site is still in use. So, too, is the large former orphanage building at Cologne-Dellbrück in Germany. In Israel, the trees Jakob planted around his farm may still be evident and, we can speculate, the wells and irrigation works he developed around Acre and elsewhere may still be in use.

As a nurse and midwife, in her missionary role and as an educator at Tatura, Charlotte left little material evidence of her work. However, for a period during the 1940s she was a prolific artist. Her artworks are now held by a number of museums or are still hung in the homes of family or descendants of Tatura internees. Invariably attractive scenes or portraits, many of these paintings have added value due to the context in which they were created and some are especially evocative of their time and place.

The most important aspect of the Ripperts' legacy may prove to be the large and eclectic collection of historical source material they left behind. With the notable exception of the First World War, all important periods of their lives are well-documented, either spread out in the archives of institutions they were associated with or contained in the two large collections left with descendants in Australia and Germany. For 'ordinary people', as opposed to the more famous individuals history is drawn to, Jakob and Charlotte have left a sizeable historical footprint. The articles they both wrote for *Der Sudan Pionier*, with their rich insights into the work of the Sudan Pionier Mission and Nubia and Egypt in the early twentieth century, are just one outstanding example of the sources they left in archival collections. Within the family collections are literally thousands of documents, photographs and the sort of ephemera from which ostensibly obscure social history can be reconstructed. They are invaluable in shedding light not just on the big developments of the twentieth century but on how these developments affected ordinary people. They also have a role to play in helping to sustain awareness of a heritage that may be on the verge of being extinguished in public memory — the story of the Palestine Germans in the 1930s, their Tatura internment and their seminal role in Australia's migration history.

Above all, Jakob and Charlotte were Christians and missionaries. It was their vocation that was ultimately responsible for the complex journey of their lives and their faith which sustained them through its hardships. In the twenty-first century, most Europeans are unlikely to look on missionary work with the same certainties as Jakob and Charlotte were inspired by when they set off for Egypt and Nubia more than one hundred years ago. Nevertheless, there is evidence that Jakob and Charlotte were open to inter-cultural understanding, formed genuine relationships with the people they worked among and thought deeply about the cultures of those they encountered as missionaries. In his own writing, for example, and in the reading he pursued until the end of his life, it is clear that Jakob was always struggling to reach an understanding beyond the limitations of his own world view. These limitations are sometimes starkly evident but this should not devalue either the commitment he and Charlotte brought to their vocation or the historical insights the story of their lives reveal about cultural interactions which are well beyond general experience or awareness.

Endnotes

1. Letter, W. J. Covell to Jakob Rippert, 27 March 1970, RPA.

Appendices

These extracts are translated, abridged versions of articles first published in Sudan Pionier Mission's journals.

A. Charlotte Wolter – 'Report 1'
Der Sudan Pionier, March 1913, p. 25

Not long ago, Ms. Z., Ms. v. M. and I paid a home visit to a former schoolchild, the now married Fatme Hassan. Fatme is barely more than 14 years old now, a petite little creature, and she hadn't been out of the house for about 1¼ years, since the day she got married. The apartment in which she lived consisted of a small, windowless, dirty room and a courtyard perhaps 4 metres long and just as wide, surrounded by high walls. She had not read again since her school days, she told us in response to our questions. We were joined by a few women from the neighbourhood who were sitting on the floor chatting and smoking cigarettes. They had no shortage of things to talk about; they immediately had all sorts of things to ask — the poor women! Everything in their lives revolves around the few, often not at all good things that can happen within such narrow, high walls as those of their houses. There is hardly any aspiration for higher things or reflection on their part. Miss Z. and Miss v. M. still talked to her and reminded her of many a word of God she had learned at school. I wonder if it has come back to life in her heart, what she once learned. After all, God's word has the promise that it will not come back empty...

My language studies have been slow so far, as all lessons were cancelled during our Christmas and New Year period and then during the Coptic Christmas period. However, I have learned many a 'Däritsch' (dialect) word through my work in the pharmacy in the mornings and the resulting contact with the natives... It is often not so easy with the women, especially the Nubian women, who either speak little or no Arabic. They usually ask me with anxious, uncertain faces in detail how they should take the medicine, whether before or after eating, how many times a day, with how much water or milk, whether hot or cold, whether it should also be soup or tea or something else, and so on. And the most complicated thing for me is always to explain to them, at their request, what the actual practice of taking it is. I swallow pills in front of them with great emphasis and apply ointment etc. Sometimes you could explain the same thing ten times, and then the success in understanding still seems doubtful to some. Others take immense pleasure in hearing me speak Arabic, which I can well understand, because I use the few words I've learned almost without permission, and I probably sometimes say them where they don't really belong. I promote the school to our little patients wherever I can. Yes, how I often wish I could speak Arabic, to be able to say the word to the women here so that it touches and moves their hearts.

B. Charlotte Wolter – 'Report 2'
Der Sudan Pionier, June 1913, pp. 46-47

Aswan, April 15, 1913 I almost feel as if time is running faster here than anywhere else in the world. My work at the hospital is now more regular. Often, a day consists of many small, little things you do. The whole thing makes up a whole day you have lived through, which then belongs to 'following Him'. We have a lot of reason to praise and thank Him when we look back on the 2½ months of hospital work. How many things have gone well beyond our expectations, and in big and small things the Lord has been our 'counsel and wisdom and strength and keeper'. In the beginning we were very much afraid that some necessary house rules would keep the patients away from the hospital. For example, that every day, but only in the afternoon from 3 to 5 o'clock, there is visiting time for the many friends and relatives and curious people, or that the patients must first take a bath and put on hospital clothes, or that only in special cases are relatives allowed to stay in the hall all day and sleep there, etc. This has all worked out well beyond expectations, and it is now rare to encounter stubborn resistance, which usually from the Copts, the country's Christians, who do not want to submit to anything and always point to their tattooed cross, believing that can achieve anything. Fortunately, there are also some very nice exceptions among them.

A difficult question for us at the beginning was the financial situation, because every patient wanted to be admitted, operated on and fed for free. Now it is the case that the Nubians, who make up the main percentage of our patients, are indeed very impoverished due to the loss of their land as a result of the dam*, and it hurts one's soul when one hears people complaining about their lost homeland. The food allowance has now been set at the lowest possible level and initially many patients were treated and fed for nothing. Gradually, people gained more confidence and realized that it was better for their health if they enjoyed the hospital's food instead of feeding themselves meagrely, and so it has been the case in recent times that we have almost constantly had all the beds and angareebs (traditional bed) occupied, all of them by patients who at least paid something and who get their food from the hospital kitchen. It was often very hard for me to see how a patient who was expected to stay in the hospital for about a week would bring bread in a dirty sack for this time, which he would then put under his bed to be gradually eaten soaked in water. It usually went mouldy by the third day, and the frugal, undemanding people would continue to eat it if we let them. How grateful they are now for the nutritious, so much better food from the hospital kitchen.

> "it hurts one's soul when one hears people complaining about their lost homeland"

For us Europeans, the way these people express themselves here often seems very strange and often very comical. For example, when a woman asks you to renew her bandage, because it is pressing on her eastern eye, or when a patient on the operating table points out to the doctor that there is still a gland to the north of the area that has just been operated on, which is causing him pain, we sometimes have to admit to ourselves with shame that we are not yet as good at keeping track of the celestial regions in every situation, day or night, as these people (even if it is often not quite true)…

Recently we had a little patient, the 11-year-old daughter of the local Bishari chief, Carona was her name. At first she behaved like a little wild cat, didn't want anything done to her and treated us all very condescendingly. How different she was in the end: still wild and often unruly, but still an obedient, sweet girl who always expressed her love for us in the most lively speeches, and as soon as I passed by, she was right by my side and put her hand in mine to ask for something. She has also decided to come to our school — I wonder if she will manage to learn to sit still? Twice now we have had members of the Bishari people in hospital, this people of whom so little is known, who keep themselves so proudly secluded and whose men are such fantastic Mohammedans. May a door slowly open to their hearts, may they gain even more trust so that God can bless them through his gospel.

*   Constructed in 1902, the Aswan Low Dam had its wall raised 5 metres in 1912.

C. Jakob Rippert – 'My Departure and First Impressions on the Mission Field'
Der Sudan Pionier, April 1925 pp. 46-48, May 1925 pp. 58-60, June 1925 pp. 70-74

The difficult time of waiting lay behind me like a dream. Anyone who has grown up as closely with the mission as I have, who has belonged to it since childhood, and then experiences the day for which one has waited so eagerly, can understand how great the joy that filled me was. Of course, as I said goodbye to so many dear people and friends, the thought ran through my heart as to whether we would see each other again down here. Alongside this was the certain hope that after faithful work and struggle there would be a reunion for us, if not here, then above in the light of eternity. The goal stood clear before my eyes — the burning desire to become a useful tool in the hands of the missionary king made me happy and strong.

I travelled over the Brenner Pass to Italy. My journey took me via Florence to Rome. I arrived there on 6 February, at 11 o'clock in the morning. A strange feeling took hold of me as I stood in front of the large train station. The sky was blue and the air so soft and warm, a spring day in Germany couldn't be more beautiful. Rome, which I had read and learned so much about, welcomed me. Green trees in front of the station, cascades that threw their water high into the air, palm trees and a lively street scene. My ship wasn't due to leave Naples until 9 February, so I had a day and a half to take a closer look at Rome. A dear friend was my guide. We stood in the Colosseum, this gigantic building with its wonderfully constructed oval, which particularly interested me as a builder. These mighty arches and vaults, piled cyclopically on top of each other from thousands of hewn stones. Past the Arch of Constantine, through the Roman Forum, to the Capitol, I will never in my life forget the impressions I received there. Walls in ruins, remains of ancient statues, white marble bodies of once great men and women, broken columns and capitals, vanished glory and splendour. What language does this field of ruins speak of the life of the once mighty Rome?

Today I understand why Italy has been the dream of German artists for centuries. The life I then encountered in the alleyways of Rome, the carefree singing and laughter, barrel organs so soft and sentimental, in between black-eyed and curly-haired children, covered in dirt, beggars, street vendors, a life and hustle and bustle that can hardly be described. I also made a short visit to the Vatican and its museums, stood in the Sistine Chapel under Michelangelo's magnificent frescoes, walked through St. Peter's Church with Michelangelo's enormous dome.

On the night of 7 February, I travelled from Rome to Naples and arrived there on Saturday morning. Naples has a very different feel to Rome. It has a somewhat oriental feel to it with its dirt, its bare houses with their many small balconies, and all the laundry flapping between the narrow streets and alleyways. I visited the National Museum, where many valuable excavations from Pompeii and Herculaneum are on display. I was amazed by this wonderful art from the time before the fall of the two cities [buried by the eruption of Mt Vesuvius in AD 79]. The works of art produced in that era are quite amazing. Magnificent sculpture, often so expressive and finely tuned. And yet nothing remains of that time except these few remnants, which speak to us of an often superhuman search for beauty and purity, for strength and light. Everywhere the religious motifs, the legends of gods and heroes in the background, and yet only a groping and searching, including getting lost in the sensual, in the earthly, and then the slow dying out of all the still great and powerful inner drives towards the noblest things. Whoever has an eye, an ear, an inner understanding, will hear a sermon of shattering force in all these places where the scanty remains of those great epochs have been gathered together. Whoever does not have a firm foundation in life, whoever has not come to the firmness of a simple and yet all-conquering faith in Jesus, must be deeply saddened by this mysterious aspiration, this mighty longing and reaching out of antiquity for eternal light, which speaks to us in all the ruins, for nothing remains of all that struggle but ruins. And all those people who believe that the beauty of art, the noble work of great spirits, is the sole content of their lives, must actually waver in their world view in the face of these last remnants of classical art. For the measure of all that is noble and the dream of the human soul for undisturbed harmony will never lie in the material, but only in Jesus alone.

At Naples I boarded the Japanese ship *Hakane Maru*. The crew were all small, brown Japanese and all were very clean and quick. I shared a cabin with two Japanese engineers. We soon became friends as fellow professionals and spoke German and English with each other. As I looked back on my past days of travel, I could only give thanks for God's help and protection on my journey; I looked ahead with a happy and grateful heart. The next morning, we sailed past the smoking Mt Etna [in Sicily]. The summit was covered in snow and looked wondrous in the rosy morning light. The journey was calm and beautiful. I sat on deck in the sun and practised my English. On 12 February we sailed past Crete, the mountain ridges covered in snow. The next morning brought us to Port Said.

Ahead of me lay Africa, my destination, the continent I have been intensely interested in since my earliest youth. It was 6 o'clock in the morning, the passport people were climbing up the gangplank, along with orange and postcard sellers, brown fellows in colourful dresses. Down below, small boats were swarming to take passengers ashore. At the back of the ship, coals were being taken on, and on two barges there was a large number of half-naked coolies running nimbly back and forth with their baskets. After going through customs and shipping my boxes on to Aswan, I travelled by train to Cairo, starting with the Suez Canal on one side and Lake Manzalah on the other.

"Ahead of me lay Africa, my destination, the continent I have been intensely interested in since my earliest youth."

From Ismailia, where the train leaves the canal, to Cairo, you travel through lovely countryside. Palm groves, villages in green fields, roads beside the railroad, traveling fellahs [farmers] with their wives in their sombre, black costumes; camels, donkeys with often two or three riders, it's funny, girls drawing water in a proud gait, elegantly carrying the water jug, laughing as they show their white, flashing teeth to passers-by, pretty, delicate faces often underneath, jewellery on hands, neck and ankles, often rings on nose and ears. And then suddenly a modern car driven by a native rattles through the authentic oriental streetscape, the dust swirls, the brown passers-by stop and grumble.

Picture after picture follows one another, and I am completely dazed by all the interesting and new things. Finally we are in Cairo, when I manage to save myself and my luggage from a storm of luggage carriers… After getting some rest, I went on a voyage of discovery. With the city map of Cairo in my hand, I walked into the Muski district of Cairo, right through the Fatimid city, then up to the old Bab el Futich, around the el Hakim mosque and back in again to the Bab en-nasr. Never in my life have I seen a more interesting and fascinating spectacle than the almost overwhelming, colourful street life of the old Fatimid city. A heavy scent of ambergris, incense and acrid smoke from the charcoal fires lingered numbingly in the air. There was shouting, singing in guttural tones, bargaining and haggling from all the stores open along the narrow streets: shoemakers and tailors, silversmiths and coppersmiths, kitchen and tea and coffee stalls, old women in their black rags squatting next to them, hawking flatbread, eggs, oranges and all sorts of things, most of them unknown to me. Swarms of flies everywhere, dust in abundance.

One is involuntarily carried away, one's heart is light and happy, it is like an intoxication that afflicts all who look into this life. There are colourful stores with cloths and carpets, merchants who wanted to drag me into their store by force and sell me huge carpets that I really couldn't have done anything with. Silversmiths held rings under my nose that could even have been used as defensive weapons in an emergency. Laughing, I thanked them and moved on.

The next day, a dear friend from the Kaiserswerth Victoria Hospital accompanied me to the pyramids of Giza. These colossal stones have defied time for thousands of years. And then the Sphinx with its dead eyes staring into infinity! We meet many strangers on donkeys and camels, they even ride close by the pyramids of Khufu. There are funny sights, such as a donkey at a gallop with a fat American on top, the little brown donkey boy with a big stick always pushing hard on the grey animal, which of course reacts very much to it, throwing its thin legs out behind and in front — that sometimes the rider loses his balance is really not to be blamed.

In the evening I caught the train from Cairo to Aswan. As it was dark, I saw very little of the landscape. On Sunday morning, 15 February, I arrived in Luxor. There I boarded the narrow-gauge train to Aswan. The journey continued along the Nile. Palm groves, villages, fields alternated with each other, Nile mud houses with their ruin-like character!

At Aswan Mr Enderlin was at the ramp to meet me. The ladies also arrived, and what a pleasure it was to see them. I received a warm welcome and we only had to walk a few steps to our mission house. This house immediately catches the eye with its beautiful façade. Now I was in Aswan, my future home. Mr. and Mrs. Enderlin showed me to my room. It is one of the most beautiful, and our dear, revered president, Rev. Ziemendorff, and [former missionary] Princess Hohenlohe-Ingelfingen, had lived in this room years ago. It is in good condition, has a lovely little balcony on the Nile side, so you can see and observe all the life and activity of the natives.

When I then took a tour of our entire estate with Mr. Enderlin and saw all the buildings, the hospital, the clinic, the school rooms, I had to say: God, how great you are. For to lose a mission station like Aswan forever would have been a great loss. And as an expert technician, I can only say that valuable, thorough German work has been done here. Even though the last 10 years [when the missionaries had been unable to return to Aswan] have made many small repairs necessary, the garden has to be replanted and the houses have to be repainted, we can only thank God that everything is still in pretty good condition. And it seems particularly valuable to me that the construction was quite good and stable by local standards, otherwise the damage could easily have been greater.

Now that I've got a good overview of all the houses and rooms and have looked at the damage, I'm going full steam ahead with making our station fully operational again. There's a lot of work ahead of me, because we can only save money if I'm able to repair most of it myself. And all my hope is always my tools, which I hope will arrive from Germany soon. A good set of tools is invaluable here, because your own work is better than native labour. Today's Egyptians don't work as cleanly and sturdily as the ancient Egyptians, and you can safely leave your European-trained eye at home when you walk through the workshops of the craftsmen here.

I took a long walk through the souk and the craft stalls here with Mr. Enderlin and got a small idea of how these people work. The fact that the German mission now has a 'Baschmahandis', an engineer, is

> "Today's Egyptians don't work as cleanly and sturdily as the ancient Egyptians…"

> "What our Expressionist painters paint 'intentionally', as expressive art, these simple Nubian sons instinctively felt from their imagination."

certainly already well known in the city and will not be appreciated by the craftsmen. You can also have some tools here, but for solid German work, these tools are not suitable. And I wish with all my heart that there were some tool manufacturers among our missionary friends [in Germany] whose hearts were warmed by the Mission King Jesus, so that they would give us some tools for blacksmithing, locksmithing, carpentry and construction work. I can use everything in future when new stations are built and new, better facilities for water and light have to be created.

I speak Arabic and Nubian at every opportunity and hope to learn the colloquial language soon.

On Friday, 20 February, in the evening, we hiked out through the dark desert, between boulders, lantern in hand, to the village of Jebbel Tokok. Soghair, our former cook, had invited us. We were to celebrate the ascension of the Prophet Mohammed, combined with a dhikr [Islamic religious exercise]. Soghair belongs to the dervish order of the Daifijja. That evening, I took a deep look into the hardship and hollowness of Islam.

Soghair greeted us very kindly and made us sit on a bench in front of the house. There was a wonderful starry sky above us, as we were sitting on the village street. Large mats lay on the ground and lanterns dangled from a crossbar, illuminating the square a little. Many men had already come and were squatting around on the ground and on benches, boys with smiling faces were running around expectantly between them. Soghair's sons, our two indigenous young servants, brought us a tea made of ginger and spruce in small glasses, which I drank with disdain, even though it was very hot and burned my tongue. A lot more tea came and each new arrival was given a small cup of it.

I took a close look at everything and discovered that the whole front of Soghair's house was painted with what must have been a primitive but highly interesting style of painting. In Germany, this would have been called Expressionism. Large ornaments were thrown onto a reddish background, divided by narrow zigzag and serpentine lines. They showed camels with triangular backs, like small pyramids, with long grotesque legs, slender necks and small heads, under palm trees and the sun disk, painted so grotesquely that I involuntarily had to think of the paintings of the cavemen. Chickens and roosters and other domestic animals were painted in colourful rows. Imagine this painted house wall as the background of the colourful scene I am trying to draw. What our Expressionist painters paint 'intentionally', as expressive art, these simple Nubian sons instinctively felt from their imagination. Many men came together under the flickering lantern light. Women could only be seen scurrying past, deeply veiled.

The dhikr, this religious exercise of the Muhammadan dervish orders, of which Mr. Enderlin wrote in the January issue of the *Sudan Pionier*, was introduced with a chant, a praise of the Prophet, sung by a man sitting on the bench with his legs crossed. They were peculiar, sad, melancholy melodies that grabbed the heart and captivated. After each section, the singer lowered his head. All was quiet, the old people hummed along quietly and nodded their heads to the beat. I felt strangely brave. The dhikr began when some more of the order came from Aswan with the insignia of the order, a large bell-shaped lamp covered with red gauze, which spread a mystical light around it. The men and boys sat opposite each other in two rows with their legs crossed and their shoes placed in front of them. At the end of the double row stood the dhikr lamp. First, the sacred books were read in a chanting tone; the whole chorus began regularly with a refrain. They sang an endlessly long song and slowly began to move their upper bodies forwards and backwards, always in time with the chanting. An old lead singer sat at the top, setting the beat, which became wilder and faster. This movement is almost transferred to the audience as they shout the name of God Al-la-hu, Al-la-hu. The Muhammadans want to get so close to God, to find God! Then the whole company stood up and everything was repeated. The movements became more and more fantastic. Soghair, who had been watching earlier, joined the line of dhikr people, and I was amazed at the speed of the old man, who was jumping along to the beat 1-2-3, about thirty centimetres off the ground.

The men's eyes rolled wildly, enraptured and entranced. One of them danced in the middle and clapped his hands to the beat. One of them collapsed, unconscious, in a frenzy, and I was amazed that more of them didn't fall over. How provocative sounded the singing of the old sheikh [elder], who apparently had a grandson, a little boy of about twelve, with him as an assistant, who occasionally joined in, with a wonderfully fine voice whose trembling tone betrayed the boy's inner emotion! Since that day, these melodies have haunted me to sleep; they are so strange that you have to listen to them again. And there is something superhuman in this desire to penetrate God's being, something devilish in the intoxication that is helped along by fragrant essences and the burning of ambergris and incense. These scents have a numbing effect.

I went home deeply shaken and thought about how important it is to bring light into the lives of these poor people and strength, real vitality, which they seek in vain within themselves. What a difficult and great task lies before us, also before the home community, which must stand behind us. How difficult it is to reach these men! Language, knowledge of the customs and traditions are required and a lot of physical strength to work and live in climatic conditions that are unfamiliar to Europeans. We go to work cheerfully; we know that God is with us and his strength will be powerful in us weak ones. And when many ask, 'What do you want out there, leave it alone?' We answer: 'The love of Christ impels us to do so.'

And therefore, dear friends at home, we call on you to fight. Take a stand on the Islam mission. Anyone who has ever had a glimpse of this misery will never forget it. I think of the work of Miss Wolter and Miss von Massenbach, where 120-150 sick women and girls sit in front of the clinic four times a week and want help! Anyone who sees these poor people in their filth and misery, these often sweet little children, so rotten in the dirt, prey to the flies, must be cold to the core if he doesn't pull himself together to help in his own way. Remember that the mission is God's will, His command. We need you to help us! I greet you all from the bottom of my heart and hope that Jesus will enliven your hearts so that you will you join in the missionary work among the Mohammedans with your prayers and your gifts.

D. Jakob Rippert – 'From the Mission Field, Ramadan'
Der Sudan Pionier, July 1925, pp. 83 – 88

Written a few months after Jakob Rippert's arrival in Egypt, this article describes his impressions of Ramadan.

There was a lively movement among our people for days before Ramadan began. It often seemed to me that many were pleased that the month of fasting was coming, but I often noticed a touch of sadness and resignation on the faces of my Arab bricklayers and day labourers when Ramadan was mentioned. Especially when they lit their beloved cigarettes, they made the remark that now we wouldn't even be allowed to smoke when Ramadan began. We also looked forward to the coming month of fasting with mixed feelings. We had 7 bricklayers and labourers with whom I was working on the old mission house to repair the damage caused by 10 years of neglect.

When fasting starts, the workers' performance decreases, as does their desire and interest in good work. Our Salih, whom I occasionally instruct to carry stones and carry sand, as he has an intense aversion to physical exertion, announced to me in good time: 'Just spare me the heavy work in Ramadan, I really can't do it then.'

And then came the day of the new moon. The sun had already disappeared behind the yellow desert mountains when a cannon shot cracked across the Nile, announcing the beginning of Ramadan.

During the month of fasting, according to the Koran: 'As soon as a person sees the new moon, fasting begins. But whoever is ill or on a journey, may fast a number of other days. Allah wishes to make it easy for you and not difficult for you to fulfil the number of days and to praise Allah for guiding you, and perhaps thanking Him for it. Abstain from your wives and eat and drink at night until you can distinguish a black thread from a white one at dawn. Then keep a strict fast until night… and do not stay with your wives, but dwell in the mosques. These are the barriers of Allah, do not approach them.'

And this is how Islam exercises its power over the hearts and bodies of the faithful. It is an achievement and a sacrifice that the Muslim makes, not eating and drinking from sunrise to sunset and having to work at the same time. Pious Muslims do not even swallow their saliva and cover their faces with a cloth so that the breath of a stranger does not touch them and make their fasting impossible. I can observe the effect of the fasting month on my workers, with whom I stand side by side on the scaffolding. Not being allowed to drink in the immense summer heat and all the dust is a torture, even a punishment for people. My bricklayers and workers are lame and sluggish, and during the lunch break they all sleep like the dead. The first few days go reasonably well, but then the work output gets less and less. People become irritable. The donkey boys, who haul sand, lime and stones to the construction site, beat the poor animals like mad. But everything is excused with the word Ramadan. If, for example, Abdu, 'the food boy', whose brain is like 'zift' (tar), as his master tells me, fails with the mortar or the stones and I get impatient because it is going so slowly, it is called Ramadan. If something doesn't work out, the 'Baschmahandis' [engineer] is reassured with the word 'Ramadan'. In general, the first lesson I have to memorize is the excellent saying that speaks to the nature of the Oriental: 'All haste is from the Shaitan [devil] and tardiness is from the merciful.'

The people who have to carry stones and sand and constantly have to deal with water and are not allowed to drink are the worst off. But they would rather suffer agony and pain than break their fast. Prayers are said several times a day and it looks strange, the praying Muslim lying on his forehead, facing east, towards the holy city of Mecca, on the grounds of the mission. Muhammed rules over the souls of his believers and it is amazing how Islam educates the masses. Even if many have become lukewarm and no longer keep the fast, they mostly bear the contempt of pious Muslims. With the exception of children, everyone submits to the compulsion. The mosques are visited a lot during this month and a lot of prayers are said. But you can feel how dead and cold all these efforts are. This huge effort to earn heaven and mercy on the Day of Judgement through all the torment and deprivation of fasting does not go any deeper.

There is very little life on Nilstrasse, which is usually very lively. Tired and disheartened, you only see a few people going about their business during the day. If you walk through the souk or bazaar, where there is usually life and activity in front of the stores, you will only see people lying on mats asleep. The carpenters lie under their workbenches in the shavings, the blacksmith next to his fire, the shoemaker in the corner of his primitive workshop, the needle rests in the tailor's shop, the cloth merchant lies peacefully slumbering next to his bales of cloth, everything is asleep. Only children run around playing. The little brown boys and cute curly-headed girls with their smudged faces from which white, flashing teeth smile at me. At the donkey stands, the donkey boys lie with their heads on the unbuckled saddles of their donkeys, which roll happily in the sand with their legs up and sleep. The shayals [porters] at the station are also asleep, lying next to piles of sacks waiting to be loaded. Only here and there is a policeman, bow-legged and weak-kneed, looking melancholically in front of him, his red fez pushed back on his head and occasionally chasing mosquitoes with a colourful handkerchief. It seems as if he is sleeping standing up.

A couple of camels trot past, grunting, reluctant, carrying little Arab boys on their backs, who don't hold back with their cane strokes. An old sheikh comes along the path. With a sweet and sour face, he rides past on his tired donkey, his long, skinny legs stretched out far from him, swaying back and forth. A hilarious caricature. Clap, clap, his cane hails on the grey animal's long ears and sets it into a faster gait. A soft desert wind blows across the Nile from Elefantine, the painfully pathetic i-a, i-a of a tortured donkey can be heard. The sakia* moans melancholically on the green shore and slowly, wearily a white sail passes by, the helmsman sitting motionless at the wheel, seemingly asleep, while his boy lies stretched out on the foredeck. The green flag with the white crescent moon flies wearily on the roof of the Mudirije [administrative building], where the poor katibs [clerks] sit sweating, half asleep, behind their dusty files, doing nothing. A stupefying fragrance wafts from the blossoming lebach trees in the chamsin and the flaming red of the tufted blossoms of some acacia trees shines beautifully amidst their lush green.**

It is only towards sunset that the fasting, sleeping faithful come to life. Women in their sombre, black costumes, barefoot or in red markubs [traditional footwear], trailing the hem of their large black shawls that hang down from their heads over their backs, hurry by. Carrying their youngest child astride one hip, bowls of food or jugs of water on their heads, which they bring to their waiting, hungry men. The cafés slowly fill up, water pipes are set up, cigarettes and matches are brought out by those who want to smoke. Our men climb down from the scaffolding, wash their heads, hands and feet according to the Prophet's instructions, rinse their mouths and noses, adjust their skimpy suits, tie their turbans anew and prepare to perform their evening prayers. Barefoot, standing upright, his face turned towards Mecca, the man murmurs his prayer, then bows forward, his hands touching both knees. He falls to the ground, touches it with his

---

"The sakia moans melancholically on the green shore and slowly, wearily a white sail passes by, the helmsman sitting motionless at the wheel…"

forehead several times in succession and mumbles a prayer. When he has finished, he gets up again and wants to go home, where steaming bowls are already waiting for him. And everything is just waiting for the redeeming cannon shot, which is fired as soon as the sun has disappeared behind the desert mountains. It's interesting to see how the water goblets are then put to the mouth on command and the spoons go into overdrive. With a greed, everything missed and deprived during the day is made up for.

If you walk through the souq after sunset, the picture of the day has changed dramatically. There is light everywhere in the stores, tea and coffee stalls and eateries. Cooks with their filled 'kitchen' on their heads, shouting 'Bänja', hurry past and praise their dishes, which often look more than dubious to Europeans. Water and lemonade vendors shout and scream in between, boys with boxes under their arms containing smoking goods shout out their cigarettes. In front of some cafes, efendis, soldiers and sheikhs sit, densely packed, smoking, sipping tea or coffee, with a board game in front of them. The passionate rhythm of the tarabukas (tambourines) resounds to the songs of those who sing or recite poetry for backshish. An old, worn-out gramophone screams its repetitive melodies like a mad parrot, speaking the Arabic words so quickly and fluently that Mr Enderlin said to me, 'you have to sing Arabic to us in the exam'. I am horrified and confess that I will probably never in my life rattle off my Arabic with such virtuosity.

Chaffirs (guards) with their antediluvian shotguns on their backs, their cartridge belts diagonally across their chests, pass by on duty. Laughter, singing, music, eating and drinking and great joy are everywhere. Thus, the believers fortify themselves for the next day of fasting, and during the night we are startled twice more by the thunder of the cannon at 3 and 4 o'clock, the sign that everyone should eat and drink properly once more, because at sunrise the fasting begins again. And so it goes on for a whole month.

Many become miserable and ill. Babies die because their mothers cannot feed them because of the fast. But none of that matters. After all, people believe that this gives them a head start on the road to perfection. It is a profound aberration of millions of tormented people who believe that they can earn the bliss of paradise by cleansing their bodies, which is actually cancelled out by excessive eating and drinking during the night. It is an abysmal delusion, behind which lies so much depravity and licentiousness.

The question of the mission of Islam is becoming increasingly urgent for the Christian West. Will we watch as the resounding religion of Muhammad takes hold of the whole of Africa and seizes so many healthy, viable peoples and tribes and presses them into its cold forms and laws, under the effect of which all deeper life and spiritual upward striving is simply crushed? I can't help but shout again and again: 'Let's go to battle, let's go to help, Christians of the homeland.' Millions are waiting for the liberating word of Jesus: 'Come to me, all you who labour and are heavily laden, and I will give you rest.' Do you want to stand idle in the marketplace, where a large part of humanity is dying in the hopelessness and joylessness of its tortured life, crushed under the weight of an empty, powerless religion, longing from the depths of its soul for the liberating power, for a hand that helps and brings new life?

* The sakia is a traditional wooden water wheel used to irrigate fields by lifting water from the Nile into canals.
** The lebach tree originally came from Asia but is not uncommon in tropical regions. The chamsin is a hot, dry and often sandy desert wind. It is known as the sirocco elsewhere in North Africa.

E. Jakob Rippert – 'My First Trip to Nubia'
Der Sudan Pionier, April 1926 pp. 38-42 and May 1926, pp. 51-55

On Monday, 4 January, Mr Enderlin and I took the evening train to Shellal to travel to Koshtamne, a Nubian village 100 kilometres south of Aswan. At Shellal we were to catch the mail steamer that connects Aswan and Wadi Halfa. We were going to inspect two houses we had been offered for the purpose of establishing a mission station in Nubia.

We were equipped with food, a kerosene stove and all sorts of things needed for a journey to a country where no white people have yet lived. This included bedding in the style of the natives, a thin mattress, blankets, a sleeping bag, a pillow, all rolled up with straps. Neither of us went with a light heart, for the first reconnaisance by Mr Enderlin and Samuel had been unsuccessful, apart from the very valuable connections they made in various places. The resistance of the natives had clearly emerged, as they were well aware of the mission's intentions in their country.

The railroad line stops in Shellal and the only means of transport, the Nile, has to be used. Shellal is a district of the Mudirine Aswan, consisting of several poor villages. The station of Shellal ends in front of a mountain consisting of huge granite blocks. The houses of the natives are clinging to the mountain slopes. The railroad leads from Aswan through the Shellal desert, through barren sandy and rocky areas. Behind the dam at the head of the reservoir is the railroad station, fenced in with barbed wire, next to the steamer landing stage. We drove out of the station through the middle of the water, i.e. to the left and right of the railroad embankment is the water of the reservoir. We were greeted by a strange sight when we left the train and boarded the steamer: the rocky mountains falling vertically into the surrounding masses of water and the narrow valleys through which the water has made its way.

The Sudan steamer consists of three ships, the steamer, a two-storey living ship with cabins above and engines below, and the large paddle wheel that moves the ship forward at the back. On each side of the steamer is a trailer, called a sandel. These are also two-storey ships, clumsily built of iron and wood. Freight is stowed below and third-class passengers above. To save money, we travel third class, which is only used by natives and poor people. At first we had climbed over bales, barrels, etc. onto the one boat with our bags. But as it was already very crowded — everyone squats on the floor on their rolled-up bed — we climbed over to the upper deck of the other boat. About forty Bishari and Arabs had already made themselves at home on this one. Our houseboat was open on all sides and the wind could blow on us, which wasn't exactly pleasant during the cold nights. There were no children or women on the boat. The Aswan court, some fat Effendis with their scribes, also sailed with us. They had booked themselves into the first-class cabins on the steamer and watched, shaking their heads and laughing, as we were the only Europeans to join the Bishari. That didn't bother us, because the journey with the sons of the desert was more interesting than in the beautiful cabins, where there were often so many little animals hiding in the beds that they could rob a person of their peace if they joined them.

We sat down on our 'beds' and watched the people and the setting sun, which sank like a ball of fire over the jagged, grey Shellal Mountains and bathed the evening sky in a rosy glow. We left Shellal at 6 o'clock. The whole ship is a floating house. Lights flared up and we sailed into the sinking evening. The Bishari wrapped themselves in their furs and blankets and first ate their very simple evening meal, which for most consisted only of dates and a sip of water. Some also had bread and onions. Everyone laid out their things for the night. Many of the Bishari took off their vests and slept under their blankets with their upper bodies bare. You have to like these men with their proud stature, their striking, sharp facial features and racy heads with their hanging black hair, which is braided into small plaits at the temples and pinned to the top of their heads in a tuft through which a finely carved stick or long spike is inserted. They all have their swords with them. They reminded me of the old crusader swords with the cross hilt at the top. They carry these double-edged steel blades, about 80 cm long, in a leather sheath. Everyone also has a small dagger with them, either in their waist belt or on their left upper arm. Then there is the goatskin water bag. Next to us, one floor below, the large bucket wheel is working. It sounds like the roaring of a mill wheel back home. Almost all the men are wrapped up in their blankets. Some are still sitting in groups and chatting. In a corner at the back, a Bishari has pulled out a harmonica and is expressing his feelings on it, just like we did as little boys at Christmas when we were given such a thing. They are very big children, these handsome brown men from the desert.

We also open our rucksacks and eat our evening meal, then we make up our 'bed' on the floor and wrap ourselves in our blankets. We talked about many things together, and I also remembered that exactly one year ago, on 4 February 1925, I said goodbye to my home congregation in the church of my home village. What a time of rich experiences and wonderful guidance from our faithful God lies between then and now. I am at the beginning of my pioneering work, which I have been looking forward to for so long. The thought of what the outcome of our journey will be weighed heavily on both of us. But trusting in our Lord who sends us, we lay down to rest.

As dawn broke, the shore of Gerf Hussein lay before us. We passed an old rock temple carved into the sandstone wall of the shore.* Gerf Hussein is a post station. Some people went ashore, including relatives of the Omda (mayor) of this village. This Omda died a few days ago in the Aswan government hospital. The relatives brought the news of his death. Suddenly a howling and wailing could be heard. Some men in the countryside, who had apparently been expecting the arrivals, tied the cloth of their turbans around their waists as a sign of mourning. The women nearby began to rage and wail, throwing sand on their heads, throwing themselves to the ground, grabbing each other around the neck and jumping. In an instant, the whole area was in motion. All the men and women came down from the houses clinging to the mountain sides. They all began to howl and moved towards the house of the deceased Omda. Soon the crowd of women could be seen dancing there. There was a scream and howl in the air that gripped the spectators to the core. Swords and staffs were waved in the air as the women danced. Mr Enderlin explained to me that this was to drive away the evil spirits. The whole desolation of the animal existence of these poor people came before my eyes. The superstition and the fear of spirits, the tremendous fear of death, became apparent. It was said that the Omda of Gerf Hussein was a good man, who enjoyed general popularity among his people. His ancestors were sheikhs to whose tombs pilgrimages are made in Nubia. Not far from the house on the hillside, five white, round domes shine side by side, visible from afar.

Two more stops and we were in Koshtamne. The riverbed widens to the width of a lake, the mountains become flatter and form plateaus. To the left and right of the flooded area, the tops of the trees and palms look out over the water. A desolate picture. All the arable land is flooded. Only bare fields of sand and stone to the left and right. The elongated villages of the natives lie in between. Difficult paths lead from village to village over field mountains and stone valleys. The dry straw from the last harvest is piled up under protruding rocks, weighed down with stones to prevent the wind from carrying it away. Before we left the ship, Mr Enderlin had a few conversations with ship people, some of whom had previously been treated by our missionary doctor, Dr. Fröhlich, and who were familiar with our mission. We went ashore in Koshtamne at half past seven in the morning and waited outside on the shore for the postal clerk from Koshtamne, to whom we were to turn.

After the mail had been unloaded, we greeted the man. Everyone looked with great interest at the two Europeans who had come ashore. After Mr Enderlin had explained to the letter carrier what we wanted, he led us with some men to a small house nearby. In front of it sat old men from the village in their black galabias [robes], all their heads twisted against the morning cold. They were waiting for the mail. The Omda of Koshtamne was also sitting among them, an old man with a grey beard. Mr Enderlin exchanged Nubian greetings with everyone. But I immediately had the impression that the men, especially the Omda, received us coldly. We were ushered into the hut, the village guesthouse. A narrow door, more like an oblong hole, led to a room in semi-darkness. There were three angareebs**, the walls were covered with blankets and cushions, and there was a stone bench on one narrow side. The floor was loose sand and there was a small fireplace on one side for making tea and coffee. We were left alone for a while. Outside, the mail was distributed and the contents of our letter to our Koshtamne confidant, a relative of Samuel Efendi, with the request to show us a house belonging to him and that of a relative working in Cairo, were discussed. The resistance of the people was noticeable, and when some came in and started talking to us, Mr Enderlin was asked: 'Why haven't you found anything in Alagi? What do you want here? There is no free house here. We can't show you the houses.' It weighed heavily on me, and I spoke to God inside as Mr Enderlin negotiated with the men, because it was clear to me that if God didn't guide these people's hearts, we wouldn't even get to see the houses. Mr Enderlin said, 'We can't and won't force you to show us the houses, but we have an order from the owners that you help us.' Excuses were made that the village chief had to be asked for permission first, etc. 'We already know what you want, you are seducers, you want to tempt our people to become Christians. We don't want you, because we have the good. And we don't need your Hakima (doctor) because our people are all healthy.' Mr Enderlin had to talk and explain a lot.

In the meantime, an old man, the owner of the inn, had made us coffee on the fire on the floor. The room was filled with acrid smoke. After we had drunk the Arabic coffee, the food arrived after a while, in a bowl of red clay, sour milk dipped in thin pieces of bread broken off large, round flat cakes. Everyone dipped into the bowl, one of the men present ate with us. You can't look at the cleanliness of the hands, nor at the preparation. The sand crunched under our teeth as we ate the bread but the sour milk tasted fine. You just have to learn to scoop it out skilfully. People watch with interest to see if you are doing it right. After the meal was over, the letter carrier said to us: 'Now we'll have a look at the houses and then a boat will take you to Dakke, where you can continue your journey.' They wanted to get rid of the foreign intruders as quickly as possible.

By now it was midday. The sun shone warmly on the bare rocks over which we walked to where one house was located. The ground had been torn up many times by the people. Building stones had been blasted out so that the flat rocky land reminded me of shell-blasted land often seen during the war. The rock is a soft, white sandstone, often interspersed with limestone. About fifty metres inland is the first row of houses, which are 3-4 m high. The door, or rather the facade, faces exactly north-west. Several houses are always built together. The individual houses surround a quadrangle, a spacious courtyard with several living rooms and a room for guests leading off it. Most of the roofs consist of split palm trunks and thin wooden beams, with mats of palm leaves, twigs and earth or Nile mud on top. There are only a few plank roofs, as wood is most expensive in this country. The roofs are usually covered with branches on which goats graze and donkeys eat from below.

The house walls and courtyard walls in Koshtamne are made of the stones that the ground yields and are still smeared with Nile mud. The shape of the houses is peculiar. One is involuntarily reminded of the pylon construction of ancient Egyptian temples. The house and courtyard are open to the east. It is the direction towards Mecca and also there is the desire to avoid too much northern air, which is very cold in winter, that influences people when building their houses. I also noticed the strange, rough clay pots in front of the houses, often over one metre high and 40-50 cm thick. I saw these as chicken coops, with a small hole at the bottom, and others were used to hold butter and food. These pots are made of Nile mud and have a lid at the top made of the same material. I also saw some pigeon houses, up to 1.50 metres high, with several holes in the top, in which pigeons perched. These holes were arranged in such a way that a funny-looking face could be seen, with eyes, nose and mouth.

We came to the letter carrier's house, where we had to sit down and drink tea while the village chief was informed. Several men came over and everyone was informed of our plans by the letter carrier. The men, mostly older ones who can no longer work as servants in the Lower Egyptian houses, were very interested in the women who were to come to Koshtamne. And they found it outrageous that they could even learn their language in Germany. It also turned out that there were sick people there, because when an old man heard us talk about a doctor, he showed his sick eyes and asked if we had any medicine with us. We had some with us, and later I gave him some drops in his inflamed eyes. With a larger group we went to the house of Achmed Salach, the cook in Cairo, who wants to rent us his house.

Like all the houses there, it looks closed on the outside. On one side there are four broken windows without shutters and a large wooden door as the main entrance. We went around the back through a 60 cm wide side gate and entered the courtyard. There are three living rooms. The ceiling is made of beams and boards, the door to the room is missing. The roof is covered with palm branches. There is a small kitchen without a roof, like all the kitchens here. The courtyard space could be partitioned off and a clinic area and room can be created. The roof of the two rooms would also have to be made of boards, as foliage and earth are no protection against the sun in the hot season. If we were to get this house, it could be made up to some extent so that Europeans could live in it, albeit very primitively.

The owner of the second house flatly refused to let us see it. Then the men took us to their new village school. These are now being built in every village throughout Nubia by order of the government. The school in Koshtamne has nine large rooms, but I don't know what they want to do with them, because there aren't enough children to fill the large classrooms. The building is built as well as the people in Nubia can. However, the windows and roof line are adapted to the sloping terrain. If you enter a room, the floor runs downhill. But that doesn't bother people. The schoolhouse is one of the few houses painted with lime paint, mostly the colour is dirty grey like the Nile mud, but bright red or blue front doors are not uncommon.

The population is poor because the few men have no work, as the fertile land is only free from the flooding water for cultivation for four months of the year. Many families live only from the money that fathers and sons working in Egypt send home. You can see sheep and goats, chickens, pigeons and a few cows. I saw the women baking bread in small ovens made of Nile mud and spinning with the house spindle. They use sheep and goat hair for this. Everything fled from us when we arrived. Even the cattle were driven away from us because they feared our evil eye. The people are enslaved by superstition.

Mr Enderlin had another opportunity to talk to the people in a serious manner. Most of them were very anxious that our missionaries would enlighten their wives. We were warned not to tell the women that a man should have only one wife: 'It is not forbidden to us, Muhammad has given us permission.' There are not many who have two or three wives, because most men are far too poor to be able to afford it. Mr Enderlin picked it up at this point and went back to the Old Testament to Adam and Eve. These arguments are very interesting to me. Mr Enderlin had the opportunity to tell the people the truth about Jesus. It was half past two in the afternoon when we got back to our rest hut. Mr Enderlin was 'all out' from the non-stop talking from the morning. But soon some people were sitting with us again.

Unfortunately, we couldn't go to Dakke as there was no boat available, because all the boats were going to Gerf Hussein for the mourning. So we had to spend the night. We slept well on the angareebs, while next to us, squatting on the ground, some men, including our old landlord, played cards deep into the night. After they left, we put the third empty angareeb in front of the door hole as a door to protect us from the cold night air. As the sun flashed over the mountains in the morning, we got ready, and before we left, our landlord brought us hot tea and the news that a boat was waiting for us. He watched us as we packed and urged us to leave quickly. He absolutely wanted to be rid of us.

We loaded our bags on our backs and headed for the beach. It was very windy and cold and the sun barely broke through the clouds. A rare sight in this country, the water lapped hard against the rocky edge of the shore and you felt like you were on the seashore. We were soon sitting in our boat, and with the good wind we made good time. However, we had to turn around when we had a northerly wind. A wonderful picture, this wide expanse of water with palm trees and treetops jutting out at the edges. Behind it are the mostly steeply rising rock faces, to which the houses are clinging like swallows' nests.

We had to land in Marua in the evening because it was pitch dark and our boatman had fallen ill. I made tea for us and a whole bunch of men who were perched like chickens on the edge of our boat. Mr Enderlin evangelized again, and a lively conversation got going. This trip to Nubia had become a real mission trip. We slept badly in our boat at night. It was cold and all sorts of 'animals', such as those found on old ships, made their appearance. The interior of the boat was simply lined with cow dung, which more or less dissolved. The journey continued at dawn. In the afternoon we had to land in Murwau because the wind had become too strong and the sky was full of thunderstorms.

Murwau lies under the Tropic of Cancer. I looked at the small village and took a walk into the black mountains. From a high mountain peak I could see far into the endless desert, all dark, gloomy mountain cones of volcanic character. The rocks clinked like iron wherever you stepped. As far as the eye can see, everything is dead; not a songbird, not a blade of grass, just a few cawing vultures and, at night, wolves, jackals and hyenas stealing their meagre food in the poor villages of the Nile. After sunset it thundered heavily and started to rain. We had to take refuge from our open boat in a house belonging to an elderly Nubian woman. We stayed the night in the little hut with seven people. Four skippers, Mr Enderlin and I on a wide angareeb, and an old woman who was on another ship. They were all curled up in their blankets on the floor. The woman was lying under the angareeb. It was raining outside. The roof, which was just palm branches and earth, was already starting to let moisture through. But we fell asleep.

In the morning, we thanked our old landlady, who had slept in an adjoining house, and boarded our boat, which had been soaked by the rain. We soon reached the gate of Kalabsha, a dangerous place on the Nile. A mountain range runs through the river, broken by the water in some places. We rowed through a gateway twenty metres wide, the notch between two mountains that stand deep in the water. I used to sail on the North Sea quite often and have experienced many things, but I have never sailed between mountain peaks before. The black mountains fall steeply, almost vertically, into the water, no wind can get through because the mountains hold it back. Our people had to row a long distance before we reached the Umm Barakat area. Here the mountains recede a little further so that the wind can catch the sail again.

There was another dangerous spot at the gate of Abiska, called the black stones. A rocky reef runs through the middle of the wide bed, broken by the water in some places. Once again I made tea and we ate the last of our provisions. At half past midnight that night, we dropped anchor off Shellal in a palm crown jutting out of the water and lay there almost until dawn. After five days we were back in Aswan at half past eight in the morning.

* While its free-standing sections were later re-erected at New Kalabsha, the rock cut temple of Gerf Hussein now lies beneath Lake Nasser.
** Angareeb – traditional Nubian bed or couch.

F. Jakob Rippert – 'First Nile Journey of the *Ischimbul*'
Der Sudan Pionier, June 1927, pp. 77-80 and July 1927 pp. 94-96

Missionary friends have asked about the journey of our missionary boat from Haifa to Aswan. The Ischimbul *was transported from Haifa to Alexandria, where Mr Rippert, accompanied by Mr Kaltenbach from Haifa, took charge.*

We left Alexandria on the morning of 25 December 1926, happy to finally be moving forward again. The legal formalities were endless. The boats [the *Ischimbul* towed a loaded barge and small sailing vessel] had been given new numbers and were registered with the river police. We had hired two assistant boatmen and a helmsman, with whom we later had some dismal experiences. We had taken a large supply of fuel, kerosene and gasoline on board. We had the engine in order, the fuel tanks filled and so we sailed for about eight hours the first day after we had adjusted the carburettor. The journey initially took us into the Mahmoudia Canal, a miserable ditch in places that connects the port of Alexandria with the western branch of the Nile. We had to navigate very carefully in passing the sailing vessels and large cargo barges, most of which were heavily laden with cotton, without causing any damage. We docked on the bank in the evening and lay moored overnight. We had to pass through many locks and lifting bridges.

You need infinite patience in this country, because the Arab takes a long time before he finally gets to work. At night, the lock keepers and their bosses could only be brought in with a mighty roar and then they were usually in a bad mood. If you wanted to pass under a bridge, you had to help pull it up yourself. Many road bridges over the canal are made of wood and are pulled up by hand. There were always several boats with us at the bridges and locks. When you are together with the native boat people for hours or days, you get a deeper insight into their lives. There are many shipmen in Egypt; they are mostly wild, rough and mean fellows who do not trust each other. Their lives revolve around wages, food and drink. It made me downright sick to have to listen to my three men talking about money and eating and drinking and bad things until late at night. The sailors of Upper Egypt are at least still Mohammedans. They observe their ablutions and prayers. But those I saw in Lower Egypt live like animals. My three people never prayed. Only in times of need did they sometimes cry out to God.

At the end of the Mahmoudia Canal is a small village called El Adf [El-Mahmoudeya]. Before you can get into the open Nile, you first have to pass through a chamber lock. We got through quite well. However, as there were many large ships in front of the lock gate, all of which wanted to enter the lock, two lock policemen drove out with us so that we wouldn't be run over by the incoming cargo steamers. But that wasn't worth much, because all the cotton barges and steamers started moving from all sides, and before we could get through, we were in the middle of it with our boats. Our policemen were shouting, raving and swearing. Ships crashed, scraps flew. In short, it was as if we had fallen among wild animals. Nothing could be done with calm and reason.

Everyone wanted to get into the lock first, out of the strong current of the branch of the Nile. In any case, I saw the worst coming for my boats, which were so small compared with the giant barges. We were completely wedged in on all sides. I stood there powerless. I could only cry out inwardly to God for help. We were stuck in a press. I could already hear the soft crashing of the side walls. It was only a matter of moments before we were finished. One of the policemen had jumped onto the cargo ship in front of us and was struggling with the helmsman to push him back. The second policeman braced himself with us against the cotton ship, which threatened to crush us. Tears were streaming down his cheeks and he howled as if a loved one was dying: 'O Ibrahim, the motorboat is sinking!' The grief and fear of this man, who had nothing to do with the boat, was so hilarious that we had to laugh about it afterwards, when the horror was over.

The steamer in front of us only had to push back 10 metres and we were helped. I shouted this to the captain of this ship, but for the time being he didn't want to help us. In those seconds I saw the work of four months, with all its responsibility, abandoned to destruction and the barge, with its valuable cargo, already taking on water from the side and sinking. At such moments, the human soul clings to God and despairs. Finally, the steamer pushed back 10 metres in front of us. We caught our breath. The engine started. One corner of our cabin was still hooked into the side of the cotton ship, and I thought the roof was gone. But *Ischimbul* held firm. She quickly took revenge and ripped open the belly of a large cotton seed sack so that the seed spilled out and fell into the water. The current grabbed us and pushed

> "Ships crashed, scraps flew. In short, it was as if we had fallen among wild animals."

us back against the boats and I had to turn and head downstream to get free. Then I steered in an arc back into the deep channel. We were in a daze and Mr Kaltenbach and I didn't talk much. Everyone thanked God for saving us and helping us at the last moment.

The *Ischimbul* had become about 1.5 centimetres 'slimmer' due to the enormous side pressure of the steamers. The cabin doors jammed and no longer closed. The strong design had already proved its worth here, as well as the double oak sideboards. Now we sailed upstream in the open Nile. It soon became apparent that our helmsman was no good. We got stuck on a sandbank and had trouble getting off. As we got stuck more often, it became easier to push off because we got used to the sad business. Our captain had no idea where the channel was. When we could sail behind other boats, we did so, but that was also our undoing a few times, because then we ended up sitting on a sandbank with them.

In the evening, we usually docked on one of the banks, made tea, ate our own supper and soon slept, because sailing makes you tired. Unfortunately, a canal that would have brought us to Cairo more safely and quickly was not open. We were therefore forced to use the open Nile to Cairo. It was a difficult journey. I had been given our helmsman in Alexandria and told that he was reliable. It turned out that the man was simply incompetent, cheeky and big-snouted, as Alexandrians usually are. I had to keep an eye on the channel myself and it was lucky that I had my friend Kaltenbach with me to operate the engine so that I could take care of the rest. I often went overboard to push the boats off the sandbank.

We made slow progress, as the Nile makes many bends on this stretch. We passed villages of fellahs [farmers] and small towns. In places the desert and the yellow sand dunes could be seen close to the banks. The engine performed well, but 60 kilometres before Qalyub, near where the old Nile barrage [weir or small dam] of Muhammed Ali is located, a sharp side current caught us and our brake lining came off the clutch disk. The propeller stopped working and we had to go ashore. We were moored off the village of Chadadbara [Al Khatatbah?]. Fortunately for us, there was a train station here and Mr Kaltenbach was able to travel to Cairo in 1.5 hours to put a new brake leather on the clutch. During the day of Mr Kaltenbach's absence, I cleaned the ship and engine and transferred some of the wood from the barge to the sailboat to make it lighter. After we reinstalled the clutch, the journey continued happily.

On 1 January 1927 we finally set sail for Qalyub. As we approached the city, it was cloudy and foggy and we could only vaguely see the bridge-like sluice wall of the barrage in the distance. About 300 metres from the city wall, a white, silver stripe ran across the Nile. As it was my first time on this section of the river, I didn't know that this white stripe was the foamy crest of the Nile crashing over a 2-metre-high barrage wall. I assumed it was a sharp side current, like the ones we had often been through. My helmsman explained: 'It's nothing, you sail through it.' We sailed on in the middle of the river. About 50 metres before the barrage, I recognized what it was. As there was still a lot of water in the Nile at the time, you could hardly see the drop from the front and there was fog over the water. Our helmsman was still heading towards the foam strip and I assumed that he was going to turn right to approach the barrage's lock, but we had already sailed into swirling waves. Gripped by horror, I thought: this person has gone mad. He was heading towards the rapids at full speed. I pushed him off the wheel and wrenched it around. But the water boiling in front of the white stripe had already grabbed us and pulled us back. With great difficulty, I managed to get past the side of the lock and into the protective lock, but so quickly that we couldn't stop fast enough and crashed hard into the iron lock gate. I was still shaking all over for several minutes. A somewhat too stormy start to a new year!

When we questioned helmsman afterwards, it turned out that he was completely befuddled, because he was a cocaine sniffer. Even his not much better boatmen were outraged by his behaviour because they knew that they too had almost been killed. If the Nile is at its highest level, it is certainly possible to sail over this artificial rapid. Nevertheless, two sailors and their crew sank there in September last year when they tried to cross the sill at night to avoid having to wait for the lock to open in the morning. In the afternoon we docked in Cairo next to the Bulak Bridge. Various necessary errands kept us in Cairo until 5 January, when we set off on our onward journey, which went well as far as Beni Suef. Suddenly our engine stopped at a small village of fellahs about an hour from the town. There was soot on the valves. A fatal story! We needed to find a mechanic in the town.

"This made me uneasy, although I didn't believe it was a theft, because Nubians don't steal."

As it was a long way, my boatman Achmed borrowed a donkey from a fellah. If I had known that morning that this donkey would bring me new misfortune, I would have preferred to walk to the town. Nevertheless, I took the youngest boatman with me into town as a donkey boy. I got off in front of the post office and told the boy: 'Hold on to the donkey until I get back.' Then I went to the station to telegraph Aswan. I soon found a mechanic and set off with him to the post office to pick up my donkey. But there was neither my boatman nor the donkey in front of the post office. We searched for half an hour, walking back and forth, to no avail. Finally, I assumed the boy had ridden the donkey back to our boat. With the mechanic, I took a carriage back to the boat. But when we reached our boat, we found neither the donkey nor its keeper. This made me uneasy, although I didn't believe it was a theft, because Nubians don't steal.

We cleaned the engine and discovered that two of the valves were bent and needed to be straightened. So I went back to Beni Suef with my native mechanic to straighten the valve spindles on his lathe. On the way to the town, we met the boatman without a donkey. I asked: 'Where did you leave the donkey?' He replied, quite distraught: 'He's up and away. The donkey kicked me in the stomach and ran off. I couldn't run after him straight away because I had to hold my stomach, which was hurting. It disappeared around a street corner and nobody saw it anymore.'

Don't let it get you down, I thought, because the donkey can't have disappeared from the earth. So I went to the police station in Beni Suef and reported the lost donkey. The police chief promised to have the donkey brought to me by the evening. However, I had my doubts about these friendly promises. When he found out that I was from the German mission, he even invited me to dinner, but I declined with thanks, as all the difficulties had made me lose my appetite. In addition to my boat's troubles, I now had to worry about a runaway donkey, which, to make matters worse, had three owners. These three people made my life very sour. One of them followed me around like my shadow. Wherever I walked and stood, I was reminded of the donkey. Evening came and of course the donkey had not yet been found. I stayed overnight in an Arab hotel after working on the lathe until ten o'clock.

My first walk in the morning was to the police station. But there was no donkey there. They put me off until the evening. So I went out to the village to at least get my boat back in order. The donkey owners soon appeared and spoke to me about the value of donkeys in general and about their donkey in particular, which was a fine specimen. To shut them up, I finally showed myself to be completely uninterested.

When the engine was almost ready, I was gripped by a strange restlessness. Our anchorage was on a steeply sloping Nile mud bank, behind which the village lay. Now I felt as if this towering wall was moving. I carried on working and thought: It's probably just nerves! When I looked again after a while, it was moving again. My boatman Achmed had now noticed it too. Without further ado, I jumped out of the boat, pulled the anchor out of the shore, winched and dragged it 20 metres forward. My crew, grumbling about this new whim, pushed the other two boats along. We were barely moored in the new location when part of the wall under which we had been lying before collapsed into the water, thundering and clapping, and new pieces kept coming in, forcing us even further away from the spot. It was quite frightening to watch as one piece of land after another detached itself from the spot, tilted over and fell with a loud clap into the water. The fact that we were able to move away from the spot in time was an act of God's kind preservation.

The women in the village started howling and trilling when they saw the masses of earth tearing down close to their houses and plunging into the Nile. When my engine was back in order, I sailed to the port of Beni Suef. Of course, I also had one of the donkey owners on board. Once there, I wanted to go to the police again with him when the other fellahs arrived with the runaway donkey. The people then told me that the donkey had been stolen from the road by thieves, but one of them, who knew where it was hiding, had returned it to the fellahs in exchange for money. In any case, I was very happy and grateful that this problem had also been solved in such a friendly way.

G. Charlotte Rippert – 'From Mrs. Rippert's Travel Diary During the Nubia Trip'
Der Pionier, May 1929, pp. 71-74 and June 1929, pp 84-87

From 25 February to 10 March, Pastor Held, accompanied by Mr Schönberger, Dr Kallenbach, Mr Rippert, his wife, Dr. Herzfeld and Miss Pohl, undertook a reconnaissance trip through Nubia. Following the decision to raise the dam, we needed to determine where in the drowning country there was the possibility of founding a new mission station.

25 February We started loading our boat at 6 a.m. on Monday morning, which is no mean feat with so little space and so many things that had to be accessible at all times. However, there was still enough comfortable seating for four people in the rear third of the dinghy and, which was attached to the motorboat on a long line. Pastor Held took the seat at the dinghy's wheel. We had the best weather all the way to Koshtamne, for which we were all grateful. After a good journey through the otherwise dangerous Bab el Kalabsha, we arrived at Shauwishkolo in the Kalabsha countryside in the evening, where we boiled off and settled in for the night on both boats.

The bank sloped steeply down into the river. On a hilltop there was a so-called 'sheikh' (not a sheikh's grave), i.e. the women had placed clay jugs on a rock slab and stuck small white flags between them, which were painted red with circles and window-like ornaments. The women go to such places on the heights, beautifully decorated, and slaughter pigeons and present their request to the 'sheikh', saying: 'Oh, honoured sheikh, do me the favour and …' The clay jugs are repeatedly filled with water. Such a 'sheikh' is prompted by a vision that someone in the village has had in his sleep, in which the place in question has been revealed to him as the abode of a saint (sheikh).

26 February A day on a boat trip like this has a very specific order. Everyone has to get up at dawn and roll up their bedding. Then everyone disappears to the shore with their wash basin. During this time my husband loads the boat, removes the night tarpaulins, overhauls the engine and the boatman cleans both boats. In the meantime, I have built myself a windbreak on the shore, as it is not allowed to cook in the boat because of all the gasoline, and my two kerosene stoves have to be put into action as quickly as possible, because in addition to a hearty breakfast of tea, porridge, bread, eggs, jam, cheese, etc., eleven canteens of one litre each have to be filled with tea or coffee and, if possible, a proper vegetable or other dish has to be cooked in a large cooking pot. Then comes the communal breakfast, usually sitting on the floor, and then the communal prayer. This start to the day usually took 1-1.5 hours. Then we quickly put some provisions in the dinghy and off we go. During the trip, I was still responsible for washing all the dishes, possibly peeling potatoes and the like. But then we got to work, i.e. observing Nubia very closely and discussing anything noteworthy with each other. If we landed, we tried to get in touch with the local population and asked them to tell us what they thought about the future. The two doctors held outpatient clinics as often as they had the opportunity, and those who were able and wanted to, visited the immediate surroundings. We usually docked for the night 1-3 hours after dark.

On 26 February, after a good trip, we arrived in Koshtamne at around 2.30 p.m. Arriving and unloading was not at all easy due to the many lovely women who immediately appeared to greet us and the sheikhs and many boys who came to my husband on the boat. It did me a lot of good to experience so much love and loyalty from all the women I knew well from before. Each of them said kind words to me about the loss of our child, and many mothers gave me their babies in their arms. The latter is a great sign of trust and love. Some of them also told me straight away about their own experiences. After all, I had shared many a joy and sorrow and worry with them in the past.

After afternoon tea, there was an immediate discussion about 'The aim, limits and purpose of our journey': to get to know the country as far as Adindan, especially the three potential future settlement sites for the Nubians displaced by the raised reservoir after three to four years, namely Alagi, Toshka and Ballana; and as far as possible to make contact with the Fadija population (Nubian cultural/language group), as early work among them is desirable.

27 February After departure at 11.30 a.m. we stop at Alagi. Three of us visit the telegraph operator's wife. I've known her for many years from Aswan, and we've all visited her from Koshtamne. The conversation with her turns out in such a way that I can give her a good little evangelical script, because she can read and write.

> "Each of them said kind words to me about the loss of our child, and many mothers gave me their babies in their arms."

In the meantime, the gentlemen get some information about the cheap, good and quick procurement of camels for the planned desert ride after the boat trip, which turned out to be unnecessary for the time being.

From Alagi we continue south. Today we have muggy, hazy weather, a south-westerly wind and in the afternoon about 60% humidity. We first sailed through an area that is still familiar to us, passing Dakke, Gurte and Maharraga. Then comes the flat landscape of Seyala, here and there only a few mountains, rising up like islands. After sunset, we dock on the rocky shore a little north of Sebua.

28 February In the morning we find prehistoric drawings on large, smooth rock faces on the shore: elephants, bulls, giraffes, ships, etc. We then saw many more of these from the boat on the rocks along the shore, especially in the Madik, Seyala and Wadi el Arab landscapes.

We soon reached Sebua, the border between the Kenuzi and the Arab region. We visited the temple built by Ramesses II, which later became a Nubian-Christian church, as can still be seen from the image of St. Peter in a chapel and all kinds of cross figures. I was particularly interested in a large cross ornament, which had exactly the same shape as today's Nubian dinar (women's jewellery). We had a serious conversation with the Arab-Muhammadan temple attendant about the cross and Christ's death for our sins and about the history of this once Christian country. The further south we went, the less the Nubians seemed to have forgotten about the latter than is the case with the Kenuzi Nubians. The temple attendant then listened attentively as Mr Schönberger preached the gospel to a beautiful circle of men on the shore after a previous polyclinic and distributed scriptures among them.

It was strange to meet Bishari here on the west bank, and even to see a Bishari at work on the banks of the Nile. Many Bishari and Ababda* have now moved their herds from their mountains to the banks of the Nile, as the lack of rain has left their herds without food. The reservoir water here at Sebua stank and was as thick as spinach. Dense, almost impenetrable bushes stood lengthwise in the shallow bank water, and here my husband was able to observe a monitor lizard (approx. 60 cm long) for the first time in freedom.

At around 4.30 p.m. we landed in Korosko, the home of one of our boatmen. We cooked, talked to the people, and encountered strong doubts among them about the implementation of the dam-raising project. There was a clinic and gospel distribution, the gentlemen distributed many gospels in Fadija dialect and Arabic scriptures. After about an hour we left this picturesque and wonderful area.

It is remarkable that so far not a single Nubian has stated with certainty where he or his village will go in the event of emigration. One could have the impression that either a large proportion of the southern Nubians in particular do not really believe in the implementation of the dam-raising project, or are trying to extract as much as possible from the government through passive behaviour. From Korosko we sailed past Dir, whose few lights could only be seen flashing in the darkness, to Quitta.

1 March Departure at 9.30 a.m., past Qasr Ibrim. Narrow, green banks, alternating with steep cliffs falling into the river. The river is not safe for shipping in these areas because of the many sandbanks. Many large and small islands, mostly well planted, and the lush date palm forests on both banks give the impression of a fertile, rich region. You can also see the wealth of the women, richly adorned with gold, proudly dragging their long black dresses far behind them. The headdress of these Fadija women is different from that of the Kenuzi women. Instead of the round forehead dinar, they wear an acute-angled, triangular gold plate on their foreheads and have many small silver rings, which look like crescent moons, woven into the many small braids so that they surround their heads like a wreath. The Fadija women wear long, wide, red pants that reach down to their ankles under their long, trailing black outer garments, which are very brightly coloured when they walk.

I was struck by the fact that no 'gabbus' [tubular mud tile roofs] have been seen in the villages since Seyala. The houses either have no roof at all, or they have reed mats or a thin slatted mud roof. The various paintings on the houses always show the cross ornament: the doors, which look like large human figures with their graphic decoration, are also peculiar. We docked in the Toshka landscape near Nega'Abdu Hille to take a closer look at the future Nubian settlement area.

We had just passed a nice, small, isolated settlement with a sakia, which Matter, our helmsman who is very well known here, told us was a settlement of Umbarakab people who had emigrated here at the time of the first damming. This was the first case I knew of Kenuzi settling under Fadija. Later, in response to my question, a Fadija farmer there told me that these Umbarakab people had asked for land, they had then been given an isolated piece of desert on the west bank, and there they were now. But they are still sitting there as strangers.

This farmer then showed us the land to be cultivated later. It is the property of the government, which also wants to provide water later on. No individual can buy the land, but the village in question is allocated a correspondingly large piece of land, which is then distributed among the villagers belonging together. A lot of the cultivated bank here in Abdu Hille was lying fallow, and the farmer explained that the Omda had once bought a machine to fetch water, but that it could not work due to a lack of coal. Between the river farmland and the land to be cultivated in the future there is a depression in which ushr bushes and tamarisks grow, evidence of water. After about 1 ½ hours of sightseeing, we sailed on to dock near Abu Simbel soon after sunset. The bank was a 2-4 metre high wall of Nile mud, which made mooring very difficult.

> "... we sailed on to dock near Abu Simbel soon after sunset. The bank was a 2-4 metre high wall of Nile mud, which made mooring very difficult ... everyone goes to visit the two magnificent rock temples"

2 March The usual boat morning program, and everyone goes to visit the two magnificent rock temples. Then on to Ballana. Around 11 a.m. we docked at Rega' Zebaida, on the west bank of the Ballana landscape, from where we pretty much reached the centre of the future fertile land inland. We set off, a couple of Nubians went with us full of interest, and one of them dug out the best soil for us in various places under a layer of about 20 cm mixed with drifting sand. It really was a large, well-formed area of several thousand feddans [acres, approx.] of good soil that we had in front of us, and there would have been a lot to achieve for companies with a lot of money and people if large tamarisk forests completely covered by drifting sand, blown away houses and large shifting sand dunes had not indicated that any effort would probably be in vain. When I asked who was going to settle here, one of our companions replied: 'The people from Toshka to Adindan, all Fadija, but no Kenuzi, no!'

We set off late in the afternoon to return to Koshtamne. A nasty wind made the journey difficult, and the heavy swell prevented us from mooring on the eastern shore near the medieval fortress of Adda. We would have loved to see the ruins of what was probably also an ancient Nubian Christian settlement. Unfortunately we could only see the ancient Nubian Christian domed tombs from a distance.

3 March We celebrated Sunday, with Pastor Held holding a long service for us. It was Mr Schönberger's birthday, which we also tried to celebrate. Three local women here were very trusting, two of them had already been to Alexandria and had lost their fear of strangers. Mr Schönberger also had a good opportunity to take close-up photographs of these women with their beautiful jewellery.

Then we continued down the Nile at a speed of 12 kilometres per hour. There are strong, shifting winds and very turbulent water. Around 5.00 p.m. we land at the village of Guneina, above Korosko. It is a purely Arabic-speaking village and is part of the Wadi el Arab. Despite a strong, sandy wind, we continued on to Korosko, where we moored in a good spot in the dark.

4 March We continue in the morning. At the high cliffs of Djebel Saba'a Dorät, there are high waves and strong winds. We stop at the rock formations in Madik around noon, then sail on to moor at the southern beginning of the Maharraga landscape. We plan to sleep under canvas on the sand on the shore. While erecting the tent, my husband is stung. After barely 10 minutes he feels ill and faints. As there were many traces of snakes and horned vipers in the sand, we were very worried. Dr Kallenbach injected anti-scorpion serum. Jakob was fine again the next morning. How grateful I am to God's grace, which prevented the worst.

5 March We arrived at Alagi around 11 a.m. Everyone except me (I already knew the area) set off to see the lower part of the wadi. For a number of reasons, including the mixed population and likely future movement of people, it was decided that Alagi would not be suitable for a future mission settlement. We therefore continued on to Koshtamne.

* The Ababda were, like the Bishari, pastoral nomads who traditionally lived nearer the Red Sea.

Bibliography

Archives

Australian War Memorial, Canberra (AWM)
Finke River Mission, Alice Springs, Australia (FRM)
Evangeliumsgemeinschaft Mittlerer Osten, Wiesbaden, Germany (EMO)
Hessisches Hauptstaatsarchiv Wiesbaden, Germany (HHStAW)
Hessisches Staatsarchiv Darmstadt, Germany (HStAD)
Lutheran Archives Australia, Adelaide (LAA)
National Archives of Australia (NAA)
Rippert/Probert Family Collection, Australia (RPA)
Tatura Irrigation and Wartime Camps Museum, Tatura, Australia (TAM)
Temple Society of Australia Archives (TSA)

Websites

Archion Shomrat: www.archionshomrat.co.il (Kibbutz Shomrat archives)
National Library of Israel Newspaper Collection: www.nli.org.il/en/discover/newspapers (including *Palestine Post* 1932-1950 and *Die Warte des Tempels* 1861-1939)
Palestine Open Maps: palopenmaps.org/en
PalestineRemembered.com
Tempelgesellschaft Freie christliche Gemeinschaft: www.tempelgesellschaft.de/de/startseite.php
Trove: trove.nla.gov.au (Australian historical newspapers)

Articles, Chapters, Theses, Manuscripts

Ball, C. and M. Buckland, 'Obituary: Reinhart Rippert', *Anaesthesia and Intensive Care,* Vol. 39, Supplement 1, July 2011, pp. 30-32

Ben-Artzi, Yossi, 'Religious ideology and landscape formation: the case of the German Templars in Eretz-Israel' in Alan R. H. Baker and Gideon Bigger (eds), *Ideology and Landscape in Historical Perspective*, Cambridge University Press, 2006, pp. 83-106

Burnley, Ian, 'Submergence, Persistence and Identity: Generations of German Origin in the Barossa Valley and Adelaide Hills, South Australia', *Geographical Research*, 48:4, November 2010, pp. 427-439.

Goldman, Danny, 'The Architecture of the Templers in their Colonies in Eretz-Israel, 1868-1948, and their Settlements in the United States 1860-1925', Thesis, The Union Institute and University, Cincinnati, 2003

Goldman, Danny, 'Fences of Hope: Headcount and a Daily Massage, Following Sketches of an Anonymous Detainee in Mazra'a Detention Camp', *Et-Mol*, 153, 2000, pp. 14-17

Gordon, Gil, 'Die Schneller Dynastie – Drei Generationen protestantischer Missionsarbeit im Orient' in H. Goren and J. Eisler (eds), *Deutschland und Deutsche in Jerusalem, Eine Konferenz in Mishkenot Sha'ananim, März 2007*, Mishkenot Sha'ananim, Jerusalem, 2011, pp. 117-136

Gur, Jana, 'The Rise and Fall of Israel's Oranges', *Tablet*, 15 December, 2020, www.tabletmag.com (21 February 2025)

Hoffmann, Brigitte, 'Unsere Verantwortung in der Welt Gedanken über die Haltung der Tempelgesellschaft zum Nationalsozialismus', Der besondere Beitrag Beilage der *Warte des Tempels*, No. 2, 1995, https://www.tempelgesellschaft.de/posts/der-besondere-beitrag-414.php (17 March 2025)

Kauschke, Adam, 'Discovering the stories of our post Second World War migrants', *Journal of Friends of Lutheran Archives*, No. 29, 2019, pp. 30–44

Kiem, Paul, 'Overlooked German Catholics of the Hunter Valley', *Journal of the Australian Catholic Historical Society*, Vol 46, 2025, pp. 28-42

Koehne, Samuel, 'Refusing to leave: perceptions of German national identity during internment in Australia, 1941-45', in Joan Beaumont, Ilma Martinuzzi O'Brien, and Mathew Trinca (eds), *Under Suspicion: citizenship and internment in Australia during the Second World War*, National Museum of Australia, Canberra, 2008, pp. 67-83

Koehne, Samuel, '"You have to be pleasing & co-operative": Australia's vision splendid for post-World War II migrants', Traffic (University of Melbourne Postgraduate Association), no. 5, July 2004

Krumeich, Gerd, 'Der Erste Weltkrieg', in *Der Erste Weltkrieg in 100 Objekten*, Deutsches Historisches Museum, Berlin, 2014, pp. 12-19

Kupke, Lyall, 'The Restoration of German Place-Names in South Australia', *Journal of Friends of Lutheran Archives*, No. 27, 2017, pp. 51-62

Lauche, Gerald, 'The development of the "Sudan Pionier Mission" into a mission among the Nile-Nubians (1900-1966)', Thesis, University of South Africa, 2015

McNamara, Andrew and Ann Stephen, 'Exile, Internment and Hirschfeld-Mack in Geelong', in Goad, Stephen et al. (eds), *Bauhaus Diaspora and Beyond*, Miegunyah Press, Melbourne, 2019, pp. 61-71

Nicosia, Francis R. J., 'National Socialism and the Demise of the German-Christian Communities in Palestine During the Nineteen Thirties', *Canadian Journal of History/Annales Canadiennes d'Histoire*, 14: 2, 1979, pp. 235-256

Pietsch, Bethany, '"Dear Sisters in the Faith": Letters of Thanks from Post-War Germany', *Journal of Friends of Lutheran Archives*, No. 33, 2023, pp. 50-75

Rippert, Klaus and Paul Kiem, 'Jakob Rippert und Albert Kahn, zwei ungewöhnliche Auerbacher und ihre Schicksale', *Museumsverein Bensheim Mitteilungen*, 89, February 2024, pp. 64-73

Rockaway, Robert, 'The Screwy History of the Modern Knights Templer', *Tablet*, 22 March 2021, www.tabletmag.com (21 February 2025)

Rutland, Suzanne D., '"Buying out of the Matter": Australia's Role in Restitution for Templer Property in Israel', *Journal of Israeli History*, 24:1, 2005, pp. 140-149

Sauer, Christof, 'Reaching the Unreached Sudan Belt: Guinness, Kumm and the Sudan Pionier Mission', Thesis, University of South Africa, 2001

Seitz, Anne and Lois Foster, 'German Nationals in Australia 1939–1947: Internment, forced migration and/or social control?', *Journal of Intercultural Studies*, 10:1, 1989, pp. 13-31

Serr, Marcel, 'Was ist bildsamer, was ist verheißungsvoller als ein Kind?' (Schneller-Familie), 7 February 2018, www.israelnetz.com (1 April 2025)

Stoll, Ted, 'Childhood Memories', unpublished memoir.

Troeger, Eberhard, 'EMO I: 1900 to 1914' and 'EMO II: 1914 to 1950' unpublished research notes, c. 2024, EMO.

Winter, Christine, 'The Long Arm of the Third Reich', *The Journal of Pacific History*, 38:1, 2003, pp. 85-108

Yazbak, Mahmoud, 'Templars (sic) as Proto-Zionists? The "German Colony" in late Ottoman Haifa', *Journal of Palestine Studies*, 28:4, 1999, pp. 40-54

Yohanni, Lior, 'Zionist identity and the British Mandate: Palestine's internment camps and the making of the Western native', *Nations and Nationalism*, 26:1, 2020, pp. 246-262

Books

Abu-Sitta, Salman H., *Atlas of Palestine 1917-1966*, Palestine Land Society London, 2010

Austin-Broos, Diane, *Arrernte Present, Arrernte Past: Invasion, violence, and imagination in Indigenous Central Australia*, University of Chicago Press, Chicago, 2009

Bongiorno, Frank, *Dreamers and Schemers: A Political History of Australia*, La Trobe University Press, Melbourne, 2022

Boyd, Julia and Angelika Patel, *A Village in the Third Reich: How Ordinary Lives were Transformed by the Rise of Fascism*, Elliot and Thompson, London, 2022

Butz, Andreas, *Bir Salem, Nazareth und Chemet Allah, Verbindungen zwischen Württemberg und Palästina anhand dreier Zweigstellen des Syrischen Waisenhauses in Jerusalem 1889- 1939*, Harrasowitz Verlag, Wiesbaden, 2023

Caillard, Andrew, *The Australian Ark: The Story of Australian Wine* (Vol. 1-3), Longueville Media & The Vintage Journal, Sydney, 2023

Evans, Richard J., *The Third Reich in Power*, Penguin, London, 2006

Frank, Doris and Renate Weber (eds), *75 Years of Templers in Australia*, Temple Society Australia, Melbourne, 2016

Gerstäcker, Friedrich, *Australia*, JG Gotta'scher Verlag, 1853 (Projekt Gutenberg-DE).

Guinness, H. Grattan, *Lucy Guinness Kumm, Her Life Story*, Morgan & Scott, London, 1907

Held, Johannes, *Anfänge einer deutschen Muhammedanermission: Rückblick auf die ersten 25 Jahre der Sudan-Pionier-Mission 1900-1925*, Verlag der Sudan-Pionier-Mission, 1925

Heuzenroeder, Angela, *Barossa Food*, Wakefield Press, Adelaide, 2020

Ioannou, Noris, *Barossa Journeys: Into a Valley of Tradition*, Paringa Press, Adelaide, 1997

Judd, Barry and Katherine Ellinghaus, *Enlightened Aboriginal Futures*, Routledge, London, 2024

Jupp, James (ed.), *The Australian People: An Encyclopedia of the Nation, Its People and Their Origins* Cambridge University Press, 2001

Kershaw, Ian, *To Hell and Back: Europe 1914-1949*, Penguin, London, 2016

Khalidi, Rashid, *The Hundred Years' War on Palestine*, Metropolitan Books, New York, 2020

Khalidi, Walid (ed.), *All that remains: the Palestinian villages occupied and depopulated by Israel in 1948*, Institute for Palestine Studies, 1992

Knapp, Peter, *1200 Jahre Bensheim*, Bensheim an d. Bergstr.: Magistrat, 1966

Konings, Chris, *'Queen Elizabeth' at War: His Majesty's Transport, 1939-1946*, Patrick Stephens, Wellingborough, 1985

Lohe, M., F. W. Albrecht, and L.H. Leske, *Hermannsburg: A Vision and Mission*, Lutheran Publishing House, Adelaide, 1977

McCullough, Colleen, *Roden Cutler, V.C.: The Biography*, Random House, Sydney, 1988

Macintyre, Stuart, *Australia's Boldest Experiment: War and Reconstruction in the 1940s*, NewSouth, Sydney, 2015

Manz, Stefan, *Constructing a German Diaspora: The 'Greater German Empire', 1871-1914*, Routledge, New York, 2014

Meinel, Herb, *Nothing Can Make Them Stumble: The Story of the Stoll/Meinel Family*, Adelaide, 2016

Mence, Victoria, Simone Gangell and Ryan Tebb, *A History of the Department of Immigration*, Department of Immigration and Border Protection, Canberra, 2017

Meyer, Charles, *A History of the Germans in Australia*, 1839-1945, Monash University, Melbourne, 1990

Morris, Benny, *1948: A History of the First Arab-Israeli War,* Yale University Press, New Haven, 2008

Neiberg, Michael S., *The Second Battle of the Marne*, Indiana University Press, Bloomington, 2008

Orlow, Dietrich, *A History of Modern Germany: 1871 to Present* (8th ed.), Routledge, New York, 2018

Passingham, Ian, *The German Offensives of 1918: The Last Desperate Gamble*, Pen & Sword Military, Barnsley (UK), 2008

Persian, Jayne, *Beautiful Balts*, NewSouth, Sydney, 2017

Rippert, Klaus, *Chronik der Familie Ripper(t)*, Gendi Verlag, Otzberg, 2022

Sauer, Paul, *Uns rief das Heilige Land – Die Tempelgesellschaft im Wandel der Zeit*, Konrad Theiss Verlag, Stuttgart, 1985

Sauer, Paul, *The Holy Land Called: the story of the Temple Society*, (trans. Gunhild Henley), Temple Society of Australia, Melbourne, 1991

Sebag-Montefiore, Simon, *Jerusalem, The Biography: A History of the Middle East*, Weidenfeld & Nicolson, London, 2024

Strähler, Reinhold and Joachim Paesler, *Nach dem Sandsturm Klart es auf: 125 Jahre erlebte Treue Gottes Geschichte und Geschichten*, EMO, Wiesbaden, 2025

Tampke, Jürgen and Colin Doxford, *Australia, Willkommen: A history of the Germans in Australia*, NSW University Press, Sydney, 1990

Tampke, Jürgen, *The Germans in Australia*, Cambridge University Press, Melbourne, 2006

Trentmann, Frank, *Out of the Darkness: The Germans 1942-2022*, Allen Lane, London, 2023

Von Dessien, Eberhard, Ulrich Ehrbeck, Eberhard Troeger, *Wasser auf dürres Land: 85 Jahre Sudan-Pionier-Mission/Ev. Mission in Oberägypten*, EMO, Wiesbaden, 1985

Wawrzyn, Heidemarie, *Nazis in the Holy Land 1933-1948*, De Gruyter Magnes, Berlin & Jerusalem, 2013

Yazbak, Mahmoud and Yfaat Weiss (eds), *Haifa Before & After 1948: Narratives of a Mixed City*, Republic of Letters Publishing, Dordrecht, 2011

– *Juncken Builders – 100 Years: a commemorative souvenir edition*, 1995

– *Dunera: Stories of Internment*, State Library of NSW, 2024

– *Fabric of Society, the Templer Journey: an embroidered history*, Temple Society Australia, Melbourne, 2009

Index

A

Ababda   171, 172
Aboriginal Australians   84, 121, 122, 127, 128–130, 148 *See also* Arrarnta
Abu Simbel   35–36, 172
Acre (Akko)   24–25, 43, 47–49, 53–56, 59, 60, 75, 84, 87, 97, 98, 114–116, 140, 151, 153
Adelaide   80, 83, 84, 88, 103, 107, 110, 111–112, 113, 121, 123, 125, 132, 135–138, 147, 149
Albrecht, Friedrich Wilhelm (F. W.)   92, 96, 101, 107–108, 121–125, 126, 128–130, 132
Alice Springs   83–84, 119, 121, 122, 125, 126, 129, 132, 153
Appinger, Gottlob   30, 32, 34, 45, 47
Armstrong, Manasse   122
Arrarnta   56, 84, 119, 121, 126, 128
Aswan   13–14, 18, 22, 25, 27–33, 35, 37, 40, 126, 148, 155–156, 157–159, 160–162, 162–163, 166, 167, 169, 170
Aswan Low Dam   13, 27, 35, 39, 156
Auerbach   vii–ix, 1–3, 7, 15, 16, 17, 37, 52, 54, 87, 89, 90, 93, 94, 96, 99, 109, 122, 146
Austin-Broos, Diane   128
Ayub, Anton   45

B

Barossa and Light Herald   152
Barossa *Deutsch*   141
Barossa Valley   56, 83, 84, 105, 135–143, 145
Battarbee, Bernice   128
Battarbee, Rex   125, 128, 129, 132, 134
Bauhaus   68
Beersheba   43
Beilharz, Richard   115
Beirut   151
Bensheim   viii, 1–4, 15, 87, 93–94, 96
Betlehem   44, 57
Bir Salem   46, 47
Bishari   13, 16, 28, 156, 163, 171–172
Blackwood, Staff Sergeant Archibald   68, 96
Bongiorno, Frank   104
Borgelt, Lou   123, 125
Boyd, Julia   78
Brandt, Karl   114–115
Burton, Roy   127

C

Cairo   1, 14, 22, 33, 35, 37, 67, 157–158, 164, 165, 168
Calwell, Arthur   66, 80–82, 103–105, 107, 132
Carmel, Alex   44, 45
Cassab, Judy   128
Chapman, Major C.   68, 96
Chemet Allah   46, 47
Chifley, Ben   104
C. O. Juncken   142, 144, 149
Cologne   89, 98
Cologne-Dellbrück   99–100, 108, 153
Covell, William (Bill) J.   151–153
Curtin, John   104
Cutler, Sir Roden   64–66
Cyprus   139, 141

D

Dammann, Julius   13–14
Darau   15, 28, 40
Darling, James   68
Der Pionier   v, 17, 33, 37, 170–172
Der Sudan Pionier   v, 15, 17, 18, 22, 25, 29, 31, 33, 41, 146, 152–153, 155–169
Deutschtum   138
Dhikr   18, 159–160
Doering, Bert   125, 127
Doxford, Colin   104
Drogemuller, Dick   126
Dunera   63, 68

E

Egypt   13, 14–15, 17–18, 22, 25, 27–41, 46, 59–60, 82–83, 89, 135, 143, 152, 153, 154, 157–159, 167
Eisenach   14
Ellinghaus, Katherine   129, 130, 134

Enderlin, Elisabeth 25, 27
Enderlin, Samuel Jakob 25, 28, 30–31, 158, 162–166
Eeucalyptus trees 45, 63, 141
Evangeliumsgemeinschaft Mittlerer Osten (EMO — Evangelical Middle East Ministries) 14–15, 26

F

Finke River Mission 83, 107, 109, 121, 123, 125, 128, 132–133
First World War vii, viii, 3, 5–12, 22–23, 24, 25, 43, 46, 49, 67, 72, 129, 136, 138, 148, 152, 153
    Second Battle of the Marne 8–11
Frank, Doris 62, 64, 87
Frederick William III (Prussia) 136
Fremantle 61, 87
Fugmann, Wilhelm 67

G

General Stuart Heintzelman 87, 103–104, 106
German POWs 59–61, 63, 74, 77
Germany 13, 14, 18, 23, 27, 28, 29, 40, 43, 46, 47–48, 52–53, 54, 55, 56, 64, 66–67, 68, 69, 73, 77, 78, 79, 81, 82, 83, 86–87, 100–101, 103, 104, 105, 106–109, 111, 113, 114, 115, 119, 122, 135, 136, 138, 139–141, 143, 146, 147, 149, 152, 153, 156, 158, 159, 165
    Post-War: 1948-1950 vii–ix, 89–99
    West Germany 93, 114–115
    See also First World War, Hermannsburg, Nazism
Gerstäcker, Friedrich 138
Ghan (train) 83, 85
Glockemann family 67, 71
Glockemann, Leo vi
Goyder, George 119
Gross, Sam 83
Guinness, Henry Grattan 13–14
Guinness, Lucy 13–14

H

Haganah 141
Hahndorf 130, 136
Haifa ix, 20, 25, 30, 32–34, 44–45, 46, 47, 49, 50, 52, 54, 59, 67–68, 71, 96, 97, 115–116, 140, 142, 143, 145, 151, 167
Halle 14, 22
Hardegg, Georg David 44

Held, Johannes 25, 33, 40
Held, Siegfried 149
Hermannsburg (Australia) 56, 83, 83–84, 86, 88, 89, 90, 92, 96, 101, 107, 109, 110, 114, 119–134, 135, 142, 143, 147, 148, 149, 152, 153
Hermannsburg (Germany) 84, 119
Higgins, Michael 56
Hirschfeld-Mack, Ludwig 68, 69
Hitler, Adolf 11, 52, 53, 77, 79, 96, 98, 146
    See also Nazism
Hoffman, Christoph 44, 76
Hoffmann, Brigitte 53
Hohenlohe-Ingelfingen, Princess 158
Hussein, Samuel Ali 13, 28, 30, 162
Hutchins, Wilfred 73, 80–82, 106

I

Imberger, Friederike 43–44
Immanuel College, Adelaide 110, 111
Ischimbul 33–34, 37, 46, 167–169
Israel v, 43, 45, 79, 108, 114–116, 133, 144, 146, 147, 151, 153
Istanbul 141
Italian internees 17, 22, 60, 61, 63
    Vagarini, Cesare 67, 68, 76
    Zerjal, Frida 69
Italian POWs 60
Italy 5, 17, 103, 156–157

J

Jaffa 43, 44, 45, 59, 74
Jerusalem 44, 46, 77, 97, 100, 115, 145, 151
Jews/Jewish ix, 46, 47, 60–61, 63, 65, 68, 75, 78, 79, 97, 98, 114, 116, 141, 146, 149
    Settlement in Palestine 43, 45, 48, 49, 52–53, 96–97, 114, 116, 141, 146, 152
    See also Dunera, Israel, Palestine, Zionist
Judd, Barry 129, 130, 134
Juncken(s) *See* C. O. Juncken
Justin, Otto Paul 23

K

Kahn, Albert ix, 47, 52–53, 96–97, 146
Kahn, Harry ix, 52–53, 96, 146
Kahn, Marie Clara ix, 52, 96, 146
Kaiserswerth Victoria Hospital 33, 158
Kaiser Wilhelm II 11

Kanimbla 87
Kantara (El Qantara) 59, 61
Karmel Mission 25, 27, 46
Kavel, August 136, 145
Kempe, A. H. 119–121
Kempe, Ludwig 119–121
Kershaw, Ian 94
Kibbutz Netser Sereni 46
Kibbutz Shomrat 48–49, 50
Kissinger, Henry viii, 94
Klemzig 136
Koshtamne 30–39, 41, 153, 162–166, 170–172
Krumeich, Gerd 11
Kumm, Hermann Karl Wilhelm 13–14

L

Lake Nasser 35, 36, 153, 166
Landara, Benjamin 122
Latz, Arthur 122
League of Nations 43
Lebanon 22, 24, 64, 100–101, 108, 116, 151
Liebler, Oskar 56, 84, 86
Lobethal 136
Lodewyckx, Augustin 138
Lutherans/Lutheran Church
    Australia 56, 83–84, 91–92, 107–109, 111, 119–121, 125, 127, 128, 133, 135, 141, 144, 149
    Germany 15, 44, 136, 138
    Palestine 44, 46, 49, 50, 53, 60, 66, 140
Lydda 59

M

Macintyre, Stuart 104
Massenbach, Gertrud von 27, 28, 31–32
Mazra'a British Camp 56, 59–60, 75, 84, 151
Meinel, Helga 140–141
Meinel, Herb 49, 139, 140–141, 143, 149
Meinel, Inge 140–141
Meinel, Maria (nee Stoll) 140–141
Meinel, Martin 56, 140, 141, 143, 149
Meinel, Werner 140–141
Melbourne 63, 68, 73, 74, 86, 87, 105, 109, 110, 113, 126, 129, 138, 146, 147
Menzies, Robert 111
Migration, Australian history 43–44, 103–111, 114
    German immigration, South Australia 136–143
    New Australian 104–105, 112, 139
    Palestine German immigration 105–106
    White Australia policy 103, 104
Missionary societies/mission movment 13, 14–15, 18, 128–130
Modra, Vic 126
Moncur, William Anderson 64
Mühlenfeld, Hans (German Ambassador) 128
Murton, Frances 107

N

Nahariya 49, 53, 54
Namatjira, Albert 122, 129, 131, 132
Namatjira, Keith 122
Nazism/Nazi Party ix, 11, 54, 69–75, 79–80, 82, 105, 114, 152
    Denazification vii–ix, 89, 93–98
    Hitler Youth viii, 94
    Kraft durch Freude (KdF – Strength Through Joy) 67
    Palestine 52–53
    Reichsarbeitsdienst 48
    Reichstreue 73, 74
    Tatura Internment Camp 67, 69–75, 77–78
Nile River 13–14, 27, 30–37, 40–41, 152, 158, 160–162, 163, 165, 166, 167–169, 170–172
Noack, Gertrud 31
Nothbaum, Franz 74
Ntaria 121, 127, 128
Nubia viii, 27–41, 82, 83–84, 135, 148, 152, 162–166, 170, 170–172
    Fadija 35–36, 170–172
    Kenuzi 35–36, 171–172
    See also Koshtamne
Nuriootpa v, 1, 2, 19, 83, 135, 137, 139, 141–142, 144–149, 152

O

Ottoman Empire 5, 43

P

Paesler, Joachim 41
Pagenstecher, Dr Hermann 22
Palestine vii–ix, 18, 20, 22–25, 24–25, 27, 28, 30, 32, 41, 43–57, 58, 59–67, 69, 74, 75, 78, 79, 80, 81, 82, 84, 87, 96–99, 105, 106, 114, 115, 116,

125, 127, 133, 135, 139–149, 151, 152
   Arab uprising, (1936-1939) 53–54
   British Mandate 43, 46, 56, 79, 106
   Jewish immigration 43
   See also Templers, Palestine
Persilscheine ix, 94, 96
Pietsch, Bethany 91
Pietzcker, J. A. 74, 75, 76
Pross family 67–68, 71, 78
Pross, Johannes 78, 142

Q

Queckenstedt, Dorothea 119–121
Queen Elizabeth (ship) 59–61, 63, 68, 140, 141
Queen Elizabeth II 113, 129, 141

R

Ramadan 29–30, 160–162
Reuther, R. B. 123, 126, 132, 133
Rippert ancestry 1
Rippert, Charlotte (nee Wolter) vii–viii, 33, 35–41, 66, 81–87, 89, 92, 101, 109–110, 122–125, 132–134, 135, 142–149, 151–154, 170–172
   Legacy 152–154
   Paintings 67–68
   Palestine 46–58
   See also Wolter, Charlotte
Rippert, Eva 1–2, 15
Rippert, Jakob vii–ix, 1–4, 22, 25, 66, 68, 74, 78, 81–87, 89–90, 93, 101, 105–106, 107–109, 122–127, 130–134, 135, 142–149, 151–154
   Christianity 4, 7, 9, 11, 15–16, 18, 29, 98, 130, 135, 142, 147, 149, 157
   First World War 7–12, 129
   Legacy 152–154
   Nazi Party membership & denazification 52–53, 74, 78, 82, 89, 94–98
   Palestine 46–58
   Palestine farm 43, 47–51, 114–116, 146, 151
      Compensation 114–116, 144–146
   Sudan Pionier Mission 15–18, 27–34, 156–169
   Tatura internment camp 63–66
Rippert, Johann Philipp 1–2
Rippert, Ludwig Immanuel (Manu) 1–3, 47–48, 49, 72, 116
Rippert, Reinhart vii–viii, 19, 37, 39–40, 43, 46, 48, 49, 51, 54, 55, 89, 94, 97, 99, 101, 103, 106, 107, 108, 109–114, 122–123, 132, 133, 136, 147
Rippert, Susanna 1–2
Rippert, Wilhelm 1–3, 40, 87, 135
Rothermel, Anna 17
Rubins, Dr 49
Rubitschung, Dr O. 66, 96
Ruff, Gottlieb 66, 67, 72, 75, 77, 78
Ruff, Helmut 48, 59, 59–64, 66, 67
Rushworth 62, 63, 65, 96

S

Sacharias-Saarelinn, Eugen 103, 113, 132
Sacharias-Saarelinn, Nina 103, 112–114
Sacharias-Saarelinn, Paul 103
Sacharias-Saarelinn, Valentina 103
Sarona 44, 45, 65, 151
Sauer, Paul 52, 53, 54, 72, 77, 81
Schäfer, Edgar 15
Scherer, Philipp 109
Schmitt, Fr Werner 96
Schneller family viii, 46, 89, 98–99, 101
   Ernst 98–99, 122
   Hermann 46, 77, 87, 96, 98, 100, 101
   Johann Ludwig 46
   Johann Ludwig Schneller School, Lebanon 100
   Ludwig 98
   Syrian Orphanage, Germany 89, 98–100, 122, 149, 153
   Syrian Orphanage, Palestine 43, 46–47, 48, 77, 100
   Theodor Schneller School, Amman, Jordan 101
Schulze, L. G. 119
Schulz, Wilhelmine Charlotte 119
Schwarz, W. F. 119
Second World War 3, 43, 53, 54, 67, 70, 72, 77–79, 87, 93, 94, 116, 139–141, 151, 152
Simpfendorfer, August 83, 107, 110
Simpson, William 78, 80
Skolar, Franz 74
Soskin, Dr 49
Spohn, Mathias 47
Stoll, Anna 140
Stoll, Anna Maria 139–141

Stoll, Christel (nee Appinger)   140–141
Stoll, Christian   49, 54, 56, 115, 140, 141, 142, 144
Stoll, Garry (Gerhard)   69, 106, 130, 140, 143
Stoll, Herta   51, 140–141
Stoll, Hulda   140, 141
Stoll, Jakob   139–141
Stoll, Katharine (nee Mader)   140, 145
Stoll, Maria   140 See also Meinel, Maria
Stoll/Meinel Family   49, 139–143
Stoll, Ruth   51, 140
Stoll, Siegfried (Fred)   106, 140
Stoll, Ted (Theodor)   78, 140, 142, 149
Stoll, Walter   51, 54, 140–141, 143
Stoll, Wilhelm   49, 78, 140, 141, 145
Stoll, Wilhelm (Bill)   140, 149
Stolz, Dr Johannes   107
Strähler, Reinhold   41
Strehlow, Carl   56, 84, 121, 126–127, 128, 129, 153
Strehlow, Ted   128
Struve, Werner   106
Sudan Pionier Mission (SPM)   v, ix, 13–18, 22, 23, 25, 27–41, 43, 46, 89, 96, 152, 153, 155–172
    foundation   13–14
Suez Canal   17, 59, 109, 157
Sulzbach, Herbert   9–11
Suter, M. A.   92
Sydney   61, 62, 105
Syrian Orphanage   see Schneller family

T

Tampke, Jürgen   104
Tanunda   136, 137, 138, 139, 143
Tatura   vii, 59–75, 77–80, 83, 96, 106, 107, 110, 139, 140, 143, 147, 149, 153
    German Military Cemetery   74
Tatura internees
    Activities and community   66–71
    Arrival   61–64
    Children and school   66, 69
    Christmas   66–67
    Repatriation   79–82
    See also Nazism
Tatura Museum   67, 70
Tel Aviv   46, 151

Temby, Henry   81, 106–107, 114, 133
Templers, Australia   77, 105, 149
Templers, Germany   44, 52–53
Templers, Palestine   44–46, 48, 52, 54, 60, 105
    Palestine Compensation   105, 114–115
Trentmann, Frank   90
Troeger, Eberhard   v, 40

U

University of Adelaide   103, 107, 111, 112

W

Wächter, Luise   56
Waldheim   44, 49, 50, 56, 116, 140, 141
Walhalla   44
Wawrzyn, Heidemarie   52, 78, 98
Weber, Renate   64
Wieland, Theodor   142, 145
Wiesbaden   14, 15, 17, 22, 23, 33, 40, 96
Wilhelma   43, 44, 57, 65
Wolter, Charlotte   14, 15, 19–25, 27, 28, 30–32, 33, 155 See also Rippert, Charlotte
Wolter, Gertrud   19–20
Wolter, Ida   19, 22
Wolter, Karl Albert   19–20
Wolter, Rudolf   19, 23

Y

Yazbak, Mahmoud   45
Yohanani, Lior   75

Z

Ziemendorff, Theodor   13–14, 158
Zionist(s)   43, 45, 47, 49, 53, 79, 116

www.ingramcontent.com/pod-product-compliance
Lightning Source LLC
Chambersburg PA
CBHW061806290426
44109CB00031B/2945